Workplace Investigations

A Guidebook for Administrators, Managers, and Investigators

Workplace Investigations

A Guidebook for Administrators, Managers, and Investigators

Donald W. Slowik

THE EVERGREEN PRESS
Evergreen, Colorado

10 9 8 7 6 5 4 3 2 1

This publication is sold or distributed with the understanding that the author and publisher are not engaged in rendering legal or other professional services. The publisher disclaims any liability, loss or risk incurred as a consequence, directly or indirectly, of the use and application of any of the contents of this publication. The information in this publication is not a substitute for the advice of a competent legal or other professional person.

Library of Congress Cataloging-in-Publication Data

Slowik, Donald W.
    Workplace investigations : a guidebook for administrators, managers, and investigators / by Donald W. Slowik. -- Evergreen, CO : Evergreen Press, 1996.
    p. cm.
    Includes bibliographical references and index.
    Preassigned LCCN: 95060623
    ISBN: 1-883342-02-3

    1. Personnel management--United States. 2. Investigations. I. Title.

HF5549.S56 1995   658.3
                               QBI95-20119

Publisher
The Evergreen Press
P.O. Box 4181
Evergreen, Colorado 80439

Printed in the United States of America

TABLE OF CONTENTS

PART I
ASPECTS OF WORKPLACE INVESTIGATIONS
BREADTH COMPONENT

CHAPTER ONE
EMPLOYMENT LAW
AND WORKPLACE INVESTIGATIONS

CHAPTER TWO
NEGLIGENCE DOCTRINE
AND WORKPLACE INVESTIGATIONS

CHAPTER THREE
EMPLOYEE DEVIANCE
AND WORKPLACE INVESTIGATIONS

PART II
THE ELEMENTS OF SUCCESSFUL INVESTIGATIONS
DEPTH COMPONENT

CHAPTER FOUR
TOOLS AND TECHNIQUES
FOR WORKPLACE INVESTIGATIONS

CHAPTER FIVE
EMPLOYER LIABILITY
AND ELEMENTS OF EMPLOYMENT LAW

CHAPTER SIX
UNICOM_{SM}
UNIVERSAL INTERVIEWING AND COMMUNICATIONS

CHAPTER SEVEN
UNIVERSAL COMPONENTS OF COMMUNICATION

CHAPTER EIGHT
UNICOM_{SM}
A TECHNIQUE FOR INVESTIGATIVE INTERVIEWING

PART III
UNICOM_{SM} INVESTIGATIVE MODELS
APPLICATION COMPONENT

CHAPTER NINE
UNICOM_{SM}
MODEL FOR PREEMPLOYMENT INVESTIGATIONS

CHAPTER TEN
UNICOM_{SM}
MODEL FOR EMPLOYMENT INVESTIGATIONS

CHAPTER ELEVEN
UNICOM_SM
MODEL FOR POST-EMPLOYMENT INVESTIGATIONS

CHAPTER TWELVE
UNICOM_SM
APPLICATION SUMMARY

WORKPLACE INVESTIGATIONS

A GUIDEBOOK FOR
ADMINISTRATORS, MANAGERS, AND INVESTIGATORS

INTRODUCTION

Employers have a duty to investigate certain complaints, including harassment, discrimination, potentially violent employees, criminal violations, and policy violations.

What exactly is an investigation? The term "investigation" is derived from its Latin counterpart, *in-vestigare*, meaning to track or trace out. A contemporary working definition of "workplace investigation" is the act or process of systematically investigating, making inquiry, or conducting an examination for the purpose of ascertaining fact regarding current or past behavior of employees. It is not just the application of common sense to a given situation -- it is a carefully orchestrated plan for gathering information. It must be conducted thoroughly and accurately, information collected must be relevant and up-to-date, and the entire process must be done objectively in order for the results of the investigation to be reliable and defensible.

The purpose of a workplace investigation is to determine whether company policies and procedures or even state or federal laws have been violated and to catalogue such evidence proving or disproving an allegation for future use. The investigator must determine the validity of complaints or charges made and whether a rule, policy, or law has been violated while keeping in mind the fact that an accused/suspected person should morally share the constitutionally guaranteed rights of a person presumed innocent unless otherwise established.

Not every workplace investigation has to do with the investigation of incidents that take place at the workplace. Contemporary human resource literature does not necessarily view preemployment interviewing and screening as an investigatory process, nor do post-employment issues for investigation receive an appropriate characterization. In fact, formal research reveals a paucity of data in the traditional realm of employment investigations. A new-fashioned approach to these enigmas is a reorganization and orderly classification of the fundamental issues and classifications of workplace investigations. From a management standpoint, this organization design offers a logical division and subsequent systemization of options for conducting any investigation within the following three areas of human resource management and responsibility:

1) **Preemployment Investigations** -- issues related to employee screening and selection.

2) **Employment Investigations** -- for issues and activities related to current employment of persons.

3) **Post-Employment Investigations** -- for issues related to a past employee beyond the scope of an employment relationship.

With this approach, any workplace investigation then can be clearly categorized into any one of the above workplace investigation classifications. A general estimation of the frequency of workplace investigations has concluded that 70% of the investigations are within the realm of preemployment screening, while 20% of the investigations are for employment matters and 10% of the investigations are in the post-employment or other miscellaneous category.

Within the realm of human resource management, today's administrators, managers, and investigators are confronted with constant trepidation and escalating risk and exposure to personal and corporate liability as new workplace torts emerge to redefine the legal doctrine of hiring, managing, and terminating employees in the workforce. The role of human resource managers and administrators has evolved over the centuries from a servant-master relationship into one of complex interaction with many diverse participants. Perhaps the most dramatic aspect of this evolutionary process has been the advent of laws and torts which govern this interactive relationship. This publication will comprehensively address the contemporary role that human resource practitioners and administrators play and, more specifically, describe an efficient systematic strategy for all categories of workplace investigations.

The UNICOM₍ₛₘ₎ **Series** -- This publication is the second in a UNICOM series in human resource development. UNICOM represents Universal Interviewing and Communications. The first publication, entitled *Universal Interviewing and Communications: A Preemployment Application,* was designed to instruct specific, industry-wide preemployment interviewing and screening techniques based on the principles of universal verbal and nonverbal communication. The text demonstrated the methodology and techniques of the UNICOM strategy, which was developed via a dual approach:

1) An eclectic assimilation and integration of over 25 years of experience in human resource and corporate loss prevention management, and

2) Research drawn from over 100 years of employment interviewing and communications literature.

The first publication is a tribute to those pioneers who contributed to the development of the universal communications philosophy, as well as a full description of how universal communication can be applied to preemployment screening and interviewing. This second of the UNICOM series has considerable semblance to the first in that, essentially, the same skills and techniques described for preemployment interviewing and screening ultimately can be applied to the interviewing and investigative process of all types of workplace investigations. This similarity actually becomes a basic strength of the UNICOM technique in that it is quite versatile and, when the human resource manager or administrator develops these skills and techniques, their multiple applications become apparent.

Much like the first, this publication is presented in three components: Breadth, Depth, and Application. The Breadth Component is a research-based module which presents a broad perspective on the legal aspects of employment law in relation to formal workplace investigations. The Depth Component provides an in-depth perspective and is a preparatory instruction module which presents the dynamics of communication related to interviewing and an efficient and proactive investigative process for workplace investigations. The Application Component introduces investigative models for preemployment investigations, employment investigations, and post-employment investigations. Each model is based on the fundamentals of the UNICOM strategy.

Part I
Aspects of Workplace Investigations

The Breadth Component presents a review of legal aspects such as employment law and the emergence of negligent torts and the pervasive problem of deviant behavior for three broad categories of workplace investigations:

1) Preemployment investigations,
2) Employment investigations, and
3) Post-employment investigations.

This component presents a comprehensive overview of the categories and types of workplace investigations that ordinarily are confronted by a human resource manager or administrator. A brief description of chapters follows:

Chapter One -- Employment Law and Workplace Investigations

This chapter presents a broad historical perspective of a century of prominent and pertinent employment legislation that illustrates how the role of human resource managers and administrators has evolved from a servant-master relationship to one of complex interaction with many diverse participants. Specific acts and laws are described from the early Civil Rights Acts of the late 1800s to current legislation. Landmark case decisions also are presented as a way to illustrate how the acts and laws have been interpreted by the courts and how precedent has been set to monitor today's workplace. It is necessary for today's human resource managers to understand and consider the information contained in this chapter as they make decisions related to formal workplace investigations.

Chapter Two -- Negligent Doctrine and Workplace Investigations

As the litigation literature indicates, there has been a proliferation of lawsuits against employers for negligent hiring, negligent retention, and negligent supervision. Each of these has emerged as workplace torts and has serious ramifications for the human resource manager and administrator, especially in the areas of formal internal workplace investigations for preemployment and employment situations. This chapter explains the emergence of torts relevant to workplace investigations and presents landmark case examples of how these torts apply specifically to the workplace investigation categories of preemployment investigations, employment investigations, and post-employment investigations.

Chapter Three -- Employee Deviance and Workplace Investigations

The decision to hire, retain, or terminate professional relationships with employees most directly is determined by employee performance and behavior in and outside of the workplace. This chapter defines employee deviance and its negative impact on the workplace. Loss prevention strategies are suggested. There is a special emphasis on drug and alcohol abuse and violence in the workplace. The correlation between drugs and family relations is discussed in terms of its effect on employee behavior in the workplace, and the chapter closes with a section on preventing workplace violence.

Part II
The Elements of Successful Investigations

The Depth Component presents preparatory instruction for an interviewer and investigator. This instruction includes the description of skills, attributes, knowledge, and abilities required of competent and professional investigators. A special section is presented on verbal and nonverbal diagnostics as well as statement analysis and practitioner impression management. This component also includes human factor analysis of investigators, complainants, and accused/suspected persons as well as management of objectivity, prejudices, and human bias. As mentioned above, much of the material presented in this component is drawn from an instructional text for job applicant interviewing and selection entitled *Universal*

Interviewing and Communications: A Preemployment Application (Slowik 1995). A brief description of the chapters follows:

Chapter Four -- Tools and Techniques for Workplace Investigations

The most significant benefit of a good internal workplace investigation is that it enables management to obtain the information it needs to manage effectively. In order to conduct a good workplace investigation, a human resource manager must strategically employ effective tools and techniques. This chapter describes the most valuable tools and techniques currently available to assist human resource managers and administrators in conducting formal workplace investigations for the areas of preemployment investigations, employment investigations, and post-employment investigations.

Preemployment Investigation Application -- Based on the premise that past behavior is predictive of future behavior, employers tend to conduct extensive investigations of applicants' work histories and personal backgrounds. For the pre-employment investigation application, a variety of preemployment selection techniques are presented. Specifically, the chapter presents an overview of popular interviewing models selected for their many attributes for successful interviewing. Secondly, the chapter discusses multiple screening methods and procedures (*i.e.*, skills and abilities tests, honesty tests, drug and alcohol tests, and background checks) and some advantages and disadvantages of their usages. This section presents a summary of these techniques in an employee screening resource table.

Employment Investigation Application -- The importance of setting employment policy is stressed in this section. The value of policy is recognized in areas such as drug and alcohol testing, performance appraisals, and avoiding invasion of privacy, sexual harassment, and discrimination. The issue of employee surveillance also is discussed in terms of legal requirements, and a chart listing the types of surveillance is presented.

Post-Employment Investigation Application -- The post-employment section focuses on the proactive premise that the best way to avoid post-employment litigation is to ensure successful employee relationships during employment. An employment termination policy is suggested as a way to avoid wrongful termination suits. The policy features such techniques as converting terminations into resignations, holding exit interviews, utilizing the preferred method of providing post-employment references, documenting employee interaction, and reviewing successful points for conducting workplace investigations.

Chapter Five -- Employer Liability and Elements of Employment Law

Based on the broad comprehensive historical perspective of employment law presented in Chapter One of Part I, this chapter presents an in-depth view of specific liabilities facing today's human resource managers and administrators. Those issues include the eight areas of potential discrimination, wrongful discharge, post-employment referencing, and other related dilemmas. These employment issues are explained in terms of employment law and illustrated by landmark cases. The primary purpose of this chapter is to offer strategies to the human resource manager for avoiding lawsuits. The seven elements of employment law designed to serve this purpose are presented:

1) Fair, logical, and defensible;
2) Consistency;
3) Legitimate business reason;
4) Documentation;
5) Multiple screening methods;
6) Understanding the human process; and
7) Expert advice.

The notion is presented that personal ethical standards must guide the decision-making process and become the basis for policy and procedures within any business operation and within any business interaction with employees, potential employees, and all others within the business realm.

Chapter Six -- UNICOM -- Universal Interviewing and Communications

This chapter presents a Behavioral Model for Verbal and Nonverbal Communication drawn from a publication entitled UNICOM -- *Universal Interviewing and Communications: A Preemployment Application* (Slowik, 1995). These chapters are designed to provide the reader with foundational information to develop and build behavioral observation techniques and interactional and management skills based on the diagnostics and analysis of verbal and nonverbal communication. The component demonstrates how these factors relate to a disciplined system for the three areas of workplace investigation. The UNICOM technique is demonstrated as a strategy designed to manage a trilogy of interactive events, which include:

1) Having a definitive understanding of the investigative objective.

2) Discerning the dynamics and the interactive behavior from the interviewee's point of view, and

3) Subsequently responding with the appropriate interactive behavior to facilitate investigation cooperation and disclosure.

The model provides an in-depth description of the cognitive interactive communication process as a method of illustrating and understanding the dynamics of the ways humans send and receive messages. It is noted that humans communicate via a dual, interactive language:

1) The language of words, and
2) The language of the body.

The actual anatomy of the UNICOM model is represented through three separate study zones depicting how each body zone is involved within the communication process. Thus, the workplace investigator is instructed to observe the communicative behavior illustrated within these body zones for the employees and witnesses who are interviewed during the investigative process.

Chapter Seven -- Universal Components of Communication
This chapter describes the dynamics of communication in terms of the conscious and subconscious ways in which we communicate. The chapter describes universal comparisons of cultural and gender communication patterns. The physiological aspects of communication are portrayed through a complete description of the central and autonomic nervous system to illustrate how emotions influence communication. An understanding of the physiology of emotions will aid the practitioner in the task of discerning truth from deception during interactions with subjects of any category of a workplace investigation.

Chapter Eight -- UNICOM -- A Technique for Investigative Interviewing
This chapter is an extension of the UNICOM Behavioral Model for Verbal and Nonverbal Communication in that it describes the techniques for interviewing and for conducting internal workplace investigations. When one understands the attributes and qualifications of a skilled practitioner, a logical task would be a self-evaluation to determine personal strengths and weaknesses in order to assist in the selection of the most needed area of emphasis in the instructional process. This chapter not only defines the multidimensional skills and attributes of a proficient practitioner but also addresses the strategies for applying the model to workplace investigations.

Part III
UNICOM Investigative Models

The Application Component introduces three investigation models for instructional purposes. This section will guide the reader through the entire process for each model in a fundamental manner. A brief description of chapters follows:

Chapter Nine -- UNICOM Model for Preemployment Investigations
This chapter presents UNICOM -- Universal Interviewing and Communication -- as an application for the preemployment interviewing and selection process. The UNICOM model is a multifaceted process of preparation, data collection, and quantitative and qualitative analysis. The model is designed for managing preemployment selection in an efficient, professional manner. It considers requirements for legal compliance, the components of communication and human behavior, and the analysis and diagnosis of verbal and nonverbal behavior.

Chapter Ten -- UNICOM Model for Employment Investigations
         Chapter Ten presents a model for employment investigation which applies
the UNICOM philosophy. The UNICOM Model for Employment Investigations is
based on the importance of understanding interactive verbal and nonverbal communication for effective interviewing, legal requirements for compliance with employment law, and the dynamics of managing the trilogy of interactive activities for
investigators. The chapter outlines a strategy for employment investigations and
discusses pertinent points of the investigative process. An extensive list of the kinds
of issues requiring investigations is presented. The attributes of an effective investigator are addressed as well as the pros and cons of interviewing cooperative, neutral, or non-cooperative witnesses. The chapter also addresses employee-generated
documentation vs. employer-generated documentation as well as the function of a
standardized form for documentation for the entire investigative process. The five
Ws (Who, What, When, Where, and Why) are suggested for consideration prior to
the investigative interview, and question formulation techniques are presented.
Points required for drawing conclusions are listed as well as recommended action
choices. The final investigation file is described, and strategies for handling an appeal are suggested.

Chapter Eleven -- UNICOM Model for Post-Employment Investigations
         Chapter Eleven presents a proactive approach to avoiding post-
employment workplace investigations. Negligent investigation is presented as a new
legal theory emerging among employment doctrine. It can be brought into action as
a result of haphazard or incomplete investigations leading to employment termination. The prevention of a wrongful discharge suit is presented as a proactive technique to avoiding negligent termination. The chapter discusses such caveats as
management malpractice, invasion of privacy, false imprisonment, discrimination,
and deviant behavior in the workplace. Specific suggestions are offered on handling
post-employment references to avoid defamation suits. To guard against post-
employment charges, companies must follow a prescribed technique for preemployment selection, hiring new employees, and advancing employees to other levels
of employment.

Chapter Twelve -- UNICOM Application Summary
         Part III concludes with a summary that presents a basic instructional al-
gorithm to assist the practitioner/investigator in appreciating the complexity of the
entire process. The chapter also includes key points from the three application
models.

APPENDICES

Several appendices have been included in this text as a resource guide for practitioners and investigators. They include the following:

Appendix A -- Glossary of Terms for Workplace Investigations

A glossary of terms related to workplace investigations is presented as a reference for the human resource manager and administrator. These terms comprise a language that describes the laws, torts, and cases which have formed precedents and guide the entire realm of workplace investigations.

Appendix B -- Common Acts of Employee Deviance

In order to enable the practitioner to be alert for deviancy in the workplace, a listing of common violations by industry-type has been provided.

Appendix C -- Bibliography: References and Suggested Readings

The bibliography contains all the references from the text as well as suggested readings from the field of workplace investigations and universal communications. This section is intended to serve as a guide in assisting the human resource manager and administrator in becoming familiar with past and current literature related to workplace investigations.

PART I

ASPECTS OF WORKPLACE INVESTIGATIONS
BREADTH COMPONENT

A formal internal workplace investigation is multifaceted and must be clearly defined as to its purpose. The chapters in Part I will address three major aspects of formal workplace investigations. Perhaps the principal concern for employers is that the workplace is governed by multiple and interrelated laws which dictate employer/employee relationships and define the rights of each. A second concern, which has relevance to both law and employee malfeasance, is the emergence of the torts of negligent hiring, negligent retention, wrongful termination, and potential predicaments related to workplace investigations. There is an increasing trend toward employer liability for acts of employees not only at the workplace but during hours away from work. Another vital matter is the pervasive problem of deviant behavior in the workplace.

Because most corporate internal workplace investigations are held to be confidential, investigative strategy and precise procedures also are kept as internal secrets. However, by reviewing the litigation literature, it becomes possible to discern these methods and to form guidelines for effective workplace investigations, and process strategy can be delineated. A common thread that runs throughout the following chapters is the revelation of legal precedence paving the way for the development of high standards for in-depth internal investigative strategy. Noted legal scholar Warren Freedman (1994) stated that:

> *Vigilance and prompt action in the form of a well-targeted internal investigation should be the order of the day when a company or corporation discovers information suggesting possible wrongdoing or misconduct on the part of a present or past officer, high level manager, or even a low level employee (p. 7).*

A case testing the quality and completeness of an internal investigation is exemplified by the following New Mexico Supreme Court Decision: Kestenbaum vs. Pennzoil Co.

Landmark Case Regarding Quality Investigation -- The 1988 New Mexico Supreme Court case of Kestenbaum vs. Pennzoil Co. established the precedence for a high quality complete internal investigation. An employee was discharged for complaints of sexual harassment, illegal conduct, and mismanagement of a ranch owned by the defendant employer. The plaintiff denied the allegations and filed suit for wrongful discharge, stating that *"without a fair investigation and consideration of the allegations and his response, he was terminated on grounds of sexual harassment for which he was innocent."* The plaintiff was awarded more than $1 million, and the court stated that the defendant had not observed the standards of good investigative practice (Kestenbaum vs. Pennzoil Co. [1988] New Mexico Supreme Court 706 P. 2d 280).

CHAPTER ONE

EMPLOYMENT LAW
AND
WORKPLACE INVESTIGATIONS

Employment Law Related to Workplace Investigations

Employment law, which has evolved since the Industrial Revolution, is the impetus for workplace investigations. The enactment and enforcement of these laws which govern the workplace must be understood from an individual basis as well as the myriad of ways in which they interrelate. To assist the reader with this task, a historical perspective of a century of prominent and pertinent employment legislation is presented in this chapter. Specific cases are outlined to illustrate the application and enforcement of employment law.

Civil Rights Acts of 1870, 1871, and 1866

The Civil Rights Act of 1870 provides that *"all persons within the jurisdiction of the United States shall have the same right in every State...to make and enforce contracts...and to the full and equal benefit of all laws and proceedings...."* While somewhat relevant to current employment law, it does not apply to claims of discriminatory discharge, it contains no limitation period in which a complaint must be filed, and back pay awards are not limited to two years. Thus, the act has very little application to contemporary employment law. The Civil Rights Act of 1871, relevant to today's circumstances, declares that:

> *every person who, under color of any statute...subjects, or causes to be subjected, any citizen of the United States or other person within the jurisdiction thereof to the deprivation of any rights, privileges, or immunities secured by the Constitution and laws, shall be liable to the party injured in an action at law....*

The section stated above is similar to the Civil Rights Act of 1866 and has been held applicable to discrimination claims independent of Title VII (Hill & Wright, 1993).

The Civil Service Act of 1883 (Pendelton Act)

The Civil Service Act of 1883, also known as the Pendelton Act, provided for the formation of a permanent, bipartisan Civil Service Commission which gave legitimacy to the idea that jobs would be awarded on the merit principle. Originally, it included approximately 10% of federal civilian employees, but was amended in 1908 to cover 60% of federal civilian workers. In 1923, the Classification Act was passed, which grouped duties and responsibilities into classes. During the 1930s, the Civil Service Commission developed job analyses specifically for the purpose of developing relevant selection tests (Douglas, *et al.,* 1989).

The Norris-LaGuardia Anti-Injunction Act of 1932

The Norris-LaGuardia Anti-Injunction Act of 1932 restricted federal courts from issuing injunctions in labor disputes. Additionally, it declared *yellow-dog* contracts (an employee-employer agreement or contract by which an employee agrees not to join a union while employed) to be against public policy, and made such contracts unenforceable in federal courts (Terry, 1988).

The Fair Labor Standards Act of 1938 (FLSA)

The FLSA established minimum wages and overtime pay for men and women, thus eliminating ultra-cheap pay in blue-collar jobs and establishing over-time law *(i.e.,* time-and-a-half for over 40 hours per week of work). Nevertheless, women legally were prohibited from performing essential features of many blue-collar jobs. The act also sets child labor standards. Finally, in 1963, the FLSA was amended by the Equal Pay Act (Douglas, *et al.,* 1989).

The National Labor Relations Act (Wagner Act) of 1935

The National Labor Relations Act was designed to safeguard the rights of workers to organize and bargain collectively, and it forbade employers from engaging in certain unfair labor practices. Forbidden practices are:

1)   Interference with employees in the exercise of legitimate union activities,

2)   Company domination of any employee organization,

3)   Discrimination against an employee because of union membership or activity,

4)   Discrimination against an employee for having filed charges or given testimony under the act, and

5)   Refusal to bargain collectively with duly-elected representatives of the employees (Terry, 1984).

The Taft-Hartley Act (Labor-Management Act of 1947)

The Taft-Hartley Act of 1947 significantly altered the Wagner Act and extended government intervention into labor relations. It confers rights and imposes responsibilities on the unions. It states that it is unfair practice for unions to:

1)   Coerce employees or employers in their choice of bargaining agents,

2)   Coerce employees or effect discrimination of employees under a union shop for any reason other than nonpayment of dues,

3)   Refuse to bargain,

4)   Engage in certain types of strikes or boycotts,

5)   Assess discriminatory fees or dues, or

6)   Engage in "featherbedding."

Equal Pay Act of 1963

The Equal Pay Act (EPA) of 1963 prohibits differential pay on the basis of sex and requires equal pay for equal work regardless of sex (*equal work* means equal skill, effort, responsibility, and working conditions). The act is enforced by the Equal Employment Opportunity Commission (EEOC), and exceptions provide that pay differences are permitted under some seniority and merit-pay systems or systems that measure earnings on the basis of quantity or quality of production. Differences also are allowed based on reasonable factors other than sex. The EPA covers only equal work and not comparable worth. However, in 1981, the Supreme Court channeled decisions for comparable worth toward Title VII, but the conflict still is unresolved. It is estimated that women earn between 60 and 70 cents on the dollar compared to their male counterparts (Gutman, 1993).

Title VII of the Civil Rights Act of 1964

On July 2, 1964, Title VII of the Civil Rights Act of 1964, as sponsored by President John F. Kennedy, was enacted to eradicate employment discrimination on the basis of race, color, religion, national origin, and sex and is the broadest of all EEO laws. Title VII was a major part of the act, but enforcement was left to the courts instead of establishing a special administrative agency. The law applies to all employers except those with fewer than 15 employees, and employment discrimination unequivocally is prohibited. Section 703(a)(1) states:

[it is] an unlawful employment practice for an employer...to fail or refuse to hire or to discharge any individual with respect to his compensation, terms, conditions, or privileges of employment, because of such individual's race, color, religion, sex, or national origin.

The law is enforced by the U.S. Equal Employment Opportunity Commission (EEOC), with few exceptions. Exceptions include employment actions which selectively discriminate because of a Bona Fide Occupational Qualification (BFOQ) that is *reasonably necessary* to the normal operation of a business.

Landmark Case Decision Regarding BFOQ -- The 1977 U.S. Supreme Court decision regarding Dothard vs. Rawlinson on the issue of Bona Fide Occupational Qualification (BFOQ) and on the disparate impact theory of discrimination was a landmark case. It involved a woman who challenged Alabama statutes and administration regulations for height, weight, and gender criteria for various positions as prison guards. The Court narrowly affirmed that the BFOQ was an exception to discrimination because of the extra danger of dormitory style housing, rather than single-cell lockup, in Alabama prisons, plus the fact that sex offenders were not otherwise segregated. In regard to the disparate impact issue of the case, the female plaintiff argued that height and weight requirements were discriminatory against women. The state, however, argued that such requirements were related to physical strength essential to performance as a correctional counselor. The Court dictated that a more direct test of physical strength was required under Title VII so as to measure the person for the job and not the person in the abstract. (Dothard vs. Rawlinson -- U.S. Supreme Court [1977] 433 U.S. 321, 97 S. CT. 2720, 53 L Ed. 2d 786).

Executive Order 11246

Issued by President Lyndon Johnson in 1965, Executive Order 11246 activated affirmative action, which applies to women and minorities. The order was amended by Johnson in 1967 and by President Richard Nixon in 1969. Finally, President James Carter, in 1978, ordered a reorganization of administrative enforcement of all federal EEO laws as well as E.O. 11246 (Gutman, 1993). Controversy and expected litigation exist currently as to whether affirmative action for minorities and women raises valid reverse discrimination charges under Title VII. The order is administered by the Office of Federal Contract Compliance Programs (OFCCP) but has common ground with the EEOC. In 1979, the EEOC published *Affirmative Action Guidelines*.

Title III -- Federal Omnibus Crime Control and Safe Streets Act of 1968

This act prohibits all private individuals and companies from intercepting the wire and oral communications of others. The law applies to all communications on cellular telephones, electronic mail, and computers. Exceptions may be considered to allow employers to monitor employee conversations on an extension of the telephone system as long as the monitoring is done in the "ordinary course of the employer's business."

Occupational Safety and Health Act (OSHA) of 1970

This act sets mandatory standards for safety and health. The 1980 amendment extends the act's provisions from the private sector to federal agencies by Executive Order 12196. Under OSHA, employers must provide a workplace free of recognized hazards. OSHA's broad coverage applies to any "person engaged in a business affecting commerce who has employees but does not include the United States government or any State or political subdivision of a State" (SHRM, 1994).

Fair Credit Reporting Act of 1970 (FCRA)

The Fair Credit Reporting Act of 1970 protects applicants and employees from the dissemination of inaccurate or misleading personal information distributed by consumer reporting agencies. The FCR Act is enforced by the U.S. Federal Trade Commission and allows employees or applicants to bring suit and claim for intentional and negligent infliction of emotional distress, defamation, and violation of applicable state labor code sections.

In regard to reference checking of job applicants, it is important for employers to know how to phrase questions, know what questions cannot be asked, and know how to handle the information received. Proper reference checking procedures will result in better hiring decisions, protect against negligent hiring, and prevent legal complaints.

Equal Employment Opportunity Act of 1972

The Civil Rights Act was amended in 1972 by the Equal Employment Opportunity Act of 1972 (EEO Act) and gave the Equal Employment Opportunity Commission (EEOC) the power to bring suit against employers in U.S. District Courts. Initially, jurisdiction over federal employee Title VII claims was awarded to the Civil Service Commission, however, in 1978 jurisdiction was transferred to the EEOC.

EEOC Guidelines -- Influenced by the EEO ruling, the EEOC issued Guidelines on Employment Testing Procedures in August 1966. These guidelines were not requirements, however. They became much more stringent in August of 1970 when the EEOC issued *Guidelines on Employee Selection Procedures,* which set up an eight-year conflict.

Finally, in 1978, the EEOC, the Office of Federal Contract Compliance Programs (OFCCP), the Department of Justice, and the Civil Service Commission reached agreement on a set of guidelines, the jointly issued *Uniform Guidelines on Employee Selection Procedures.* These guidelines contain detailed instructions on how to demonstrate validity, allowing employers to use *content validity* where appropriate. In the event of adverse impact, the employer must look for equally valid procedures that have less adverse impact. The guidelines apply not just to written tests, but also to all selection procedures (*i.e.*, interviews, review of experience or education from application forms, work samples, physical requirements, and evaluations of performance) used to make employment decisions (Douglas, *et al.,* 1989).

Landmark Case Regarding Racial Discrimination -- A landmark ruling in the case of Griggs vs. Duke Power Company established the precedent on how the courts would treat Title VII. Duke Power Company historically had practiced open racial discrimination by employing blacks only in the labor department, where all workers were paid less than workers in the white departments. However, in answer to Title VII, the company opened jobs in all departments to blacks, but required a high school diploma for employees transferring from labor jobs to other departments.

An additional requirement for new employees was to obtain satisfactory scores on two professionally prepared aptitude tests: the Wonderlic Personnel Test and the Bennett Mechanical Aptitude Test. When blacks brought discrimination suits, the U.S. Supreme Court ruled in criticism of the *professionally developed ability test*. The case left employers free to use tests, but limited their usage in regard to an adverse impact on minorities (Griggs vs. Duke Power Co. [1971] 401 U.S. 424).

Landmark Case Regarding Burden of Proof -- Further clarification of the burden of proof precedent was the 1981 U.S. Supreme Court case involving the Texas Department of Community Affairs vs. Burdine, in which a female plaintiff had shown a *prima facie* case of discrimination in being rejected for a position. The court determined that the burden of proof then shifts to the defendant to rebut a presumption of discrimination by producing evidence that the plaintiff was rejected or someone else was preferred, for a legitimate, nondiscriminatory reason. If the defendant accomplishes this, the burden of proof shifts back to the plaintiff, who must show that the reasons offered by the employer were not the true reasons for the rejection decision (Texas Department of Community Affairs vs. Burdine, U.S. Supreme Court [1981] 450 U.S. 248, 101 S.Ct. 1089, 67 L Ed. 2d 207).

During the early 1970s, it was determined that, nationally, only 55% of employers were using employment tests compared to an estimate of 90% in 1963. It is projected that the future use of preemployment tests will mirror the 1960s trend because of the proliferation of wrongful discharge and negligent hiring law suits, which place an increasingly important burden on employers to make careful hiring decisions (Douglas, *et al.*, 1989).

The Pregnancy Discrimination Act of 1978 (PDA)

The Pregnancy Discrimination Act defines virtually any discrimination based on pregnancy and protects women who seek abortions, covers abortion as a disability if there is potential danger to the mother, and covers as a disability medical complications to an otherwise uncovered abortion. The act does not, however, require employers to employ fertile women in jobs that require exposure to chemicals that create a substantial and/or imminent health risk for the unborn. The act has resulted in employers forming a fetal protection policy (Douglas, *et al.*, 1989). The act is under 701(k) of Title VII and is governed by the EEOC (Gutman, 1993).

Landmark Case Regarding Pregnancy Discrimination -- Another landmark case in 1983 involved a U.S. Supreme Court decision regarding the Newport News Shipbuilding and Dry Dock Company vs. EEOC. The company's health insurance plan provided female employees with hospitalization benefits for pregnancy-related conditions but provided less extensive pregnancy benefits for spouses of male employees. The court ruled that the plan discriminated against male employees in that it excluded pregnancy coverage from an otherwise inclusive benefits plan (Newport News Shipbuilding and Dry Dock Company vs. EEOC, U.S. Supreme Court [1983] 462 U.S. 669, 103 S.Ct. 2622, 77 L Ed. 2d 89).

Civil Rights Act of 1991

The Civil Rights Act of 1991, signed into law on November 21, 1991, represents two years of negotiation between Congress, President George Bush, and other interested parties. It significantly expands the rights of job applicants, employees, and former employees who bring discrimination suits to court, and it extends new protections, making jury trials and limited punitive damages available under Title VII (Asquith & Feld, 1993).

The enforcement agency is the EEOC, and the act covers employers with 15 or more workers. It provides a schedule of limits for each claim for punitive and emotional injury damages (*i.e.*, depending upon employer size) for claims which are not based on race:

exempt	-	fewer than 15 employees
$50,000	-	15 to 100 employees
$100,000	-	101 to 200 employees
$200,000	-	201 to 500 employees
$300,000	-	more than 500

The Age Discrimination in Employment Act of 1967

Another law prohibiting employment discrimination was the Age Discrimination in Employment Act of 1967 (ADEA), which forbids discrimination against applicants or employees over age 40 and also is vested in the EEOC. The act enjoyed bipartisan support in Congress; the Senate passed it 91-6 and the House voted 377-27.

ADEA also was supported by Presidents Ronald Reagan and George Bush (Gutman, 1993). ADEA states that an aggrieved party must file a charge with the EEOC within 180 days of the alleged unlawful employment practice and has two advantages not available under Title VII:

1)   ADEA cases are tried by a jury instead of by judges as in Title VII cases, and

2)   The plaintiff can receive liquidated damages in addition to back pay (Douglas, *et al.,* 1989).

Exceptions to ADEA are related to the Bona Fide Occupational Qualification (BFOQ) when it is *necessary to the basic operation* of a business. Differentiation is based on reasonable factors other than age, the terms of a bona fide seniority system except in the case of retirement, and *bona fide executives* who are exempt because of their executive positions.

Landmark Case Regarding Age Discrimination -- The Hodgson vs. First Federal Savings and Loan Association case involved a 47-year-old woman who was denied a job as teller. The Labor Department investigation revealed that a personnel officer labeled the woman as *too old for teller.* The job order with an employment agency requested a "young man" between the ages of 21 and 24 and none of the 39 persons hired for the teller job during the year was over 40 years old. The court prohibited the bank from any further violations of the Age Discrimination in Employment Act and ordered back pay for the plaintiff (Hodgson vs. First Federal Savings and Loan Assoc. [1975] 455 F.2nd 818, 5th Circuit).

Vocational Rehabilitation Act of 1973 (Handicap Discrimination)

Section 503 of the act requires employers to take affirmative action to employ and advance in employment qualified handicapped individuals. Employers with 50 or more employees and federal contracts awarded in excess of $50,000 are compelled to write an Affirmative Action Plan.

Section 504 of the Rehabilitation Act of 1973 prohibits a federally funded program from discriminating against a handicapped individual solely on the basis of the handicap (Douglas, *et al.,* 1989). The statute states:

No otherwise qualified individual with handicaps...shall, solely by reason of her or his handicap, be excluded from the participation in, be denied the benefits of, or be subjected to discrimination under any program or activity receiving Federal financial assistance or under any program or activity conducted by any Executive Agency or by the United States Postal Service.

A handicapped person is defined as one who:

1)   Has a physical or mental impairment which substantially limits one or more of such person's major life activities,

2)   Has a record of such an impairment, or

3)   Is regarded as having such an impairment.

An Affirmative Action Plan is not required but involves similar anti-discrimination requirements. A handicapped individual may bring a court action on his own behalf if he believes Section 504 has been violated (Hill & Wright, 1993).

The act is enforced by The U.S. Department of Labor, Office of Federal Contract Compliance Programs (DOL-OFCCP), and there are no exceptions.

Landmark Case Regarding Rehabilitation Act -- A 1987 U.S. Supreme Court case of School Board of Nassau County, Florida, vs. Arline involved a school teacher as plaintiff who was afflicted with tuberculosis, a contagious disease. The Court ruled that she was a *handicapped individual* within the meaning of the Rehabilitation Act and therefore could not be dismissed from employment solely on the basis of her handicap (School Board of Nassau County, Florida, vs. Arline, U.S. Supreme Court [1987] 107 S.Ct. 1123).

Privacy Act of 1974

This act prohibits federal agencies from revealing certain information without permission from the employee. Employees are given the right to inspect records about themselves held by the federal government and to make corrections and copies (SHRM, 1994).

Employee Retirement Income Security Act (ERISA) of 1974

This act requires that employees be informed about their pension and certain other employee benefit plans "in a manner calculated to be understood by the average employee." It provides controls and vesting standards for pension plans and sets a minimum standard of funding that ensures the financial soundness of the plans (SHRM, 1994).

Vietnam Era Veterans' Readjustment Assistance Act of 1974

This act forbids employment discrimination against veterans and all disabled veterans of the Vietnam era (August 5, 1964, to May 7, 1975). The act ensures that all organizations with government contracts take affirmative action to employ and advance in employment such individuals. The enforcement agency is the U.S. Department of Labor, Office of Federal Contract Compliance Programs (DOL-OFCCP). The act covers employers with government contracts in excess of $10,000 with no exceptions.

Immigration and Naturalization Act of 1966

This act covers the hiring of resident aliens and new or prospective immigrants.

Immigration Reform and Control Act of 1986

The Immigration Reform and Control Act (IRCA) of 1986 states that all employers must verify the eligibility for employment of newly hired employees by having them complete Form I-9, Employee Eligibility Verification Form. Employees are required to demonstrate, after acceptance of a job offer, documentation of the right to work and documentation of identity. Employers must then verify the information provided in the I-9 form, and copies of the verification documents must be retained with the I-9 form. These records must be retained by the employer for a period of three years after the hiring date or one year after the employment termination date. The primary purpose of the act was to prevent the employment of illegal aliens and to penalize employers who hire undocumented aliens. The enforcement agency is the Special Counsel's Office, United States Justice Department. All employers are covered with no exceptions.

The Drug Free Workplace Act of 1988

President Ronald Reagan issued an executive order in 1986 which mandated developing a program for achieving a drug-free federal workplace. In 1988, the Drug Free Workplace Act was passed to require holders of contracts and grants from the federal government to take a number of steps to keep drugs out of the workplace. It does not require testing.

Mandate for a Drug-Free Workplace

In 1986, the federal government began testing civilian employees for drug use after an executive order was issued which mandated the development of a program for achieving a drug-free federal workplace. The order was issued by President Ronald Reagan, and many state and local governments followed suit, passing similar measures. The executive order called for all federal agencies to set up programs to test workers in sensitive positions for illegal drug use and to establish a voluntary drug-testing program for all other employers.

The U.S. Department of Transportation began random drug testing of employees in safety-related jobs in 1987. In 1988, the U.S. Department of Health and Human Services adopted scientific and technical guidelines for drug-testing programs and established standards for certification of laboratories engaged in urine drug testing for federal agencies.

Drug-Free Private Sector -- Within the private sector, by 1988, almost half of the Fortune 500 companies were screening for drugs as a condition of employment, and the practice is becoming increasingly common. The federal government also is reaching into the private sector with drug-testing regulations. For example, in 1988 the U.S. Department of Transportation (DOT) proposed random drug testing of commercial airline employees, and the Federal Railroad Administration also proposed rules requiring random drug testing programs for railroad companies (Douglas, *et al.,* 1989). In 1991, the DOT published a *Drug Testing Procedures Handbook*, which contains an employers' guide to the DOT final rule, a guide for medical review officers, and a guide to urine specimen collection procedures (Asquith & Feld, 1993).

Landmark Case Regarding "Probable Cause" -- U.S. Supreme Court decisions in 1989 upheld mandatory drug testing for railroad and U.S. Customs Service employees. The Skinner vs. Railway Labor Executives Association case involved Skinner's challenge to the Department of Transportation regulations requiring drug testing of railroad employees involved in train accidents or who violated safety rules. The Court supported the governmental need to ensure the safety of the traveling public against the intrusion into an employee's privacy by upholding the legality of the testing (Skinner vs. Railway Labor Executives Association, U.S. Supreme Court [1989] 109 S.Ct 1402).

Landmark Case Regarding Drug Testing -- A second case involved the National Treasury Employees Union vs. Von Raab and the regulations that made drug tests a condition of placement or employment. The court deemed the testing program reasonable for jobs that:

1)   require the employee to have direct involvement in drug interdiction or enforcement,
2)   require the employee to carry a firearm, or
3)   require the employee to handle "classified" materials that might fall into the hands of smugglers.

(National Treasury employees Union vs. Von Raab. U.S. Supreme Court [1989] 109 S. Ct. 1384).

Worker Adjustment and Retraining Notification Act of 1988

This act, often referred to as the WARN Act, requires employers with 100 or more employees to give a 60-day advance notice of a plant closing or a mass layoff affecting 50 or more employers or one-third of the work force at one site within 30 days (SHRM, 1994).

Omnibus Transportation Employee Testing Act of 1991 (OTETA)

OTETA, signed into law on October 28, 1991, calls for drug and alcohol testing of transportation industry and employees in safety-sensitive positions. The new law expanded the number of transportation workers who are required to be tested from 4.5 million to 6 million, by the addition of interstate truck drivers (Asquith & Feld, 1993).

The Employee Polygraph Protection Act of 1988

The Employee Polygraph Protection Act of 1988 prohibits private sector employers from using polygraphs, voice print devices, and other related technologies in the selection of employees. Exceptions to the ban are employees in the government, the FBI, the Defense Department, and the Energy Department or other such individuals who work under contract to federal intelligence agencies. The Employee Polygraph Protection Act is enforced by the Wage and Hour Division of the Department of Labor (Douglas, *et al.*, 1989).

Impact of the Employee Polygraph Protection Act (EPPA) -- EPPA essentially eliminated polygraph testing by private employers and increased the need for a scientific means of detecting dishonesty in the workplace. Written honesty tests, often referred to as paper-and-pencil honesty tests, currently are a multimillion dollar industry. It is estimated that about 3.5 million written honesty tests are given annually in the United States with 15% to 20% of Fortune 500 Companies using them. Primarily, the tests are used for preemployment screening in work settings where employees have access to cash or merchandise (*i.e.*, retailers, financial institutions, warehouses) and for positions such as clerks, tellers, cashiers, and security guards (Douglas, *et al.*, 1989).

The Americans with Disabilities Act (ADA) of 1990

The Americans with Disabilities Act of 1990 (ADA) extended protections under Title VII of the Civil Rights Act of 1964 to all handicapped individuals and is regulated by the EEOC (Jones, 1993). The act was signed into law by President Bush on July 20, 1990, and it became effective in July of 1992. J. G. Allen (1993) noted that the ADA was hailed by disabled advocacy groups as the *emancipation proclamation of the disabled.* For employers, however, it created apprehension because of its legal and economic implications. It dramatically restricts most preemployment medical screening and sets up a number of ramifications for other preemployment screening and interviewing. For example, it is noted that the MMPI, often is given to police officer candidates to screen out individuals who manifest personality disorders and therefore may be deemed unfit to carry guns. With the ADA, however, job applicants, who have personality disorders of sufficient severity to be disabling within the realm of ADA, may not be screened out on the basis of their disabilities, or otherwise discriminated against, unless they pose a significant risk to the health and safety of themselves and others (Asquith & Feld, 1993).

ADA Prohibits Discrimination -- The ADA lists the following forms of discrimination for employers to consider:

1) Limiting, segregating, or classifying disabled persons;

2) Participating in contractual relationships that effectuate discrimination;

3) Enacting standards, criteria, and methods of administration that effectuate discrimination;

4) Excluding or denying jobs or benefits because of a relationship to individuals with disabilities; and

5) Using qualification standards, employment tests, and all other selection criteria that effect discrimination.

In the event that a qualified individual is discriminated against in violation of the ADA, there are numerous remedies. The act provides temporary or preliminary relief, such as temporary restraining orders, permanent injunctions, additional back pay, and equitable relief. An employer may be liable for the employee's attorney's fees if found to be in violation (Hill & Wright, 193).

ADA Impacts the Interview Process -- There are a number of other ways in which the ADA impacts the interview process. This impact should be noted in the types of questions that may and may not be asked and the care that the practitioner must take during the interview process to accommodate ADA-protected applicants.

For example, an interviewer may only inquire about a person's ability to perform specific job-related functions. Interviewing author William Swan (1989) recommended a formula that is both legal and sensitive: *"State the job requirements as clearly as you can and then ask the candidate a closed-ended question"* (p. 268). ADA applies, with no exceptions, to employers with 15 or more employees, and Title D employment, state and local governments (Title II), accessibility accommodations (Title III), and telecommunication systems for the deaf (Title IV).

ADA Impacts the Employee Supervisor -- Under the Americans with Disabilities Act, supervisors who discriminate against employees with disabilities may be liable personally for damages. ADA considers supervisors to be "agents" of an organization. Thus, for companies employing 15 or more workers, the supervisor must guard against discriminatory behavior. A federal district court in New Jersey has ruled in this regard and this is significant in that it extends ADA liability to individual supervisors as well as to the employer (HR News, 1995, p. 12).

Landmark Case Exemplifying Supervisors' Liability Under the ADA -- Precedent was set in a New Jersey federal court case involving a pending lawsuit against an employer and two individuals. A female employee, who was diagnosed with cancer after she was hired, filed the complaint because she had been passed over for 10 promotions over four-and-a-half years. Following surgery for her cancer, the employer ordered her to return to work within two weeks and refused to give her time off for further treatments. She also was demoted and received negative comments regarding her medical condition in her performance evaluation. She claimed that two supervisors made harassing comments about her medical condition as well. The court followed the rulings of other courts to allow suits against individual supervisors who have taken discriminatory action outside the scope of their employers' policies (Bishop vs. Okidata, Inc. [1994], No. 94-1931 DCNJ 10/3/94).

Family and Medical Leave Act of 1993

Under the Family and Medical Leave Act of 1993, employers are required to continue an employee's health care coverage when the worker is on leave. Failure to do so could result in penalties for non-compliance. This act applies to all private, state, and federal employers with 50 or more employees within 75 miles of a given workplace. To qualify for eligibility, an employee must have worked at least 12 months for the employer and 1,250 hours in the previous year. Eligible employees are entitled to a total of 12 weeks of leave during any 12-month period for one or more of the following:

- Birth of a child;

- Placement of a child for adoption or foster care;

- Caring for a spouse, child, or parent with a serious health condition; or

- Serious health condition of the employee.

The employer must continue the employee's health benefits during the leave period. Following the leave, the employee must be able to return to the same job or a job with equivalent status and pay. Limited exceptions may apply to certain highly compensated employees. Employees may be asked or required to apply vacation, personal leave, and sick days before using unpaid leave. An employer who violates the act will be liable for wages and benefits the employee has lost and any monetary losses plus interest. An employer who has not acted in good faith will be liable for double damages. The courts also can order reinstatement or the promotion of an employee (SHRM, 1994).

Agency Law

A brief discussion is presented here on the description of agency law to illustrate the distinction between the employer/employee relationship and the employer/independent contractor relationship. The first noted distinction is that all employment laws apply only to the employer-employee relationship. For example, the statutes that govern social security, withholding taxes, workers' compensation, unemployment compensation, workplace safety laws, and other similar laws apply only to the employer/employee status. These laws do not apply to an independent contractor (Clarkson, *et al.,* 1991).

Summary of Employment Law

This chapter has presented a broad historical perspective of a century of prominent and pertinent employment legislation which illustrates how the role of human resource managers and administrators has evolved from a servant-master relationship to one of complex interaction with many participants. Specific acts and laws are described from the early Civil Rights Acts of the late 1800s to current legislation. Landmark case decisions also are presented as a way to illustrate how the acts and laws have been interpreted by the courts and how precedent has been set to monitor today's workplace. It is necessary for today's human resource managers to understand and consider the information contained in this chapter as they make decisions related to formal workplace investigations.

CHAPTER TWO

NEGLIGENCE DOCTRINE
AND
WORKPLACE INVESTIGATIONS

This chapter explains the emergence of common-law tort theories relevant to workplace investigations and presents case examples of how these torts apply to three specific areas of workplace investigations: preemployment, employment, and post-employment. The key common-law concepts presented here are:

1) Negligent hiring,
2) Negligent retention,
3) Negligent supervision,
4) Negligent investigation,
5) Defamation,
6) Invasion of privacy,
7) Constructive discharge, and
8) Retaliatory discharge.

The Tort of Negligent Hiring

Under the negligent hiring doctrine, an employer can be held liable for acts by the employee which are foreseeable, even if the employee exceeds the scope of his or her authorized duties (Gregory, 1988).

> *"Liability for negligent hiring arises only when a particular unfitness of an applicant creates a danger of harm to a third person which the employer knew, or should have known, when he hired and placed this applicant in employment when he could injure others" (Fallon vs. Indian Trail School, 1976, p. 101).*

Negligent Hiring Criterion

Five points must be documented for an employer to be held liable for negligent hiring:

1)   An injury must be shown to be caused by an employee acting under the auspices of employment,

2)   The employee must be shown to be unfit,

3)   The employer must be shown to have known about the unfitness,

4)   The injury must be shown to be a foreseeable consequence of hiring the unfit employee, and

5)   The hiring of the unfit employee must be shown to be the proximate cause of the injury (Branch, 1988; Green & Reibstein, 1988; Gregory, 1988; Schmitt, 1980).

Each of these five points is discussed below:

Auspices of Employment -- The first point, auspices of employment, refers to the fact that it must be shown that an injury was caused by an employee of the defendant acting under the auspices of his or her employment, *i.e.*, while on the job or acting as a representative of the employer. While not often a source of dispute, several cases have focused on whether an employment relationship existed at the time of injury. For example, the case of Giles vs. Shell Oil (1985) involved a shooting death by a service station attendant. However, it was shown that the attendant was not an employee of the parent company, because control over the individual's day-to-day operation was not exercised.

Another case, Lear Siegler, Inc., vs. Stegall (1987), involved an individual who brought a negligent hiring suit against an employer because of an accident with an employee driving a company car. The negligent hiring cause of action was not brought because the employee was commuting from home to work and, therefore, the tortious act did not occur while the employee was working or "acting under the color of employment." In a third case, Bates vs. Doria (1986), a deputy sheriff raped and assaulted an individual, but the county was not held liable for injuries because the employee was off duty, was not in uniform, and was not conducting activities related to employment.

This point of inquiry raises many questions about defining auspices of employment. Many jobs have a fair amount of autonomy associated with the positions, and the individual job holder often is the key determiner of job duties and decisions. Thus, these jobs do not have clear-cut boundaries of employment. For instance, sales positions often require socializing with clients outside the office and outside the 9-to-5 context. Similarly, the roles of professions such as doctors, lawyers, and university professors, take on many contexts while the persons remain on duty.

> **Landmark Case Regarding "under the auspices of employment"** -- In Coath vs. Jones (1980), the court issued a ruling that a negligent hiring suit could be brought where a former employee raped a customer. The rapist, representing himself as a customer of an ex-employer, gained access to the victim's house. The victim was unaware that the rapist was no longer an employee. The court stated: *"where the employer had created a special relationship, whereby his customers admit his employee into their homes, then the employer may be required to give notice or warning to the customer that the employee is no longer employed"* (Coath vs. Jones, 1980, p. 1250).

Unfitness of the Employee -- Fitness as an employee is described by S. Rynes and B. Gerhart (1990) as an elusive concept. In employment terms, fitness may be defined as to how an individual's knowledge, skills, and abilities relate to the requirements of a job. They noted, however, that courts have said negligent hiring carries fitness beyond immediate job-relevant factors to what might be construed as universally desirable characteristics of employees, *i.e.*, honesty, even temperedness, and those positive characteristics associated with law-abiding citizens. This is apparent in the case of Pruitt vs. Pavelin (1984), in which the employee's unfitness was a propensity to lie in a job where honesty in dealing with clients was important.

Foreseeability -- Perhaps the most frequently disputed issue in negligent hiring is the issue of foreseeability, or the existence of a duty owed by the employer to the injured party (Green & Reibstein, 1988; Schmitt, 1988). The courts question whether the employer reasonably could have discovered an employee's incompetence and, if the incompetence was known, whether the employer could have foreseen the act that led to injury as a result of hiring. As an example, in the case of Focke vs. United States (1982), the court did not find it foreseeable that a social work associate would engage in sexual contact with family members of hospital patients because his job duties were limited to essentially clerical tasks, and there should have been only limited, administrative contact with the family.

While the courts have held that it is not essential that an employer should have foreseen the precise injury resulting from a negligent act, the employer, however, is held to the standard of exercising the degree of care in selecting an employee that a reasonably prudent person would exercise, in view of the consequences that might be expected to occur if an unfit individual were hired. An example is illustrated in the case of Malorney vs. B&L Motor Freight, Inc. (1986), in which a hitchhiker was sexually assaulted by a truck driver. The driver had been informed in writing at the time of hiring that he was not to pick up hitchhikers. The employer maintained that it had no duty to investigate the employee's criminal record, which indicated previous sexual assaults on hitchhikers, because it was not foreseeable that he would pick up hitchhikers. However, the courts ruled that the employer had a duty to investigate the prospective employee's background because the driver was given an over-the-road vehicle with a sleeping compartment, and the employer should have known that truckers are prone to give rides despite company regulations. Therefore, the court ruled that the employer should have foreseen that the unfitness could lead to injury.

Landmark Case regarding "Foreseeability" -- In the case of Ponticas vs. K.M.S. Investments, the employer was found to have negligently hired a resident manager who sexually assaulted a tenant. The employer was held liable for negligent hiring for failure to inquire properly into the background and references of the apartment manager who was provided with a pass key that facilitated entry into the victim's apartment. The court stated that *"an employer has the duty to exercise reasonable care in view of all the circumstances in hiring individuals who, because of the employment, may pose a threat of injury to members of the public"* (p. 907). Positions that involve access to homes or involve public safety require a more thorough background check, or what has often been termed a "special duty to care" (Ponticas vs. K.M.S. Invs. [1983] 331 N.W.2d 907 Minn.)

Proximate Cause -- A negligent hiring claim cannot be made simply on the charge of a duty to investigate employee fitness. Additionally, it must be shown that the negligent hiring was the proximate cause of the injury. It must be shown that the injury appears to be the reasonable and probable consequence of what the employer did or not do in the hiring process (Green & Reibstein, 1988).

Understanding the Concept of Negligent Hiring -- It is imperative that human resource managers understand the concept of negligence in hiring before loss prevention programs are established in order to avoid such charges. Negligent hiring liability is defined as *"the failure to exercise reasonable care in the selection of an applicant, in view of the risk created by the position."* This means that employers must adequately screen individuals before hiring (Bates, 1988).

Employees who engage in criminal, violent, or other wrongful acts, during and after work hours, are among the greatest concerns in today's corporate world. In the past, corporate employers only have been considered responsible for an employee's behavior at the workplace and during working hours. Recently, however, a number of court decisions have found employers liable for negligent hiring and/or negligent retention of dangerous individuals. Such incidents leading to these charges include: the murder of fellow employees; rape and murder of a housing resident; sexual harassment of a fellow employee; physical assault that included hitting and kicking customers; theft of gold; and even one incident where an airline boarding agent, who tested positive for the AIDS antibody, bit a passenger (Green & Reibstein, 1988).

The New Terms -- In the past two decades, courts and juries have become the ultimate personnel directors of the U.S. workplace (Mullaney, 1989). New terms have been legislated into the vocabulary of the employment field, as well as numerous implications and ramifications that result in considerable dilemmas. The terms fraud, defamation, negligent hiring, negligent retention, negligent supervision, and negligent investigation all play a new role in how personnel directors must conduct themselves in the employee selection and retention process.

The primary concern of this chapter is to document actual court decisions that have deemed an employer or company liable for the subsequent criminal behavior of an employee, even when the crime occurred miles away from the workplace and during the employee's free time.

Corporate Costs of Negligent Hiring

"Parent Corporation Ordered to Pay $5 Million damages for Fatal Assault by Paroled Employee" (Green & Reibstein, 1988, p. 8). This headline is representative of the costs of negligent hiring. Some plaintiffs have asked for as much as $12 million while others have even settled out of court for as little as $440,000 for a murder conviction (Green & Reibstein).

The commonalty of these cases is that the employer was charged with *negligent hiring* or breaching the duty to make an adequate investigation of an employee's fitness before hiring the worker. In some cases, the employers also were charged with *negligent retention*, which is the breach of an employer's duty to be aware of an employee's fitness and to take corrective action through retraining, reassignment, or even discharging a worker (Silver, 1987).

These emerging tortious theories have even reached into the pockets of the Boy Scouts of America, as in the case of a Boy Scout who was shot in the neck with a gun owned by a camp employee. The Boy Scout organization was held liable for employing a dangerous individual in spite of the fact that the person was the boy's uncle (Silver, 1987).

History of the Emergent Negligent Hiring Doctrine

The evidence cited above represents a convincing evolution of a commanding theory of negligent hiring. The development of the negligent hiring doctrine began with the common law fellow servant rule designed to absolve an employer from liability if an employee was injured due to negligence, carelessness, or intentional misconduct of a fellow employee. However, exceptions to the servant rule turned toward the recognition of an employer's duty to provide a safe workplace, which included the duty to hire safe employees (Minum, 1988).

A subsequent 1914 railroad incident expanded the employer's responsibility beyond the scope of the workplace when an employee attacked another worker with a knife. Then, in 1933, an assistant manager of a Woolworth Five-and-Ten-Cent Store pushed a customer over a counter, causing the woman to injure her back. The store was held liable for not providing a safe condition, which included employing competent and law-abiding servants. The negligent hiring doctrine was expanded again in 1954 when an apartment building tenant was shot by a maintenance employee.

Negligent hiring was furthered, beyond the area within an employer's immediate control, in another apartment incident, when a man delivering groceries assaulted a woman. The grocer was held liable for reasonable care in the employment of delivery men (Minum, 1988).

Duty to Investigate -- Under the negligent hiring doctrine, employers are obligated to conduct a reasonable investigation into a prospective employee's background to determine qualifications and trustworthiness for the particular position (Marderosian, 1985). The duty to investigate each applicant's employment background, references, and possible criminal record, to determine the person's fitness for a position of trust or to work with other personnel, becomes more imperative than ever. Rulings also have balanced the duty to investigate against the costs and difficulty of obtaining such records.

To date, a court precedent has at least found no liability if an employer makes adequate inquiry or otherwise has a sufficient basis upon which to rely that an actual criminal record inquiry may not be necessary. This ruling, of course, is based solely on whether or not the job entails special duty to the public, or, in other words, the nature of the risk posed by an employee's possible unfitness for certain positions. For example, if an employee is given a passkey to apartments or living quarters, the employer has a duty to thoroughly investigate the employee's fitness to hold such a position of strong trust (Silver, 1987). The courts have placed high duties especially on landlords and apartment complex owners who must use reasonable precautions in the safeguard of premises and preventing crimes against the tenants (Haerle, 1984).

This precedent was broadened in the Minnesota case of a resident apartment complex manager who used his passkey to enter a female tenant's apartment and rape her at knife point. Both the owner and operator of the complex were found liable for negligent hiring, because the employee had a record of conviction for burglary and aggravated robbery. At the time of the rape, the employee was on parole and under the supervision of the Minnesota Department of Corrections. The victim was awarded $75,000 for personal injuries and her husband $15,000 for loss of consortium (Haerle, 1984).

Case Examples

More specific negligent hiring, retaining, and supervising employee precedents have been established which involve elderly and disabled patients in relation to health care settings (Spain & Spain, 1989).

Girardi vs. Community Hospital of Brooklyn (1988) -- Girardi's 79-year-old mother was a comatose patient at the community hospital when she was sexually assaulted by a hospital orderly. The incident was observed by a nurse who did not report it for two days because of fear for her own safety. The patient died approximately two weeks following the assault, and the surviving daughter sued for wrongful death and negligent hiring. The court granted her request for pain and suffering but could not find evidence that would indicate negligent hiring (Spain & Spain, 1989).

Corker vs. Appalachian Regional Healthcare, Inc. (1989) -- Corker was a 34-year-old mentally retarded patient raped by an employee of the above hospital. Corker and her mother filed suit against the hospital for negligence in hiring, retaining, and supervising the employee. It was learned that the hospital had been informed by a previous employer that the charged employee had displayed inappropriate behavior with female patients. In addition, the director of nurses had failed to follow hospital policy and order a physical examination of the victim. The hospital administrators failed to provide prompt notification to the police and the victim's family and had concealed information regarding a previous sexual assault on another psychiatric patient by the employee on the same shift. The case was settled out of court with confidential terms (Spain & Spain, 1989).

Moore vs. St. Joseph Nursing Home, Inc. (1990) -- This was a case that involved negligence and failure to warn. An employee was dismissed by the nursing home after 24 disciplinary infractions, which included acts of violence. The employee then obtained employment with Maintenance Management, listing the nursing home as a former employer on his application. Subsequently, Moore, a Maintenance Management security officer, was brutally murdered by the employee. Moore's estate filed suit against the nursing home for failure to warn Maintenance Management of the employee's violent tendencies. The nursing home representative stated that they had been contacted for a reference but, according to their policy they only provided dates of employment (Green & Reibstein, 1992).

Deerings West Nursing Center vs. Scott (1990) -- Scott was an 81-year-old woman who was attacked, punched in the face, and knocked to the ground by a male employee as she paid an early morning visit to her elderly brother, a patient at the nursing home. After learning that the employee was not even a Licensed Vocational Nurse (LVN), as he stated on his application, and that he had 56 prior convictions, Scott sued the nursing home for negligence in hiring. Since the nursing home had failed to verify the employee's background, the jury awarded Scott $35,000 in actual damages and $200,000 in punitive damages (Green & Reibstein, 1992).

North Houston Pole Line Corp. vs. McAllister (1983) -- This case underscored the need to check the driving record of an employee. In this case, a man was hired as a driver for a telephone pole company. After his first week on the job, he hit several cars when driving too fast to stop behind stalled traffic. The employer had failed to check the employee's driving record. An after-the-fact check revealed that the employee had received at least five speeding tickets in the previous 18 months. The jury ruled that the employer's conduct endangered the lives of others, assessed $250,000 in punitive damages, and awarded the injured plaintiff $250,000 in compensatory damages. Also, the truck driver was assessed $50,000 in punitive damages (Green & Reibstein, 1992).

Negligent Retention

Negligent retention occurs when an employer keeps an unfit employee on the job who later commits a crime related directly or indirectly to the job. If this employee, in a position to commit a violent or criminal act, is not properly supervised, the result is *negligent supervision* (Supervisory Management, 1990). Thus, a heavy burden is placed on employers to not only thoroughly investigate, but, in the case of lack of evidence of criminal background even after concentrated effort, it is imperative to secure affirmation statements attesting to the potential employee's honesty, trustworthiness, and reliability (Marderosian, 1985).

In a case of stolen gold, precedent was set whereby the employer was held liable for negligent hiring after a cursory investigation of a prospective employee. In this case, a part-time security guard was responsible for two major thefts of gold and was instrumental in arranging a third theft with other perpetrators. Upon employing the guard, the security firm requested the employee's police records but did not contact character references listed nor query previous employers about his honesty and trustworthiness. A previous employment incident with the guard involved a theft of money from a vending machine (Green & Reibstein, 1988).

It was established that, because of the serious nature of the employee's intended service in the security industry, a detailed inquiry into the applicant's background was required to satisfy the reasonable care standard. Further, it was established that the employer had a continuing duty to retain in service only those employees who were proven fit and competent. The court indirectly indicated that the security guard should have been dismissed for the vending machine incident, before further opportunity for theft occurred (*i.e.*, meaning negligent retention) (Marderosian, 1985).

A 1989 lawsuit was filed against Appalachian Regional Healthcare, Inc., for negligence in the hiring, retention, and supervision of an employee. The employee had raped a 34-year-old mentally retarded patient of the defendant hospital. The plaintiff filed suit for this incident, and, because the hospital had allowed the employee to continue in his position even after the attack, the court ruled it further increased the victim's emotional stress (Bates, 1992).

Noted legal authority Norman Bates (1992) further advised that the degree of care used or the effort made in pre-screening and hiring employees must be proportional to the risk created by the position to be filled. He noted that the relative risk depends upon the position to be filled rather than the applicant or the job title. For example, one focal point should be access, that is, an employee's access to such items or situations as master keys, children, elderly or disabled persons, private homes, narcotics, patients, explosives, dangerous chemicals, weapons, ammunition, and nuclear power (Bates, 1988).

Negligent Investigation

As the doctrines of negligent hiring, negligent retention, and negligent supervision have emerged, a new legal theory known as negligent investigation has come to the forefront. As reported by Waterman and Maginn (1993, p.85) *"even in the most clear-cut cases, conducting an investigation is a delicate initiative, because of the potential of invasion of privacy, coercion, defamation and even false imprisonment."*

The Decision to Investigate -- Certain allegations are clearly mandated for investigations, *i.e.*, sexual harassment, racial discrimination, or any area governed by employment law. However, in other cases such as an employee's behavior not governed by law, it becomes the employer's choice to conduct an internal investigation.

Informal Investigations -- Matthew Bender (1993) noted that the scope of an investigation will vary from case to case. In certain cases, the employer may need to conduct a nominal or informal investigation, *i.e.*, in the event an employee violates a clearly articulated attendance or tardiness policy. In this regard the employer should:

- Determine if the employee was or should have been aware of the rule or policy,

- Determine if the infractions were accurately documented,

- Determine if there were mitigating circumstances that had been previously granted in similar cases involving other employees.

In cases involving an employment termination decision rather than a mere reprimand, the employer should consider the likelihood that an employee may challenge the decision and the subsequent monetary liability. In this regard, the employer should conduct a thorough investigation and review the results prior to making the decision to discharge an employee. The burden of a formal comprehensive investigation may be quite insignificant when compared to a potential legal challenge. Formal investigations are appropriate:

1)   For self-audit and prevention purposes meant to keep employees honest;

2)   In pre-disciplinary measures, prompted by a grievance;

3)   When suspicions of serious wrongdoing exist; and

4)   Because of a lawsuit or legal charge.

This section will define the caveats of negligent investigation and will present selected case examples to exemplify the seriousness of conducting complete, accurate, and high quality negligent investigations.

Investigation Guidelines -- Matthew Bender (1993) offered a number of guidelines for employers to consider in conducting a proper formal investigation. These caveats are listed below.

- The investigation should be based on the presumption that the accused/suspect is not guilty, especially if the investigation involves a discharge or termination of employment. It therefore is suggested that the investigator should be a person other than the immediate supervisor who dismissed the employee.

- Keep the investigation plan flexible. The investigator should consider all relevant facts in a particular case, not just facts recognized to be advantageous to the company. The investigator also should be prepared in the event the investigated employee presents previously unknown exculpatory evidence or claims.

- The investigator should invite an objective third-party point of view to ensure that the investigation has been conducted fairly. Thus, an investigation must not only be fairly conducted but must be made to appear fair to everyone, even to those who have no knowledge of the circumstances or facts related to a particular disciplinary action or investigative decision.

Invasion of Privacy

Invasion of privacy is protected by statutes, constitutions, common law, or by medical or other privacy laws. Within the realm of common law, there are four distinct theories for recovery on the basis of invasion of privacy. Three of these directly relevant to investigations are:

1) Public disclosure given to private life,
2) Placing in a false light, and
3) Intrusion into another's seclusion.

Each of these is described below:

Public Disclosure Given to Private Life -- An investigating company is prohibited from publicizing certain information about an individual's private affairs. If a company publicizes information that is considered highly offensive to a reasonable person and not of legitimate concern to the public, it may face financial recovery for such a violation to the common law right to privacy.

Placing in False Light -- An investigating company is prohibited from publishing or disseminating false information regarding an employee. Even though there may be no injury to the mislabeled employee's reputation, the company may face recovery for invasion of privacy.

Intrusion into Another's Seclusion -- The common law recognizes that each person is entitled to a private physical space and private psychological space. If an employer's investigation violates another's personal space in a manner that is highly offensive to a reasonable person, the employer may face recovery for invasion of privacy.

Intentional Infliction of Emotional Distress -- An investigating company is compelled to be sensitive to the emotional state of the person being investigated. If an investigation is conducted in an extreme and outrageous manner, the employer may risk the liability of intentional infliction of emotional distress. The investigator must guard against verbal or physical harassment, accusations of dishonesty, or any alleged wrongdoing during any investigative interview.

Assault and Battery

Battery is intentional harmful or offensive touching, while assault occurs if an employer creates a reasonable fear in an employee that the employer is going to touch the employee in a harmful or offensive way. An investigator must follow investigative policy, especially in the areas of employee misconduct, exposure to toxic substances, and drug and alcohol testing, to avoid assault and battery charges. The Singer Shop-Rite vs. Rangel (1980) case example illustrates how an employee can recover damages for assault and battery during investigation.

> **Landmark Case of Assault and Battery During Investigation** -- An employee of a grocery store was subjected to an interrogation during an investigation into a disappearance of company funds. The employer brought suit against the employee for embezzlement, and the employee claimed that he was assaulted by two investigators of the company. A jury awarded the employee $15,000 in damages on the assault and battery claim. The employer appealed, contending that the workers' compensation law provided the employee with his exclusive remedy, because the assault and battery was committed by a fellow employee. The appellate court rejected that argument and upheld the previous award. It ruled that an employer cannot avail itself of the workers' compensation defense where its own investigators committed an assault and battery during an investigation. (Singer Shop-Rite vs. Rangel [1980] 174 N.J. Super. 442, 416 A.2d 965 [APP. Div.], cert. denied, 85 N.J. 148, 425 A.2d 299).

Defamation

In recent years, there has been an abundance of defamation actions filed against employers regarding a broad range of employment-related situations, *i.e.*, performance evaluations, workplace investigations, disciplinary warnings, terminations, post-employment references, and administrative proceedings before workers' compensation and unemployment boards (Green & Reibstein, 1992). While workplace investigations are mentioned above as a category for legal action, the reader should recognize that all of the other categories under legal consideration also require an internal investigation.

Defamation is defined as a communication that tends to harm the reputation of another so as to lower him in the estimation of the community or to deter third persons from associating or dealing with him. Three components, reported by M.F. Hill and J.A. Wright (1993), are necessary in order for a statement to be considered defamation:

1)   It must be communicated to someone other than the plaintiff,

2)   It must be false, and

3)   It must tend to harm the plaintiff's reputation and lower his or her esteem in the community.

As a tort, defamation may arise in the course of an internal investigation, but states differ in their laws dealing with libel and slander. R. D. Freedman (1993) warned that employers should avoid speaking or publishing statements about an employee's personal affairs that are not job related or relevant to the particular investigation. He cited the case of Jacron Sales Co. vs. Sindorf in which the plaintiff-former employee alleged that a telephone conversation between the plaintiff's new employer and the vice-president of the defendant (former employer) implied that the plaintiff had stolen merchandise during his employment. The trial court directed a verdict for the defendant employer on the grounds of "qualified privilege." However the Maryland Court of Appeals reversed the decision (see the landmark case decision on the following page).

Qualified Privilege -- Elements of "qualified privilege," as reported by Hill and Wright (1993), are:

1)   Good faith by the defendant,

2)   An interest or duty to be upheld,

3)   A statement limited in its scope to the purpose,

4)   A proper occasion, and

5)   Publication in a proper manner and to proper parties only with a "need to know."

Landmark Case Regarding "Qualified Privilege" -- The Supreme Court of Alabama regarding Reynolds Metal Co. vs. Mays stated: *"Where a party makes a communication, and such communication is prompted by duty owed either to the public or to a third party, or the communication is one in which the party has an interest and it is made to another having a corresponding interest, the communication is privileged, if made in good faith and without actual malice....The duty under which the party is privileged to make the communication need not be one having the force of legal obligation, but it is sufficient if it is social or moral in its nature and defendant in good faith believes he is acting in pursuance thereof, although in fact he is mistaken"* (Reynolds Metal Co. vs. Mays [1989] Alabama Sup. Ct. 547 So. 2d 518, 5 IER 1820).

Landmark Case Regarding Defamation Related to "Qualified Privilege" -- "The adoption of a negligence standard in cases of purely private defamation hardly introduces a radical concept to tort law. The application of the negligence standard in tort cases is so well established that juries safely can be expected to comprehend the term when applied in defamation cases. We hold, therefore, that a standard of negligence, as set forth in Restatement (Second) of Torts 580B (Tend. Draft No. 21, 1975), which we here adopt, must be applied in cases of purely private defamation. Section 580B states: *'One who publishes a false and defamatory communication concerning a private person, or concerning a public official or public figure in relation to a purely private matter not affecting his conduct, fitness, or role in his public capacity, is subject to liability, if, but only if, he (a) knows that the statement is false and that it defames the other, (b) acts in reckless disregard of these matters, or (c) acts negligently in failing to ascertain them.'* It is to be noted that under the negligence statement which we adopt here, truth no longer is an affirmative defense to be established by the defendant, but instead the burden of proving falsity rests upon the plaintiff, since, under this standard, he already is required to establish negligence with respect to such falsity. We hold that proof of fault in cases of purely private defamation must meet the standard of the preponderance of the evidence. This is a quantum of proof ordinarily required in other types of actions for negligence, and is apt to be more readily understood by juries" (Jacron Sales Co. vs. Sindorf [1976] Maryland App. 350 A.2d 688).

"Qualified privilege" is limited to employee work habits and how well the employee performed on the job, and the disclosed information must be limited to employment concerns and only in response to a request by a potential employer for a recommendation or statement.

False Imprisonment -- The internal investigation process typically requires private interviewing, and, if the employee is detained or restrained, an action for false imprisonment may arise. The term, "false imprisonment" is defined for these purposes as the intentional confinement of an employee by an employer. To meet the conditions of false imprisonment, the employee must be confined within a definite physical boundary. It is irrelevant as to whether there is some means of escape, and the employee must realize that he or she is confined (Freedman, 1994).

The following case exemplifies false imprisonment and involves a 17-year-old female employee who filed false imprisonment charges against a loss prevention manager.

Landmark Case Regarding False Imprisonment -- In the case of deAngelis vs. Jamesway Department Store, a New Jersey Court awarded $110,000 to an employee who had been detained for a four-hour interrogation for an alleged theft. The loss prevention manager who conducted the investigative interview raised his voice, slammed his fist on the desk, and put his face close to hers. He also told her that she was to remain in the room until she confessed to the crime of theft (deAngelis vs. Jamesway Department Store [1985] NJ 501 A.2d 561).

Malicious Prosecution -- A legal action regarding malicious prosecution is based on a number of facts:

1)   That the employer instituted criminal proceedings against the employee,

2)   That the criminal proceedings terminated in favor of the employee,

3)   That the employer had no probable cause to institute the criminal proceedings in the first place, and

4)   That the employer was motivated primarily by some purpose other than bringing an offender to justice.

Thus, the action for malicious prosecution can only be brought after a criminal proceeding has been terminated (Freedman, 1994).

Landmark Case Regarding Malicious Prosecution -- In the case of Wainauskis vs. Howard Johnson Co., the criminal proceedings instigated by the employer charged the employee with theft of monies. The employee stated that she had not worked on the day of the theft and that others also knew the combination to the safe. While the first jury could not reach a verdict, a second jury acquitted the employee and awarded her $100,000. The jury found that the employer had initiated criminal proceedings with undue haste and without adequate internal investigations on insufficient grounds and without probable cause (Wainauskis vs. Howard Johnson Co. [1985] Pa. Super. Ct. 488 A.2d 1117).

Legality of Search and Surveillance

Federal and state statutes, constitutions, and common law rights to privacy dictate the limitations on search and surveillance. The Council on Education (1994) reported on the legality of the following methods of search and surveillance.

Surveillance -- It is suggested that an attorney be consulted before initiating an off-the-job surveillance procedure. In some cases, if the employer can prove there is a business-related reason for the investigation, it may be deemed permissible to conduct off-the-job surveillance.

Searching Work Areas -- It is suggested that the employer have a policy on searches in the employee handbook in order to alleviate the expectation of such privacy on the part of employees. It is further suggested that the employee sign the statement acknowledging an awareness of the policy. While the courts consider the reasonable expectation of privacy of the employee and the grounds for a search, such policy could justify an employer's search of desks, files, or other personal work areas if an employee is suspected of theft or other misconduct.

Wiretapping -- Wiretapping is prohibited by Title III of the Federal Omnibus Crime Control and Safe Streets Act of 1968. The law applies to communications on cellular telephones, electronic mail, and computer transmissions. However, an exception allows an employer to monitor employee phone conversations by listening on an extension to the telephone system, as long as the monitoring is done in the "ordinary course of the employer's business." In this regard, it is suggested that the employer inform all employees of the "business reason policy" to monitor phone calls and computer usage.

Polygraph Examinations -- The use of polygraph examinations are limited by the Federal Employee Polygraph Protection Act. Polygraph testing generally is restricted to preemployment screening for government employees and those involved with certain security positions.

Employment-At-Will

Employment-at-will is the concept that an employer may terminate a professional relationship with an employee at any time for any reason -- with or without cause -- unless prohibited by law or an employment contract (SHRM, 1994). The employment-at-will doctrine originated in the English Industrial Revolution when the employee and employer were free to terminate the employment relationship for any reason at any time. The doctrine was favored by the employer, but the employee had no sense of job security. With legal recognition of labor unions and substantial public criticism, the doctrine has seen a multitude of changes, over the years, which have led to near abandonment of the rule. Today, most state courts have supported the "good faith and fair dealing" rule, and most employer-employee relationships are defined on a contractual basis. Dissatisfaction with the employment-at-will doctrine was perhaps the greatest factor leading to the advent of employee handbooks and other written personnel policies of the employer (Freedman 1994).

Thoroughness of Investigation -- Reasonable investigation, as determined by the circumstances of the employment, has indeed had other problems with inconsistent court rulings. Hospitals have been required to conduct exhaustive investigations before hiring, while another employer was not held liable for an employee's molestation of a child when an investigation would not have revealed a previous conviction for sodomy (Haerle, 1984).

There are no hard and fast rules for the obligatory extent of investigation on the part of the employer. However, the degree of thoroughness, as a reasonable investigation is defined, becomes greater with each tortious employment case that enters the courtroom. The decision to hire a questionable or potentially dangerous person is followed by a contingency obligation of negligent retention (Minum, 1988).

Standards of Proof

An investigator should not hesitate to reach a conclusion for fear of being wrong. It should be remembered that few issues are black and white and that decisions regarding an investigation may need to be based on the relevant facts gathered against the foundation of the investigator's experience. While no one requires the conclusions to be right, the investigator must clearly document a good faith investigation. However, it is imperative that the investigator be cognizant of the three levels of burden of proof:

1) Beyond a reasonable doubt,
2) Clear and convincing evidence, and
3) Preponderance of the evidence.

Each standard of proof briefly is discussed below:

Beyond a Reasonable Doubt -- For criminal cases, the burden of proof is on the state prosecution to prove the guilt of an accused/suspect beyond a reasonable doubt. Therefore, in a criminal case, if the prosecution produces evidence beyond a reasonable doubt on each element of the crime, to the point where a *prima facie* case has been established, the defendant can be convicted, unless he or she accepts the burden of introducing evidence that challenges or reverses the evidence.

Clear and Convincing Evidence -- It is noted that the term "presumed innocent" is not necessarily a presumption. It merely implies that the defendant has no burden of proof to prove himself or herself innocent. In a criminal case, the state has the burden of proving each element of a crime beyond a reasonable doubt. M. Bender (1993) noted that, in civil cases, the burden of proof is on the employer. The employer is obliged to convince the fact-finder that there was "just cause" for a disciplinary action. In regard to employee dismissal, the employer's burden of proof is summarized as follows:

The most frequently cited reason for imposing the burden of proving "just cause" upon the employer is a sociological argument that the employer can impose no greater penalty than termination and thus it has a social obligation justifying this action (Mansfield, 1977).

Thus, suspicions of misconduct, even though supported by circumstantial evidence, generally are insufficient to justify an employer's action.

Preponderance of the Evidence -- Preponderance of evidence relates to civil litigation where the burden of proof is on the plaintiff. Preponderance of evidence is somewhat less than proof "beyond a reasonable doubt" and "clear and convincing evidence."

Preemployment Legislation vs. Negligent Hiring
The negligent hiring doctrine is complicated by legislation that contradicts an employer's responsibility to thoroughly investigate a potential employee's history of honesty.

Dilemmas of Employment Selection -- It is challenging to come to a realization and understanding of all the dilemmas created by legislation that limits, inhibits, or prohibits the preemployment process as a means for screening for the potentially criminal-minded applicant. This information is vital to managers because it will form the necessary basis for setting future employment selection guidelines and procedures. New hiring guidelines essentially will contain the terms thoroughness, duty to investigate, tortious acts, hiring privacy, workplace privacy, and also will address privacy outside the workplace. This information especially is vital for planning protective services for the elderly and disabled.

The Paradox of EEOC and Negligent Hiring -- The Equal Employment Opportunity Commission was established to enforce Title VII of the Civil Rights Act of 1964 and has become the cornerstone of anti-discrimination laws in the United States (Wendover, 1989). Besides Title VII, the EEOC administers the Equal Pay Act, the Age Discrimination in Employment Act, a portion of the Rehabilitation Act, and the Americans with Disabilities Act (Gutman, 1993).
Both corporate and private personnel departments face a paradoxical situation in that the doctrine of negligent hiring dictates some specific responsibilities for the employer in the hiring and retention of trustworthy, safe-minded employees, but the EEOC effectively inhibits the preemployment screening process, and, essentially, contradicts the theory of negligent hiring and retention.
Perhaps the greatest contradiction to the negligent hiring doctrine is that the EEOC has certain restrictions regarding an employer's possible requirement that applicants or employees have no previous arrest record. It states that it is unlawful to reject an applicant on the basis of conviction of a crime unless the crime was substantially related to job responsibilities. While an applicant convicted of embezzlement could be refused employment as a bookkeeper, a convicted rapist would not

necessarily be refused a position as bookkeeper (Wendover, 1989). In this situation, if the convicted rapist is hired as a bookkeeper and rapes again, either committing the crime at the workplace or assaulting a fellow employer outside the workplace, it is possible that the employer may be held liable. However, the employer does not have the right to not hire the potential rapist as a bookkeeper.

Prevention of Negligent Hiring -- Noted employment consultant Robert W. Wendover (1993) provided a comprehensive list of steps to take in screening candidates to protect against negligent hiring:

1) *Review applicable federal, state, and local laws to ensure your process conforms to all such laws.*

2) *Comply with federal, state, and local fair credit reporting laws if a credit check is conducted.*

3) *Look for gaps in employment and other suspicious or unusual entries in the candidates' applications.*

4) *Call each reference listed on the application.*

5) *Obtain a signed waiver and consent form from each applicant to conduct a full reference check.*

6) *Document all information received, including licenses, diplomas, and certificates, as well as efforts to obtain this information if it was not available.*

7) *Require all employees who have served in the armed forces to provide a copy of their DD Form-214 stating they were discharged honorably.*

8) *Decide whether it is appropriate to conduct a criminal records search in view of the job being filled.*

9) *Do not offer employment until screening and testing has been completed.*

10) *If appropriate, require a physical examination of the applicant. Make sure the applicant consents to the examination, and that all procedures comply with the Americans with Disabilities Act.*

11) *Even if an employee is transferring within the organization, reexamine his fitness for the new position* (p. 21).

Employer Liability for Acts of Employees

An employer can be held liable for acts or omissions of an employee.

Tort of Interference With the Employee Relationship -- Generally speaking, the tort of interference with the employment relationship arises in the following employment situations:

1)   Where a former employer provides an unfavorable post-employment job reference that results in the rejection of the employee for a new job,

2)   Where a supervisor interferes with an employee's job performance or causes the employee's termination from employment,

3)   Where an employer seeks to enforce a noncompetition provision in the employee's contract of employment, or

4)   Where the defendant who is a competitor of the employer procures the discharge of the employee.

However, it legally is justifiable for an employer to provide truthful information or honest advice about a former employee, even though the employer may intentionally cause the prospective employer not to offer the job to the employee (Freedman, 1994).

Post-Employment Liability

Investigations during post-employment may stem from wrongful discharge or defamatory post-employment references.

Landmark Case of Employer Interference -- In the 1986 Geyer vs. Steinbronn case, a Pennsylvania jury returned a verdict of $100,000 in compensatory damages and $50,000 in punitive damages in favor of an employee who did not get a job with a prospective employer. In this case, the employee had sought a security position with another company. During a routine investigation of his employment reference, the former employee's supervisor told the investigator that the former employee had been fired, that the former employee was the subject of an investigation into check forgeries, and that the investigative report had been turned over to the district attorney's office. The former employee filed suit for interference with prospective contractual relations and defamation. It was found that the employee had not been fired, and the "forgery matter" was never referred to the district attorney's office (Freedman, 1994).

R.M. vs. McDonald's Corp. (1991) -- This illustrates the need to contact references listed by the applicant. In this case, a 37-year-old man, was referred to the McDonald's restaurant chain by the Colorado Division of Vocational Rehabilitation. He previously had been convicted for child molestation and was on parole. The agency had failed to inform the fast food chain of the employee's criminal conviction, and the manager of the restaurant failed to contact all references listed by the applicant. The employee subsequently assaulted a 3-year-boy in the restaurant restroom. The boy's parents sued the fast food chain for negligent hiring and sued the State of Colorado for failing to provide an appropriate applicant. The jury found the State of Colorado to be 55% at fault, and the fast food chain to be 45% at fault. Damages were assessed at $210,000 (Green & Reibstein, 1992).

Landmark Case Regarding Defamatory Post-Employment References -- In the case of Frank B. Hall & Co. vs. Buck, a salesman called "a zero" in a post-employment reference was awarded $1.9 million, which included $1.3 million in punitive damages. An investigator was hired to learn what the insurance company was saying about the salesman who had been fired. One of the salesman's former co-workers reported that the salesman was *"untrustworthy...not always entirely truthful...disruptive...paranoid...hostile and was guilty of padding his expense account."* Another former co-worker stated that the salesman was *"horrible in a business sense, irrational, ruthless, and disliked by office personnel."* He also described the salesman as "a zero." The Court stated that it was reasonable for the jury to have found that the personal verbal attacks on the salesman were false and defamatory to the extent they injured his reputation. (Frank B. Hall & Co. vs. Buck, 678 S.W.2d 612 Tex. Ct. App. [1984], cert denied, 472 U.S. 1009 [1985]).

It has been documented that employers have been held liable for former employees. In another Minnesota case of a fired employee who raped a customer, the employer was found liable for not warning customers of the ex-employee's violent propensities. However, there have been some inconsistencies in court interpretations in that a parking lot owner was not held liable for a parking lot attendant's assault on a customer (Haerle, 1984).

Employer's Right of Discharge -- Warren Freedman (1994) reported that, over the centuries, the employer's right of discharge or termination increasingly has been restricted by court decisions and federal and state statutes. Terms such as termination in "bad faith" and termination for "good cause" have come to be an employer's downfall or justification for post-employment suits. At any rate, an employee who is discharged as a result of an internal investigation or other act violating his privacy rights may have a claim for contract damages for wrongful termination of employment. This was the case of Rulon-Miller vs. IBM (1984), where the employee's right of privacy was acknowledged in the employer's policies but disregarded by the employer's conduct surrounding the employee discharge. A case representing "bad faith" termination is seen in Zaretsky vs. New York City Health and Hospitals Corp. (1991), where the discharged employee showed that his termination had been made in bad faith, and the employer's failure to hold a hearing was a violation of his due process rights.

On the other hand, discharge or termination for "good cause" is the employer's justification.

> **Landmark Case Regarding "Good Cause" Discharge** -- In the case of Clutterham vs. Coachman Industries, Inc., the plaintiff had been employed by the defendant for seven years when the parties entered into a written employment contract which contained a termination clause that authorized either party to terminate on 30 days' written notice. Several months later, the plaintiff was discharged on the grounds that sales of the product had declined, and the employer had determined to consolidate its operations elsewhere. The trial court granted summary judgment for the employer, finding that there was good cause for the termination due to the depressed industry conditions. The appellate court affirmed, stating that *"courts must take care not to interfere with a legitimate exercise of managerial discretion....Nothing suggests that, in making the business judgment to reorganize its marketing operations, respondent had a duty to consider appellant's economic interest and try to preserve his job...."* (Clutterham vs. Coachman Industries, Inc. [1985], 169 Call. App. 3d 1223).

Other circumstances for an employer to discharge an employee for just or good cause are found in the areas of absenteeism or tardiness, insubordination, misconduct, unsatisfactory performance, moonlighting, horseplay, fighting, off-duty misconduct, dress and grooming codes, seniority rules, and work slowdowns and stoppages.

Illegal Terminations

Certain types of employment terminations which may be considered illegal are constructive discharge, retaliatory discharge, and involuntary or coerced retirement. Each is defined below:

Constructive Discharge -- Constructive discharge occurs when the employer creates a working condition that is so intolerable that the employee is forced into involuntary resignation (SHRM, 1994).

Retaliatory Discharge -- An employment termination might be considered retaliatory if it is the result of an employer "punishing" an employee for engaging in a protected activity. These activities might include:

1)   Filing a discrimination charge;

2)   Opposing unlawful employer practices; or

3)   Testifying, assisting, or participating in an investigation, proceeding, or litigation against the employer under any of the labor relations, OSHA, workers' compensation, or unemployment compensation acts.

A charge of retaliatory discharge becomes valid if an employee can prove that he or she was engaged in a protected activity and subsequently was discharged, and that a causal connection exists between that activity and the discharge (SHRM, 1994).

Involuntary Retirement -- If an employee takes involuntary retirement because he or she was offered a choice of early retirement, demotion, or dismissal, the employer may be sued for age discrimination. For a charge to be valid, employees have to prove that they were coerced into early retirement because of unlawful age considerations. However, employers may be protected from such charges if they can prove the following:

1)   That they provided accurate information about the plan and benefits,

2)   That they provided honest information about future job prospects with the employer,

3)   That they allowed sufficient time for employees to make considered decisions,

4)   That they assured employees that the offers might freely be declined (SHRM, 1994).

Layoffs Without Lawsuits -- Whenever an employer considers discharging or laying off employees, great care must be taken so as not to violate the employees' rights. Often times, a high-quality internal workplace investigation is the key to preventing post-employment lawsuits.

Summary of Negligent Doctrine
As the litigation literature indicates, there has been a proliferation of lawsuits against employers for negligent hiring, negligent retention, and negligent supervision. Each of these have emerged as workplace torts and have serious ramifications for the human resource manager and administrator, especially in the areas of formal internal workplace investigations for preemployment and employment situations. Thus, a more recent tort has emerged, called negligent investigation. This chapter explained the emergence of common-law tort theories relevant to workplace investigations and presented landmark case examples of how these torts

specifically apply to workplace investigations. The interrelatedness of preemployment screening and hiring and the evolution of the negligent hiring doctrine specifically was emphasized.

CHAPTER THREE

EMPLOYEE DEVIANCE
AND
WORKPLACE INVESTIGATIONS

Defining Employee Deviance

Employee deviance is described here as any counterproductive behavior that may cause, either directly or indirectly, loss of resources, assets, profits, goodwill, and/or time to the employing company. While there are numerous categories of employee deviance, specific to occupation and industry, Appendix B of this text illustrates the common acts of employee deviance for some notable and highly populated industry groups. A review of the deviant behaviors for these representative groups can assist the human resource practitioner or investigator in assimilating the vulnerabilities and risks inherent for other groups and occupations not listed.

The Impact of Employee Counterproductive Behavior

The negative impact of deviant or counterproductive behavior in the workplace can be observed in a number of areas. The two most obvious are loss of productive time on the job due to absences, tardiness, or even a negative attitude toward work, and shrinkage or internal theft of cash or merchandise. Both of these aspects are manifestations of employee dishonesty.

The Cost of Employee Deviance -- The cost of all forms of employee dishonesty (*i.e.*, substance abuse, tangible theft, lost time, and related legal entanglements) is estimated to be more than $300 billion each year. This counterproductive behavior also is costly in an intangible way in that it degrades overall productivity by negatively impacting morale, distracting productive workers, heightening turnover, and driving away those who do not want to associate with it (Kuhn, 1991).

Dishonesty in the Workplace -- Dishonesty in the workplace has reached epidemic proportions and costs American industry $50 billion a year. Besides this extraordinary loss, it is estimated that approximately one-third of all business failures are due to employee theft and dishonesty. The third appalling note is that approximately 40% of employees are dishonest in the workplace (Rafilson, 1991).

Retail establishments tend to suffer the greatest losses, approximately $817 million annually, while financial institutions experience internal thefts of $382 million per year. The U.S. Department of Commerce estimates that total losses nationwide amount to 1% of the Gross National Product and is increasing 15% per year (London House, 1986).

A recent National Retail Security Survey, that reports on 423 retailers, revealed that employee theft represents the largest source of loss and accounts for an average of 38% of all store losses (Zalud, 1991). According to the National Business Crime Information Network, American businesses in 1988 lost $200 billion to cash and merchandise thefts committed by employees (Shepard & Dustin, 1988).

A 1993 National Retail Security Survey (NRSS) revealed that employee theft is the most significant source of shrinkage. The study involved 386 respondents who represented 23 different retail segments. The survey reported a specific composite of theft that attributed 40.7% to employee theft, 33.7% to shoplifting, 18.2% to administrative error, and 7.4% to vendor fraud (Hollinger, *et al.*, 1993).

The total loss, however, can be estimated only in a subjective manner, but that estimation is, of course, much higher than the aforementioned figures. Research indicates that only about 20% of all employee theft is detected and that almost half of all employees at some time steal to some degree. Additionally, it has been discovered that theft-prone people are attracted to jobs that offer greater theft opportunity (Kuhn, 1991).

Jack L. Hayes (1994), a specialist in inventory shrinkage control and loss prevention, noted that retailers lose eight times more merchandise to dishonest employees than to shoplifters. Hayes recommended that prevention of undesirable individuals from entry into the workforce has proven time and again to be an effective way of controlling internal theft. He especially recommended such preemployment screening practices as skilled interviewing and drug and honesty testing.

Loss Prevention Strategies

The Hollinger NRSS (1993) study, mentioned above, examined 52 different loss prevention strategies, which were grouped into four classifications: preemployment integrity screening, employee awareness programs, asset control policies, and loss prevention systems. Each of these practices are discussed below:

Employee Integrity Screening -- The survey inquired about the utilization of 14 different employee integrity screening techniques. Past employment verification was the most commonly employed technique (87%), multiple interviews ranked second (72.5%), and personal reference checks ranked third (66.1%). The verification techniques ranking between 45% and 25% were: criminal conviction checks (44%), credit history checks (40.2%), driving history checks (35.8%), pencil-and-paper honesty tests (31.9%), and education verification (28.8%). Only 21.8% used drug screening.

Loss Prevention Awareness Programs -- Nine different loss prevention awareness programs were cited. The top three programs were reported to be discussion during orientation (71.8%), periodic programs (63.2%), and bulletin boards/posters (58.8%). Training videos (48.4%), honesty incentives (38.3%), anonymous telephone hotlines (35.8%), and newsletters (35.5%) were secondary choices. Only 25% or fewer used paycheck stuffers and audio training tapes.

Asset Control Policies -- The most widely used approaches to preventing inventory shrinkage were the use of various types of asset control policies. The 10 most popular types of controls are ranked in order: refund controls (86.5%), void controls (80.6%), merchandise receiving controls (75.9%), controlled access to cash (72.5%), interstore transfer controls (69.7%), price change controls (67.9%), employee package checks (59.1%), unobserved exit controls (57.3%), trash removal controls (55.2%), and point-of-sale exception reports (53.9%).

Additional Forms of Workplace Deviance -- Besides worker theft by stealing, there is another type of workplace deviance -- production deviance, which essentially includes counterproductive behavior such as sabotage, not being at the job, or not performing assigned duties. R.C. Hollinger and J.P. Clark (1983) believed that the same factors used to explain worker theft are equally good predictors of counterproductive behavior.

Combating Employee Theft/Deviance -- Perhaps the best theft prevention technique is the relationships between workers. Hollinger (1982b) reported that if employees *"signal that theft is unacceptable and will not be tolerated, much lower levels of theft are observed"* (p. 29). Another technique might be in providing employee incentives, such as a profit-sharing plan, in order to provide a psychological effect of linking the employees' actions directly to the profitability of the company (Hollinger, 1989).

Drug and Alcohol Abuse Defined

The United States Department of Justice defines illicit drug use as the use of prescription psycho-therapeutic drugs for nonmedical purposes or the use of illegal drugs. In fact, some experts define illicit drug use as drug abuse, while others believe drug abuse is illicit drug use that results in social, economic, psychological, or legal problems for the user. People take drugs mainly for the effects they produce (*i.e.*, mood change, excitement, relaxation, pleasure, stimulation, or sedation). Heroin is taken to reduce pain, cocaine produces excitement, marijuana provides feelings of excitement and intoxication, and stimulants increase alertness (U.S. Dept. Justice, 1992).

Cost of Drug and Alcohol Abuse -- It is estimated that the economic cost of drug abuse in the workplace is $30 billion per year, and the National Institute on

Drug Abuse reported that drug and alcohol abuse costs the United States nearly $100 billion in lost productivity each year. It has been determined that drug users have three times as many accidents as non-users, are absent from work two-and-one-half times more than non-users, and have three times the medical costs of non-users. They are seven times more likely to have their wages garnished, are more likely than non-users to steal company and co-worker property, and are more likely to experience strained relationships with other employees (Douglas, *et al.*, 1989).

It has been reported that alcohol abuse alone costs $71.5 billion annually in lost productivity and absenteeism, and drug abuse costs $34 billion. The National Institute on Drug Abuse (NIDA) estimated that between 500,000 and 750,000 people use heroine regularly and that approximately 17 million people are alcoholics (Shepard, *et al.*, 1989).

Impact of Drug and Alcohol Abuse in the Workplace -- Drug and alcohol abuse, both on the job and in employees' private lives, has a significant impact on the business world and national economy. At least 50 train accidents have been linked to drug and alcohol abuse and have left 37 people dead, 80 injured, and more than $34 million in property damage (London House, 1986). Some major costly effects on productivity of individual drug/alcohol users are listed below. Drug abusers are:

1) At least three times as likely to be involved in an accident (*i.e.*, work-related or at home),

2) Likely to have more than twice as many absences of eight days or more,

3) Likely to receive at least three times the average amount of sick benefits,

4) At least five times as likely to file workers' compensation claims,

5) At least seven times as likely to be the target of garnishment of wages,

6) Likely to function at about 65% or less of one's work potential, and

7) More apt to participate in employee counterproductive behavior.

Employers' Concerns Regarding Drug and Alcohol Abuse

Workplace-related drug use is a great concern for employers, especially in the areas of safety, productivity, and health.

Safety -- The greatest concerns for safety are centered around high-precision or high-risk occupations such as air traffic controllers, airline flight crews, railroad workers, truck drivers, energy workers *(e.g.,* miners and nuclear power plant workers), construction, medical care (*e.g.,* doctors and nurses, emergency paramedics, and laboratory technicians), law enforcement, firefighters, and the military.

Productivity -- The greatest concerns for productivity center around poor work performance, such as shoddily manufactured products; badly considered decisions; and slow moving, understaffed business or services. Absenteeism, sickness, and turnover also reduce productivity. Worker relationships also are jeopardized by drug abuse in that it causes mood changes and leads to unreliable and sometimes dangerous worker relationships where workers depend upon one another in teamwork.

Health -- Another central concern for employers is the increasing costs of health care which tend to grow even more with drug- and alcohol-related health problems. It is not difficult to realize how closely worker health is tied to worker productivity and safety of the workplace in that drug use may result in greater absenteeism and tardiness, illness, injury, legal incidents, and family problems. The U.S. Department of Justice (1992) reported that drug and alcohol abuse can harm the health of users. A list of possible harmful affects are:

1)   Death;

2)   Medical emergencies from acute reactions;

3)   Exposure to HIV infection, hepatitis, and other diseases resulting from intravenous injections;

4)   Injury from accidents related to drug impairment;

5)   Dependence or addiction; or

6)   Chronic or physical problems related to illness or debilitation.

Violence in the Workplace

At one time, violence in the workplace was considered to be only in the realm of deviant behavior. Currently, violence is becoming commonplace and may be occurring in epidemic proportions. The Reuter Business Report (Reuter, 1993) noted that, last year alone, there were 750 homicides and an estimated 300,000 acts of violence at the workplace, which cost employers $4.2 billion and imposed untold trauma on workers and management. Research attributes the high level of workplace violence to dramatic changes resulting in employment-related stress, drug and alcohol abuse, and external conflicts such as marital and family problems

Employment-Related Stress -- The corporate trend of the 1990s has been a dramatic *downsizing,* which has created a large subset of displaced workers. Those workers who have perpetrated homicide and violence at the workplace are reported to have become so overwhelmed with feelings of futility that they emotionally explode.

Drugs, Alcohol, and Violence -- Drugs and violence are linked in multiple ways. It has been reported that many of those who have perpetrated violent acts in the workplace have used and abused drugs and alcohol. It is suggested that such abuse has resulted in distorted and even hallucinated thinking that leads to such violent behavior. Drug and alcohol abuse also is strongly correlated to crime in that addictions cause people to steal to support the habit, and personal morals and values deteriorate. The profiles of drugs described above have two commonalties: overdosage can result in death, and most drugs tend to produce violent behavior.

Workplace Violence Stemming from Family Problems

A number of homicides at the workplace have involved marital partners and boyfriend/girlfriend relationships. It is surmised that, since legal restraining orders often keep violence out of the home, the violence is then diverted to the workplace, where the perpetrators more easily can gain access to their targets.

Also, it is recognized that people who suffer violence in the family setting often become problems in the workplace. Researcher Janet Deming (1991) reported that, in 1981, it was estimated that business losses from absenteeism related to family violence ranged from $3 to 5 billion annually and $100 billion in abuse-related medical costs. She reported that a Minnesota-based HMO determined that between 60 and 80% of its chemical dependency treatment patients also suffered from family-related violence. Deming also referred to studies by the National Institute of Mental Health, which indicate that 20 to 50% of American couples have violent marriages.

Judith Boyd (1994) of Kaiser Permanente filed a similar alarming report and stated that every 15 seconds someone is a victim of domestic violence. She also noted that, in one year in the 1990s, American family violence resulted in 4,000 deaths, 21,000 hospitalizations, 28,700 emergency room visits, and more than $44 million in direct care costs. One out of two women experiences at least one episode of physical abuse in a relationship, one out of five women experience serious ongoing physical abuse, and one out of three women who present themselves at emergency rooms are victims of domestic violence. It is not difficult to realize that the ramifications of family violence present costly and challenging problems in the workforce.

Drugs and Family Relations -- Drug use also can have adverse affects on family relationships and finances. Specifically:

1)   Large expenditures for drugs drain family economics,

2) Drug and alcohol abuse draws from essential emotional support for the user's partner and children,

3) Drug and alcohol abuse limits participation in household and family activities,

4) Drug and alcohol abuse results in the user's failure to provide an adequate role model for children, and

5) Drug and alcohol abuse limits the ability for a family to accumulate wealth and family equity (U.S. Dept. of Justice, 1992).

Employee/Client Violence -- Another type of workplace violence occurs in hospitals, nursing homes, board and care homes, daycare centers *(i.e.,* for children or elderly), and other institutions that provide services for children, the elderly, the sick, and the disabled. With increasing frequency, professional and paraprofessional caretakers are perpetrators of violent acts such as physical abuse, rape, verbal abuse, and inadequate care. For a comprehensive report on such abuse, see *Crimes Against The Elderly* (Slowik, 1993). This aspect of workplace violence is mentioned here as a grim reminder of the importance of understanding the doctrine of negligent hiring and negligent retention and the inherent value of adequate preemployment testing and screening.

Research on Violence in the Workplace -- Psychiatrist Dr. Paul Deitz (1994) reported that multiple-murder incidents are occurring at the workplace at the rate of three per month. Concern for workplace safety led to the study *Fear and Violence in the Workplace,* by N.K. Friedrichs and associates, which was commissioned by the Minnesota-based Northwestern National Life (Carlson, 1993). The study was based on a representative sample of 600 full-time U.S. workers. It reported that one out of four American workers was attacked, threatened, or harassed on the job during the previous year. Several other findings were cited in the study:

1) More than 2 million Americans were physically attacked while at work during the past year, 6.3 million were threatened, and 16.1 million were harassed.

2) Of the workers surveyed, 15% indicated that they have been physically attacked on the job at some time during their working life, and 21% said a co-worker had been threatened with physical harm during the past year.

3) One in six attacks on the job involved a lethal weapon.

4) Physical attacks were twice as likely to come from a customer than a co-worker or stranger.

5)   Harassment was considered to be more psychologically damaging than physical attacks and resulted in comparable levels of illness or injury. These victims were more than twice as likely to not report the incident.

Profile of Violent Offender -- The typical workplace killer presents a different sociological profile than the typical murderer. The workplace murderer typically is described as a disgruntled, middle-aged white male weapons' buff who tends to blame others for his downfall and abuses drugs and/or alcohol. He generally is a loner who identifies more with his job than any relationship and may be considered a religious fanatic. It is noted that this type of person often shows signs of imbalance and, before the violent incident, makes threats which tend to go unnoticed by managers and fellow workers.

Risk Taking and the Workplace

Two other forms of deviance that create concerns in the workplace are employee risk taking and gambling. The degree of safety at the workplace can be measured by the degree of employee awareness of danger and commitment to avoiding or preventing accidents. While risk taking is the cause of almost all accidents, Dr. Willem A. Wagemarr (1992), a professor of Experimental Psychology at Leiden University, the Netherlands, noted that behaviors leading to accidents occur at three levels: operational (*i.e.*, routine shop-floor behavior), tactical (*i.e.*, incidental decisions), and strategic *(i.e.*, planning and long-term decisions). He advised that, while errors at all levels lead to accidents, a conscious evaluation of risks can be expected only at the strategic level. To support this logic, Wagemarr states that the answer to the question, *"Are those directly involved in the causation of accidents misperceiving or knowingly accepting risks?"* should be *"no,"* because they function at the operational level. However, the answer to a more general question, *"Are accidents preceded by misperception or conscious acceptance of risks?"* should be *"yes."* Wagemarr (1991) states that *"risk communication, when aimed at a decline of accident rates, should be directed at the strategic level"* (p. 280).

Dr. Baruch Fischhoff (1985, p. 29) made the observation that *"people disagree more about what risk is than about how large it is."* It was proposed by Yates and Stone (1992) that the critical elements of risk are:

1)   Potential losses,
2)   The significance of those losses, and
3)   The uncertainty of those losses.

These researchers also pointed out two major classes of risk-taking behavior: deliberative, in which the person literally decides how to act and weighs risk against other factors, and non-deliberative, in which the person does not take risk into account, as if risk taking were inadvertent.

Gambling and the Workplace

It was explained by E.C. Devereau (1968) that systematic treatises on gambling are sadly lacking, and there are but scattered bits of useful knowledge and theory. P. Bromiley and S.P. Curley (1992) noted that gambling as a pathological behavior, and the legal aspects of it, have been extensively researched. Devereau (1968) stated that existing treatments are speculative, impressionistic, and moralistic and tend to be employed without adequate data.

It is beyond the scope of this publication to fully examine the literature, limited as it is, on both risk taking and gambling. There still is much to learn about the nature of risk-taking behavior and how to improve its effectiveness. It is, however, imperative to mention that the excessive use of drugs and alcohol has a great influence on an employee's cognitive, functional level at the workplace and leads to a high level of risk taking which directly impacts safety at the workplace.

Preventing Workplace Violence

As with all behavior, it is recognized that the best predictor of violence is a person's previous history of violence. Perhaps the best prevention is not to hire the person in the first place (Deming, 1991; Reuter, 1993; and Stuart, 1992). California attorney William W. Floyd (1993) suggested:

> *The keys to avoiding workplace violence are taking preventive steps to avoid hiring individuals who have the potential for violence and investigating and taking prompt action at the first sign of potential problems in this area* (p. 3).

A comprehensive understanding of the impacts of drug and alcohol abuse and the interrelationships with crime and violence, will, perhaps, lead practitioners to strongly consider a preemployment drug and alcohol testing protocol. Personality tests may reveal a person's propensity for violent behavior, and, of course, an extensive background and reference check include an investigation regarding any past antisocial and violent behaviors. All of these tactics serve as proactive preemployment screening techniques to avoid hiring those applicants with the propensity for deviant behavior.

Summary of Employee Deviance

This chapter has defined employee deviance and its negative impact on the workplace. Loss prevention strategies were suggested, and a comprehensive table of common acts of employee deviance is presented in Appendix B. Special emphasis was made on drug and alcohol abuse and violence in the workplace. The correlation between drugs and family relations was discussed in terms of its effect on employee behavior in the workplace. The chapter closed with a discussion on preventing workplace violence.

PART II

THE ELEMENTS OF SUCCESSFUL INVESTIGATIONS
DEPTH COMPONENT

The Depth Component serves as preparatory instruction for an interviewer and investigator to conduct complete and effective internal investigations. The section presents five chapters having the following instructional objectives:

1)   To present some major tools to be utilized by the interviewer and investigator, *i.e.*, methods of screening and methods of interviewing;

2)   To describe the elements of employment law that specifically relate to areas that dictate the protocol for internal investigations;

3)   To portray a behavioral model for verbal and nonverbal communication and describe the major body zones involved in the communication process;

4)   To describe communication as an interactive process and present a psychological and physiological explanation of verbal and nonverbal behavior in relation to truthful and deceptive communication; and

5)   To portray the skills, attributes, knowledge, and abilities of a competent professional practitioner or investigator.

CHAPTER FOUR

TOOLS AND TECHNIQUES
FOR
WORKPLACE INVESTIGATIONS

This chapter presents an overview of the tools and techniques available to assist human resource managers and administrators in conducting internal workplace investigations in three particular areas: preemployment, employment, and post-employment matters.

Legal authorities Hart and Houck (1992, p. 4) have pointed out that the most significant benefit of a good internal investigation is that it enables management to get the information it needs to manage effectively. They state:

> *Any defects in the investigation identified in the corporation's organizational structure of procedures, or any problems with staff, can be corrected. Ill-trained, negligent, or corrupt employees can be educated, disciplined, or discharged as the case may be. In short, the investigation provides management with an important tool to identify fundamental changes necessary to ensure the corporation's future well-being. Any investigation, of course, is not without risks. As indicated, the investigation may uncover information requiring disclosure. It may also reveal that important management personnel, significant to the corporation's success, are involved in potential wrongdoing. In addition, it can disrupt business operations, hurt employee morale and bring bad publicity. Frequently, however, such negative consequences are inevitable in any event. Indeed, delay in dealing with a problem often exacerbates it. A properly conducted investigation, however, allows management to seize the initiative, forestalls any implications of a cover-up, and provides control over the timing and manner of any disclosure or publicity. Also, the investigation may*

*reveal that no problem exists or is less severe than feared,
thereby lifting a cloud that hangs over the corporation and permitting normal operations to resume.*

Preemployment Selection Process

Based on the premise that past behavior is predictive of future behavior, employers tend to conduct extensive investigations of applicants' work histories and personal backgrounds. To accomplish this task, a number of techniques are employed in order to gain the most information from each applicant. Among these techniques are preemployment interviews, preemployment testing, and background and reference checks. A comprehensive review of nearly a century of research on personnel selection can be found in *Universal Interviewing and Communications: A Preemployment Application* (Slowik, 1995), while brief descriptions of these approaches are presented here.

Preemployment Selection Interviewing

The term *"interview"* is derived from its French counterpart, *entrevoir,* meaning to have a glimpse of or to see imperfectly. A contemporary working definition of preemployment selection interviewing can be understood as a dialogue to gather information for the purpose of evaluating the qualifications of an applicant for employment. This definition suggests that the selection interview involves much more than the face-to-face meeting. Although one of the least sophisticated methods, the interview is the one that most organizations heavily rely upon to select employees. There has been a recent trend toward an integrated approach to interviewing which has resulted in models proposed by Schmitt (1976), Avery and Campion (1982), Dreher and Sackett (1983), Dipboye (1982), and Dipboye and Macon (1988). These approaches incorporated three components of an interview into one framework, that is,

1)   Social process,
2)   Information processing, and
3)   Outcomes of the interview.

The following section is a brief description of a number of some popular contemporary models which contain many attributes for successful interviewing. They are reviewed in chronological order:

The Evaluation Interview Model -- The model for conducting the Evaluation Interview was developed by Richard Fear (Drake, 1982, and Fear & Chiron, 1990) and is highly structured and controlled by the interviewer. It is designed to enable a manager to make an informed, confident, hire or not-hire decision. It begins with a brief introduction which aims to minimize small talk and interruption by the applicant. The planned interview then explores the candidate's life history and is controlled by asking the applicant self-appraisal questions that follow a specific sequence allowing the applicant to talk while the interviewer gathers facts and other data. This procedural format is meant to allow the interviewer to see some indication of the applicant's social perceptivity.

The Executive Interview -- A second behaviorally structured model employs the psychology of perception of emotions, motivation, and background and is designed to provide answers to problems of morale and motivation. The process is complex and involves a dynamic interchange which builds up with reaction leading to response, then back to reaction. The interviewer directs, paces, and times the process while encouraging the interviewee to talk as spontaneously as possible, providing a social interaction designed to bring into historical focus that which has contributed to the present (Balinsky & Burger, 1959).

The Kinesic Interview Technique -- Described by researchers Frederick Link and D. Glen Foster (1980), the Kinesic Interview Technique serves as a diagnostic approach to evaluate, observe, and analyze what is seen during the interview. It primarily is used to gain information from someone who intentionally is not disclosing adequate or accurate information. The underlying concepts of the kinesic method are based on stress and the resultant symptoms or signs kinetically manifested from stressful situations. These symptoms are seen in both psychological and physiological realms. This model recognizes that behavior is anything a person says or does and that *"everything means something"* but that *"no one behavior means anything by itself."*

The Situational Interview -- As developed by researchers G.P. Latham, L.M. Saari, E.D. Pursell, and Michael Campion (1980), the Situational Interview is based on the theory that future performance of applicants can be predicted from knowledge of their goals and intentions. The first step involves analyzing a job using the critical-incident procedure and selecting those incidents that best represent dimensions of performance for questioning. The process poses hypothetical situations, and applicants are evaluated on behaviorally anchored rating scales containing possible answers and benchmarks for evaluating applicant responses.

The Tailored Selection Interview -- The Tailored Selection Interview, introduced by James G. Goodale (1982), is a semi-structured interview tailored to a specific job. It requires acute awareness of EEO law and is meant to meet both the interviewer's and applicant's objectives of information giving, information receiving, and testing of personal chemistry. The interview is conversational to encourage discussion, and it requires the interviewer to focus, probe, listen carefully, and evaluate. It is essential that the interviewer be aware of eye contact, body language, and voice.

The Casework Interview Model -- The Casework Interview Model, developed by Annette Garrett (1898-1957) of Smith College, requires a unique, humanistic approach (1982). This method is pertinent for such professionals as attorneys, physicians, nurses, newspaper reporters, police officers, members of the clergy, counselors, credit personnel, certain personnel managers, and employees of the human service spectrum. It requires the interviewer to assume leadership throughout the interview by unobtrusively directing it and by deciding when to listen, when to talk, what to observe, and how to interpret. This leadership style is based on the premise that intellectual understanding is barren unless accompanied by emotional understanding.

The Cognitive Behavioral Interview Model -- The Cognitive Behavioral Interview Model emphasizes the internal mental processes that occur when a person is stimulated by an external force -- that is, when people exhibit a behavioral reaction to certain stimuli (Dubrin, 1988). This model, developed by Tom Janz and associates, is based on the principle: *"The best predictor of behavior/performance is past behavior/performance in similar circumstances"* (Janz, Hellervick, & Gilmore, 1986, p. 32).

The Patterned Behavioral Description Interview (PBDI) -- The PBDI is related to the Cognitive Behavioral Model but follows the critical incident framework for questions by asking *"What did you do to overcome the crisis situation?"* (Janz, 1982; Opren, 1985).

Structured Integrity Interview -- The Structured Integrity Interview, developed by Charles Wilson (1988), employs structured questions about how the applicant hypothetically would respond to scenarios related to theft and dishonest behavior in the workplace. Michael McDaniel (1988) describes the instrument as one of the most promising new strategies in personnel interviewing because of much higher validity levels than the traditional interview (Jones & Terris, 1991a).

The In-Depth Selection Interview Guide -- The In-Depth Selection Interview, designed by Bradford D. Smart (1989), is applicable to all interview situations and utilizes a structured interviewer guide which includes a detailed application form and a rating scale summary. The guide contains specific questions, based on the job application form, to produce revealing responses regarding education, work history, plans and goals, management style, and interpersonal relations skills. The model is designed to be complete and consistent in that all interviewers ask the same prescribed, chronologically guided questions, and answers are recorded in the appropriate blanks of the interview schedule. The guide avoids legally forbidden questions and is designed to obtain a natural, warm dialogue directed by the interviewer.

A Scientific Interviewing Approach -- Described by Frank MacHovec (1989), the Scientific Interviewing Approach requires the interviewer to act as a serious researcher in considering every contact with another person. The scientific strategy combines interviewing and interrogation in a specialized manner that evaluates the many facets of past and present truth. It is impersonal, objective, organized, and meticulous.

The Integrity Interview for Personnel Selection -- The Integrity Interview for Personnel Selection stems from nearly a half century of interrogation and interviewing practices developed by John E. Reid and Associates (1993). The primary function of the integrity interview is to discern truth or deception by learning the "Who, What, Where, When, and How" (*i.e.*, factual information) in a non-accusatory, conversational manner. This method differs from interrogation in that an interrogation is designed to obtain an admission of guilt. The Integrity Interview provides guidelines and techniques to analyze an interviewee's verbal behavior in conjunction with simultaneous nonverbal behavior. The interviewer is advised to be wary throughout the interview process of behavioral clusters which include dynamic or static postures, protective or open gestures, and illustrative gestures as opposed to grooming gestures.

Multiple Screening Methods
The major preemployment screening methods utilized by human resource practitioners are described below:

Systematic Interview -- The preemployment interview is perhaps the single most important screening tool. Also, interviewing may be the most challenging and difficult screening tool to master and administer. Consider the dual objectives of an interview. The interviewer's goal is to gather as much accurate information as possible for the selection decision, while the interviewee's goal is to present the most positive information and behavior in order to gain the position. Thus, the applicant is presenting the *best face,* which may or may not be the *real face,* and therein lies the basic challenge to the interviewer.

Skills and Abilities Tests -- Skills and abilities tests are designed to test an applicant's knowledge and skill in a certain area. Aptitude tests are designed to determine an applicant's innate ability in specific areas, and intelligence tests measure an applicant's ability to reason and think. Interest tests are designed to find an applicant's likes and dislikes, and psychological tests provide a psychological profile of the applicant.

Honesty Tests -- G. Hanson (1991) reported that paper-and-pencil honesty tests, or integrity tests, represent the new weapon in the business war against internal shrinkage. These tests, usually used for preemployment screening to ascertain a job applicant's veracity and potential productivity, have become the latest wrinkle in the privacy testing battle. Honesty or integrity tests are designed to profile an applicant's behavior and thinking and have successful rates of predicting future behavior based on past behavior. Written honesty tests are legal in almost all states. Massachusetts prohibits honesty testing of employees, and California, Delaware, Idaho, Maryland, Washington, and Wisconsin have some restrictions in regard to honesty testing. The practitioner who selects honesty testing as a part of the employee selection process should obtain a copy of the 1990 *Model Guidelines for Preemployment Integrity Testing Programs*, published by the Association of Personnel Test Publishers. It is important that practitioners who utilize honesty testing be qualified and understand:

1)   What the integrity test is designed to measure;

2)   The importance of consistency in the testing process;

3)   The importance of confidentiality of test results and record keeping;

4)   Retention and security practices;

5)   How the test scores will be used within the selection process;

6)   How to use scores properly and consistently;

7)   The importance of a comfortable, appropriate testing environment;

8)   What to say, as well as what not to say, to applicants being tested;

9)   How to answer applicants' questions; and

10)   The procedure for testing.

Advantages of Paper-and-Pencil Tests -- Paper-and-pencil tests have proven validity and reliability, and can be one of the least discriminatory of all assessment tools. Other advantages of paper-and-pencil tests are:

1)   The tests are rather inexpensive to administer,

2)   The tests can be administered in a group setting,

3)   The test provider generally also offers specific expertise and guidance on how to administer the tests and how to interpret scores, and

4)   The tests can be recommended for certain aspects of the preemployment screening process in terms of tested high validity and reliability.

Disadvantages of Paper-and-Pencil Tests -- Such testing currently is under a great deal of controversy. While not illegal in most states, tests must be selected and monitored carefully to avoid possible discrimination against any applicant. Some major disadvantages to these tests include:

1)   An applicant may become stressed and not perform to the best of his/her ability,

2)   An applicant may know by experience and intuition the correct answer to choose in order to score high on a test,

3)   Some tests require special scoring and interpretation, and

4)   Some tests do not actually measure what they are meant to measure.

Procedural Testing Safeguards -- A preemployment practitioner, in order to feel confident in the utilization of tests for employment screening, should evaluate the selection criteria with the following questions:

1)   Will every applicant be tested with the same test?

2)   Does the test measure significant responsibilities for the job?

3)   Does the test predict job performance?

4)   Does the test pose an adverse impact on a protected class?

5)   Is the test environment comfortable and consistent every time?

6)   Does the test contain an appropriate language level for everyone?

7)   Is the test scoring accurate?

8)   What percentage of total applicants pass?

9)   What percentage of minority applicants pass?

Reference Checks -- Employment law places limitations on what an employer may and may not ask an applicant or a former employer as a reference source during the screening process. It generally is known that former employers may provide you with as little information as possible. Therefore, it is essential for the practitioner to know which questions may not be asked, how to phrase questions, and how to handle information received from reference checks. Be sure that all reference checking is completed in the same manner for each applicant, and be sure that all reference checking complies with the law.

Criminal Background Checks -- Most jurisdictions provide employers considerable freedom in determining whether a prospective employee has been convicted of a crime. In some circumstances, federal and state law may require employers to check a prospective employee's arrest or conviction record. These employment circumstances may include individuals who will be involved in daycare or child care, certain positions within financial institutions, those who carry weapons, and those with access to drugs and other medications. It should be noted that the EEOC has determined that the use of conviction records has an adverse impact on Hispanic and African Americans. Thus, under Title VII and most state anti-discrimination laws, employers' use of conviction records must be based on *business necessity*. Conversely, employers can be held liable when an employee with a history of a certain criminal behavior commits a similar crime during employment, after work hours, and sometimes even after employment is terminated.

A criminal history search includes a national fugitive search via a national database to determine if the subject is wanted by any law enforcement agency. Also included in the report are all felonies and related misdemeanors for the past seven years and all outstanding warrants from any law enforcement agency.

Civil Litigation Reports -- In addition to a criminal background check, a civil litigation report will show whether an applicant has a history of civil lawsuit involvement. These reports generally contain dates of action, the nature of civil cases involving the applicant, and the outcomes of any civil cases.

Federal Record Search -- A federal record search will reveal any criminal cases such as mail fraud, drug trafficking, civil rights violations, or any violation of federal criminal law. All information for criminal background reports can be obtained from public records maintained by the state and county courts.

Driver's Record Check -- A motor vehicle report can be obtained from the state Department of Motor Vehicles and is especially important for companies that hire people who drive company vehicles or their own vehicles on company business. Driving record reports show arrests, violations, and convictions for the past seven years, and information in these reports may implicate substance abuse and/or other behavioral problems. Also, a motor vehicle report can provide cross-reference information for criminal searches. Specific information contained on a motor vehicle report includes: date of birth, address at renewal, previous state of residence, physical description (*i.e.*, weight, height, and color of hair and eyes), driving restrictions, violations, convictions, accidents, and license validity.

Credit Checks -- The Fair Credit Reporting Act of 1970 (FCRA) protects applicants and employees from the dissemination of inaccurate or misleading personal information distributed by consumer reporting agencies. The FCRA imposes certain restrictions on the reporting credit agency and the user of a consumer report.

If an adverse employment decision is based on a consumer report obtained from a reporting agency, ordinarily the employer must notify the applicant within three days after the report has been requested by the employer. The applicant must be given the name and address of the reporting agency.

Paradigm Model for Change -- A 1994 Minnesota law concerning background checks on employees/applicants may represent a paradigm model for change. If other states follow suit and pass similar legislation, the act of conducting background checks will become considerably more burdensome for employers. The law, effective January 1, 1994, requires employers to provide written notice to applicants/employees of the employer's right to request additional information on the nature of a consumer report. The notice must disclose that the report may include information obtained through personal interviews in regard to the individual's character, general reputation, personal characteristics, or mode of living. An additional requirement is a statement of the right to dispute and correct any errors in the report. Also, the notice must contain a box for the employee or applicant to check if he wishes to receive a copy of the report. The report must be provided to that person within 24 hours of receipt. If an employer takes adverse action against the applicant/employee because of what is contained in the report, the employer must notify and advise the person of the fact, the right to obtain a copy of the report, and the right to dispute and correct errors.

This Minnesota model will require employers to develop a separate attachment for those applicants on whom reports will be obtained. It is suggested that employers also provide the disclosure to any applicant referred by an employment agency since such agencies typically conduct investigative reports before referral. Also, to avoid discrimination, employers are urged to request investigative reports on all applicants, if any reports are obtained at all. The employer's use of credit information may be restricted by Title VII of the Civil Rights Act of 1964 if employment decisions based on such a report disparately impact minorities or other protected groups.

Credit reports generally contain information on debt load, payment history, liens, judgments, collections, and bankruptcies. Also included is information on current and previous addresses, current and previous employers, dates of employment, monthly salaries, and the applicant's social security number. The procedure for obtaining credit information is simply to pay the fee and order the credit check from a reputable credit reporting agency.

Social Security Number Trace -- A social security number check can divulge whether a candidate has other social security numbers or has, or is using, an alias. It can confirm or dispute the accuracy of other information, such as current and previous addresses of the user and past employment data obtained from the resume or interview. To obtain a social security number report, a formal request in writing may be addressed to:

Director, Locator Service
Social Security Administration

6401 Security Blvd.
Baltimore, MD 12135

Employment and Earnings Report -- Employment and earnings reports can be directly obtained from government sources. These reports provide detailed summaries of the applicant's earnings from the past one, five, or 10 years.

Verification of Education -- Research has disclosed that a high percentage of job applicants falsify educational credentials through the use of counterfeit reproductions of diplomas or altered transcripts, impersonating legitimate degree holders, claiming to have degrees and credentials without supporting documentation, and other false claims on the resume. It therefore is advisable to verify such reports with said university and college registrars to obtain official transcripts and information about actual degrees obtained, years of attendance, major areas of study, grade point average, and any periods of probation.

Professional License or Certification Verification -- It is imperative that a human resource practitioner verify the professional certification of an applicant. Certification and licensing are required for the teaching profession, and medical licenses are necessary for all employees in the health care field. The practitioner should consider verification of certification for the welfare of students and patients, and also because of the negligent hiring doctrine.

Military Records -- The Freedom of Information Act of 1967 provides authorization for employers to access information regarding military records. Such reports include: branch of service, dates served, status, and honorable or dishonorable discharge. Military records are located in 15 different cities around the country.

Medical Examinations -- Health examinations are designed to determine an applicant's physical abilities and limitations. Drug and alcohol testing may be considered within the realm of medical examinations. ADA prohibits preemployment medical examinations, but post-offer or employment entrance examinations may be given, if required, as a condition of employment and if consistently and uniformly applied to all applicants. Such medical examination results must be kept confidential, separate from regular personnel files, and available only to those with a need to know.

Workers' Compensation Claims History -- In tandem with a medical examination, the human resource practitioner also may wish to obtain a workers' compensation claims history. If the job requires physical exertion, it may be important to consider whether a potential employee may be susceptible to injury. Typically, a compensation claims report reveals such information as: all claims filed, dates, nature of injury, the employer, and whether the claim was upheld or denied.

Employee Screening Resource Table
    The Employee Screening Resource Table, Figure 4.1, which follows, lists the most widely used screening methods with their comparable attributes, advantages, and disadvantages.

Figure 4.1
EMPLOYEE SCREENING RESOURCE TABLE

Screening Method	Attributes	Advantages	Disadvantages
Preemployment Polygraph	Time for exam off job site	Discourages dishonest applicants	Illegal for most business
		May result in actual admissions	May offend applicants
			Questioned validity
			Requires trained examiners
Structured Selection Interview	Generally part of screening plan	Inexpensive	Difficult to determine truthfulness
		Shows promise	Questioned validity
Reference Checks	Time consuming	Verifies information	Questioned validity
		May increase truthfulness	Misconduct can be undetected
			May obtain only negative information
Criminal Background	Obtainable from vendors	Complete and verifiable	Not all criminals are on record/known
			Must be job relevant
Credit Checks	Fast but costly	Relevant to financial need and fiscal responsibility	Relevance of debt not clear
			Must meet EEOC law
Honesty Tests	Adaptable to screening procedure	May discourage dishonest applicants	Not all tests valid
		No adverse impact	Scores can be misrepresented
		Highly valid	Tester must be trained
		Not offensive	Not legal in all states
Graphology	Faddish Complicated scoring	None identified	Questioned validity Difficult to standardize

Employment Considerations

The following should be kept in mind regarding invasion of privacy issues:

Invasion of Privacy -- The expectancy of privacy by employees and the increasing tendency for employers to monitor employee workplace behavior has created a good deal of tension and has resulted in litigation by employees against employers claiming violations of statutory, constitutional, or common law rights of privacy. Legal authority R. Howe (1991, pp. 387-388) warned that:

> *While it is true at this point in the evolution of the law the balance of power rests with the employer, it is equally clear that legislatures and courts are beginning to weigh in on the side of the employee....Employers should recognize that the best way to minimize or avoid costly privacy litigation and unduly restrictive legislation is to approach employee privacy rights proactively. If they do not, employee privacy rights could be the dominant employment issue of the 1990s, just as the erosion of the employment-at-will doctrine dominated the 1980s.*

Carol Berg O'Toole (1994) recommended that employers implement a search policy and obtain employee voluntary consent prior to any search. The policy should set forth search procedures that minimize the intrusion on privacy and should ensure that employees are informed that refusal to submit to the search may lead to disciplinary measures, including discharge. Searches should be conducted in a reasonable manner and should not be conducted in front of customers or other employees or with excess force or improper detention.

Drug and Alcohol Policy Regarding Invasion of Privacy -- A major concern in regard to drug and alcohol testing is a potential invasion of privacy. There are several precautionary measures a practitioner may take to ensure that invasion of privacy is prevented for potential employees:

1) Set reasonable standards and objectively measure employees against them;

2) Collect only information that is relevant to the job, and do so in the least intrusive manner;

3) Advise employees in advance about how information is to be collected and why and how it is to be collected. Guarantee that the information will not be disseminated to anyone without their consent; and

4) Provide employees the opportunity to review their records and to correct any inaccuracy.

Drug and Alcohol Testing -- While the Drug Free Workplace Act does not mandate testing for any employer, it has become increasingly utilized in the public sector as a screening technique. Complete confidentiality is a requisite for any employer who utilizes drug and alcohol testing, and test results and any information obtained during testing should be treated the same as other medical records in the employer's possession. An alternative to drug testing might be to establish a strong Employee Assistance Program (EAP) that includes a drug-abuse policy. Typically, an EAP has a policy that considers workplace substance abuse, supervisory training, employee orientation, drug and alcohol education and awareness, and assessment and referral.

AIDS Testing Policy -- The practitioner should be advised that there is a growing body of law that makes it unlawful to discriminate against employees with AIDS. It is recommended that employers not test applicants or current employees for AIDS unless they are involved in the health-care service. It also should be noted that mandatory testing is illegal for employers covered by the Americans with Disabilities Act or state handicap discrimination laws and state AIDS laws.

The Centers for Disease Control released new guidelines in 1991 which emphasize the need for strict infection control measures and urged all health-care workers who perform invasive procedures to undergo testing for AIDS and Hepatitis B (HBV). Those who test positive are requested to voluntarily stop performing invasive procedures. There is a significant need for employee education in regard to AIDS. A corporate AIDS policy can be helpful in a number of ways and should be based on the scientific and epidemiological evidence that people with AIDS or the HIV infection do not pose a risk of transmission of the virus to co-workers through ordinary workplace contact.

Sexual Harassment

With increasing complaints of sexual harassment in the workplace, consultant Stephan Anderson (1992) recommended that companies establish a strong policy for preventative and remedial actions to handle sexual harassment claims. He suggested that companies strive to create a harassment-free work environment by enlisting the following "nevers."

1)   Never condone sexually oriented jokes within the workplace;

2)   Never take offense to any complaint or consider it a nuisance;

3)   Never dismiss an accusation;

4)   Never ignore a complaint because the alleged act occurred several years ago;

5)   Never attempt to dissuade an employee from complaining about sexual harassment;

6)   Never try to resolve complaints -- consult the company's legal department;

7)   Never evaluate the seriousness of the complaint on hearsay, partial information, or only by talking with the allegedly harassed employee;

8)   Never remove an employee who complains as a way to rid the company of the problem;

9)   Never take action until an investigation is completed;

10)   Never attempt to influence the results of an investigation involving a complaint against top management; and

11)   Never avoid taking action because the allegedly harassed employee asked that nothing be done.

Surveillance of Employees

Noted legal expert Carol Berg O'Toole (1994) suggested a variety of business reasons to justify employee surveillance:

1)   Misappropriation of trade secrets;

2)   Investigation claims of workplace harassment;

3)   Guarding against negligent hiring and negligent retention;

4)   Controlling health-care costs;

5)   Accommodating an employee's physical or mental handicap;

6)   Providing a safe work environment;

7)   Verification of time worked; and

8)   Detecting and controlling such employee malfeasance as theft, inefficiency, drug and alcohol sale and use, corporate espionage, fraudulent activities, violence, and conflicts of interest.

It is estimated that theft and equipment vandalism costs employers in excess of $3 billion annually, while criminal computer transactions amount to more than $1 billion a year (O'Toole, 1994).

 Surveillance Techniques -- Surveillance of employees can take many forms (See Figure 4.2). While employers may be tempted to initiate surveillance of employees for reasons such as monitoring deviant behavior in the workplace, most states limit the ability of employers to engage in surveillance activities (Freedman, 1994).

Figure 4.2
SURVEILLANCE AND INFORMATION METHODS

Ability and aptitude testing	Marriage license records
Aerial surveillance	Military records
AIDS testing	Off-duty surveillance
Binoculars	Photograph surveillance
Briefcase inspection	Polygraph testing
Cameras	Public health records
Cellular phone interception	Real estate records
Computer monitoring	School records
Cordless phones	See-through walls/ceilings
Credit data	Social security records
Debit cards	Strip searches
Divorce proceedings	Tax records
Dressing rooms	Telephone books
Education records	Truth serum
Electronic eavesdropping	Undercover informants
Electronic fund transfers	Video display
File/desk searches	Terminals
Hair tests	Voice stress analysis
Implantation of devices*	Voting records
Infrared surveillance	Workers' comp. files
Insurance company records	800 toll-free tip lines
Locker room searches	

* Implantation of devices into humans to monitor psychological and physiological changes and to control or regulate an employee's biological system.

Performance Appraisals

 The manner in which an employer appraises employee performance may have a direct bearing on preventing discharge lawsuits. The definition of a workplace performance appraisal is the process that measures the degree to which an employee accomplishes work requirements. Employment attorney Rita Risser

(1993) reported that the performance-appraisal document actually can serve as a legal document in the event of a lawsuit. Appraisals of performance are meant to accomplish three purposes:

1)   Provide feedback and counseling,

2)   Allocate rewards and opportunities for advancement, and

3)   Assist in determining employees' aspirations and planning developmental needs.

It is imperative for human resource managers and administrators to be aware of legal constraints that may impact performance appraisals since an inappropriate appraisal, if used for an employment decision such as selection, compensation, or development, may lead to a case of illegal discrimination. Therefore, all performance procedures and documentation must be specific, objective, accurate, and consistent (SHRM, 1994).

Legal Requirements of Performance Appraisals -- Performance appraisals are included among the employment practices covered by Title VII of the Civil Rights Act, which prohibits discrimination in employment practices based on sex, race, color, religion, or national origin. The Pregnancy Amendment of 1978 made it illegal to discriminate because of pregnancy, childbirth, or related conditions. Thus, a lawsuit may result if employers use informal and subjective measures for performance appraisals. Uniform guidelines issued by the EEOC specify that performance appraisals must be job-related and must meet the following legal requirements.

1)   Absence of evidence that might infer discrimination,

2)   Evidence that proves the validity of the appraisal,

3)   Formal evaluation criteria that limit subjective responses,

4)   Personal knowledge of and interaction with the rated employee,

5)   A review process that prevents one manager from directing an employee's career, and

6)   Equitable treatment of all employees (SHRM, 1994).

Progressive Discipline -- It is important for human resource managers and administrators to have a progressive discipline policy which explicitly states the kinds of conduct that are serious enough to justify immediate termination without a warning. The policy also should allow for documenting interviews and decisions related to unsatisfactory performance appraisals or disciplinary measures taken against an employee.

The Legality of Surveillance

Title III of the Federal Omnibus Crime Control and Safe Streets Act of 1968 is designed to serve as a comprehensive ban on eavesdropping, wiretapping, and electronic surveillance by persons other than law enforcement officials. Exceptions can be considered when one party to the communication has given prior consent, or where the interception is under color of law or for a criminal purpose, or where the interception is over a telephone extension used by employers in the ordinary course of business (Freedman, 1994).

Legal Ways to Observe Employees -- While there are many methods an investigator or human resource manager can use to monitor or investigate employees, Senior Human Resource Manager James Vigneau (1995) described five legal ways to observe employees. These are:

1) Electronic surveillance,
2) Stationary surveillance,
3) Moving surveillance,
4) Undercover surveillance, and
5) Investigative interviews.

Each method is explained in detail in the following section:

Electronic Surveillance -- The electronic method of surveillance involves photography or video images taken in the workplace or public areas. The cameras may be in full view or may be hidden. This method does not include voice recording or photographic images where a reasonable expectation of privacy exists, such as in a restroom or a person's home.

Stationary Surveillance -- The stationary surveillance method involves a multitude of means ranging from a manager watching employees to an investigator hidden in a car or van observing an area. To avoid invasion of privacy, these methods may not be used in areas of expected privacy such as a restroom or a person's home.

Moving Surveillance -- A moving surveillance is described as an investigator following a subject from place to place, either in a vehicle or on foot. Advantages of this method are that it can cover more ground and it allows for traveling outside the workplace. Again, this method may not be applied in a restroom or a person's home.

Undercover Surveillance -- With the undercover surveillance method, a covert investigator is placed in the workplace to observe and report employee behavior and interaction. This method may be very effective in some circumstances but there is a financial and operational risk involved. The method is expensive and time consuming, and it has the potential for severely negative employee reaction if the operative or spy is discovered. Such situations may lead to distrust by employees and may create an atmosphere for retaliation.

Investigative Interview -- The investigative interview is not necessarily a surveillance technique but serves as a direct-contact method to gather information and to observe an employee's verbal and nonverbal reaction to a confrontation. By conducting investigative interviews properly, a company can send a clear message to employees that it is committed to high ethical standards and maintaining a safe, secure workplace. It is essential that the interviewer strictly adhere to provisions of existing employment and case law. Such interviews must be conducted by skilled, knowledgeable, and competent professionals. Particularly, the interview must be voluntary; there should be no coercion throughout the entire interview process. The employee should be made comfortable and given access to a telephone and be allowed to take a break or leave at any time. J.D. Vigneau (1995) warned that, even though an employee in this situation does not have a Sixth Amendment right to be represented in an investigative meeting, such a right may indeed exist under a collective-bargaining agreement. At any rate, the investigator should provide an opportunity for the employee to call or be represented by an attorney during the investigative interview.

Vigneau (1995) explained that the interview may be tape recorded to preserve the true nature of the interview and its integrity. If tape recorded, it should include the employee taking an oath, followed by his or her sworn written statement which explains to a company representative or investigator what happened and how she or he was treated. Such a record may avoid legal issues, especially if the employee later claims duress or coercion or alters descriptions of events from those described on the recording.

Computer Monitoring -- While it is noted that employers have been monitoring employees ever since the Industrial Revolution, today's computerized systems have dramatically expanded opportunities to secretly and continuously monitor employees. M. Traynor (1994) noted that, in an effort to curb computer crime, 30% of companies with 1,000 or more employees have engaged in searching employee computer files, voice mail, electronic mail, or other electronic communications for incrimination. To date, there are no statutes that specifically address workplace electronic monitoring (Freedman, 1994). Representative Pat Williams and Senator Paul Simon are sponsoring legislation to require that workers be notified in advance of most monitoring. It also is meant to curb surveillance of e-mail, bathrooms, and locker rooms and would impose civil penalties, enabling workers to sue (Hanson, 1994).

Post-Employment Considerations

Perhaps the best way to avoid post-employment lawsuits is to terminate employment situations in a successful manner. Chances are that if the employer and employee part company on good terms there will not be a follow-up lawsuit. Some methods to employ to ensure successful employment situations are discussed below:

Termination Policy -- Many times, the unsuitability of an employee does not become apparent until he or she has worked for several months or even years. A reminder here is that negligent retention should be a consideration if an employee presents an unreasonable risk of foreseeable harm to the employee's co-workers, customers, or other third parties with whom the employee may come into contact. Negligent training or supervision also may become a problem in these instances. Ronald Green and Richard Reibstein (1992) have offered some practical suggestions to assist employers in minimizing their potential exposure for negligent supervision and termination of unfit employees.

- Investigate employee complaints of workplace misconduct or harassment immediately;

- Conduct a complete and prompt investigation of the complaint and decide whether the employee is unfit to remain on the job or if disciplinary action may be more appropriate;

- An employee suspected of misconduct should be carefully supervised to avoid any further acts of misconduct;

- Training for managers and supervisors should be provided about how to handle complaints and the legal prohibitions on sexual and other forms of harassment;

- Take affirmative action steps to limit alcoholic beverages to employees at employer-hosted functions, and insist that no alcohol be served to an intoxicated employee;

- Provide alternate transportation for employees who have been drinking at employee-sponsored activities;

- Reassign employees who have exhibited difficulty in controlling their tempers to positions with little or no customer or client contact; and

- Reevaluate an employee's fitness in the event he or she is changing jobs within the organization, especially if the nature of the new job is different from the old job.

Converting Terminations into Resignations -- One of the most frequent lawsuits connected with terminations from employment is defamation. Often, an employee becomes disgruntled or feels hostile toward former employers and supervisors. A most effective manner to terminate employment is to offer the employee an opportunity to tender a resignation instead, if the circumstances permit. Of course, not all termination events and employee acts provide this flexibility. This process may lead to a more amicable separation and should include a proper waiver and release of all potential claims an employee may have against an employer. Some specific suggestions are offered by Green and Reibstein (1992) to ensure that the best interest of the employer are being served:

- Employees should be advised that a voluntary resignation may assist them in their attempts to obtain new employment;

- Outplacement assistance may help induce the employee into resigning;

- Employees should be advised that voluntary resignation in the face of certain discharge will not preclude them from receiving unemployment benefits; and

- Carefully document all circumstances related to an employee's separation including the opportunity to resign in lieu of being terminated.

Exit Interviews -- An exit interview conducted in the proper manner will help insulate the employer from potential lawsuits. During the exit interview, it is advisable to have the terminating employee sign appropriate waivers and releases. Green and Reibstein provide some practical suggestions to assist the employer with significant legal implications of such releases.

- An employer should seek inside or outside legal counsel in preparing waivers or releases;

- Severance pay may be offered to ensure that the release is enforceable as a matter of law;

- The release should be in the employee's native language, or translation should be provided if necessary;

- Allow the employee the opportunity to review the proposed release with an attorney;

- Allow ample time for the employee to consider signing a release; and

- Do not force or coerce any employee into signing a release.

Post References -- When employers are hiring, because they wish to minimize their potential for liabilities for negligent hiring, they seek complete reference information regarding applicants. But, when employers are providing that reference information, they seek ways to avoid liability for defamatory post-employment references. Some suggestions for caution in providing post-employment references are offered by Green and Reibstein (1992).

- Have a written post-employment reference policy and have all supervisors and managers follow the policy;

- Obtain the former employee's consent to disclose employment data;

- Obtain a release from the former employee waiving all claims against the employer in connection with the disclosure of employment data;

- Carefully document all requests for references, including who made the request, how it was made, and what information was given;

- Avoid oral requests for reference information and verify the party requesting information as one who has a bona fide need to know;

- If possible, limit the information provided to prospective employers to verification of dates of employment and positions held by the former employee;

- References should be limited to clear objective facts -- do not offer opinions;

- Do not provide second-hand information about an employee, but refer the questioner to persons with firsthand knowledge of the employee's employment performance; and

- If a favorable employment reference has been promised to a former employee, an unfavorable reference should not be given.

Documentation of Employee Interaction

James Vigneau (1995) forewarned human resource managers and investigators that all employee-employer interaction should be documented. All documents should be created in contemplation of future litigation or outside review.

Conducting Successful Investigations

Carol Berg O'Toole (1994) listed 12 contributing points to a successful workplace investigation:

1)   Investigations should be conducted quickly after the allegation arises;

2)   Investigations must be thorough;

3)   The investigator should not give specific information but should listen and ask open-ended and non-leading questions;

4)   The investigator should describe in general terms the exact process being undertaken, including the time frame and possible range of outcomes;

5)   The investigator should describe the competing interests including the accused/suspected employee's right to due process and privacy;

6)   The investigator must make a written report of the interviews and incorporate information into signed affidavits, if necessary;

7)   The investigator should refrain from promising things that can't be delivered, especially about confidentiality;

8)   The investigator should ask the accused/suspect to explain his or her side of the issue;

9)   The investigator ferrets out specific information such as: dates, places, individuals involved, and actual observations;

10)   The investigator is not obligated to inform the accused/suspect who will be interviewed and what will be asked in subsequent interviews;

11)   The investigator keeps a current list of those persons interviewed and allows flexibility for adding or eliminating future interviews; and

12)   The investigator's report is kept to document the employer's efforts and for future situations involving the same individual investigated.

Tools and Techniques Summary

The most significant benefit of a good internal workplace investigation is that it enables management to obtain the information it needs to manage effectively.

In order to conduct a good workplace investigation, a human resource manager must strategically employ effective tools and techniques. This chapter describes the most valuable tools and techniques currently available to assist human resource managers and administrators in conducting formal workplace investigations for the three areas of preemployment investigations, employment investigations, and post-employment investigations.

Preemployment Investigation Application -- Based on the premise that past behavior is predictive of future behavior, employers tend to conduct extensive investigations of applicants' work histories and personal backgrounds. For the pre-employment investigation application, a variety of preemployment selection techniques were presented. Specifically, the chapter presented an overview of popular interviewing models selected for their many attributes for successful interviewing. Secondly, the chapter discussed multiple screening methods and procedures (*i.e.*, skills and abilities tests, honesty tests, drug and alcohol tests, and background checks) and some advantages and disadvantages of their usage. This section is summarized in an employee screening resource table.

Employment Investigation Application -- The importance of setting employment policy was stressed in this section. The value of policy is recognized in areas such as drug and alcohol testing, performance appraisals, and avoiding invasion of privacy, sexual harassment, and discrimination. The issue of employee surveillance also was discussed in terms of legal requirements, and a chart listing the types of surveillance was presented.

Post-Employment Investigation Application -- The post-employment section focused on the proactive premise that the best way to avoid post-employment litigation is to ensure successful employee relationships during employment. An employment termination policy is suggested as a way to avoid wrongful termination lawsuits. The policy featured such techniques as converting terminations into resignations, holding exit interviews, utilizing the preferred method of providing post-employment references, documenting employee interaction, and reviewing successful points for conducting workplace investigations.

CHAPTER FIVE

EMPLOYER LIABILITY
AND
ELEMENTS OF EMPLOYMENT LAW

Threat of Employee Lawsuits

Today's employer, human resource manager, and investigator face an increasing threat of employee lawsuits related to discrimination, wrongful discharge, post-employment referencing, and other related dilemmas. Chapter One of Part I presented a comprehensive historical perspective of employment law and serves as a broad background for an in-depth perspective on how human resource managers and investigators can guard against those potential lawsuits presented in this chapter.

The Civil Rights Act of 1991 significantly expanded the rights of job applicants, employees, and former employees who bring discrimination suits to court. It extends new protections, making jury trials and limited punitive damages available under Title VII. The Civil Rights Act of 1991, Sec. 105(a)(i), states than an employer practice is deemed unlawful if adverse impact is demonstrated and the respondent *"fails to demonstrate that the challenged practice is job related for the position in question and is consistent with business necessity."*

Proving Discrimination

There are two ways employees can prove discrimination:

1) *Disparate treatment,* or intentional discrimination, or
2) *Disparate impact,* or unintentional discrimination.

An example of disparate treatment would be to ask an applicant: *"Do you have any children?"* and then refuse to hire anyone with children. An example of disparate impact, while much more subtle, would be a job requirement, such as that employees must be at least 5'6" tall, which would exclude certain groups. Many women,

Hispanics, and Asians might claim discrimination because they tend to be shorter than either white or black males.

Disparate treatment requires a motive which, of course, is a private event that must be inferred from an employer's actions. It is complicated, however, by what might be considered negative action such as a demotion that could be motivated by legitimate business reasons such as ineptitude.

Eight Areas of Potential Discrimination

Discrimination law outlines eight distinct areas of protection for employees and applicants.

National Origin Discrimination -- The national heritage of others should be respected. It is for this reason that it is illegal to discriminate because of the country from which persons or their ancestors originate. It must be apparent that Persians and Hispanics, who are of the white race, are covered under the national classifications, as are Italians, Russians, South Americans, and anyone from any other country.

Citizenship Discrimination -- Equal treatment for immigrants is required by law. Thus, it is illegal to discriminate against qualified applicants because they are not citizens if they are legally authorized to work in this country.

Racial and Color Discrimination -- It is important to value cultural diversity in the workplace, and the Civil Rights Act of 1964 makes it illegal to discriminate against any race. It is illegal to advertise and recruit on the basis of race and sex, and the word-of-mouth referral system must be checked for discrimination practices. Screening practices, such as testing and background checks, also may have adverse impact on minorities.

Landmark Case Regarding Race or Color Discrimination -- In EEOC vs. Atlas Paper Box Co., the Sixth Circuit U.S. Court of Appeals found that not one African American office worker was hired at the company over a period of 15 years while 121 white office workers were hired, and 29 of those 121 did not meet the required minimum test score. It also discovered that test scores had been favorably adjusted for some white workers, but no test scores of African American workers had been favorably adjusted. The court held that a violation of Title VII of the Civil Rights Act of 1964 was committed: Discrimination based on race or color cannot be tolerated (EEOC vs. Atlas Paper Box Co. [1989], 6th Cir. 868 F.2d 1487).

Sex Discrimination -- To avoid sex discrimination claims, a company simply must ensure that men and women be treated equally. The Equal Pay Act of

1963 states *equal pay for equal work.* An exception to the rule is a *bona fide seniority plan* that would allow an employer, for example, to pay more to a man than to a woman doing the same job. A second exception states that more experience can become a criteria for paying a male or female more. However, human resource executives are cautioned about basing pay solely on the applicant's salary history. A potential company policy that does not pay applicants more than 15% over their last salary may be discriminatory if one applicant, who was female, came from a low paying position. Sex discrimination involves seven issues that are either sex specific or sex dominant: state protective laws, height/weight criteria, pregnancy benefits, fetal protection, sex plus discrimination, benefits unrelated to pregnancy, and two forms of sexual harassment.

Freedman (1994) reported that discrimination based on sex is a common experience, for women are known to be victims of practices giving them lower wages, less life insurance paid by the employer, fewer fringe benefits, and less leave time.

Landmark Case Regarding Sex Discrimination -- In the case of Martin vs. Texaco Refining & Marketing, Inc., a California Superior Court jury awarded a female employee $17.6 million in damages for being passed over for promotions when managerial positions were created in the company (Martin vs. Texaco Refining & Marketing Inc. [1991] Cal. App. Dept. Super Ct).

Religious Discrimination -- Discrimination based on religion stems from the history of the nation, which was founded on freedom of religion. Complicated issues may arise from religious expression at the workplace. For example, some religions prohibit work on Saturdays, and other religions require special attire that may not meet the company dress code. Reasonable accommodation becomes the answer to most of these situations.

Landmark Case Regarding Religious Discrimination -- In the case of Draper vs. U.S. Pipe and Foundry Co., two employees were discharged when they failed to report for work on a Saturday. The Sixth Circuit U.S. Court of Appeals found that there had been no reasonable accommodation to the employees, and that there was no undue hardship for the employer; therefore the employer was at fault (Draper vs. U.S. Pipe and Foundry Co. [1992] 6th Cir. F.2d).

Pregnancy Discrimination -- The Pregnancy Discrimination Act prohibits virtually any discrimination based on pregnancy and protects women who seek abortion. Abortion is covered as a medical disability if there is potential danger to the mother, and is covered as disability for medical complications to an otherwise uncovered abortion. The act does not, however, require employers to hire fertile women for jobs that require exposure to chemicals that create a substantial and/or imminent health risk for the unborn. A fetal protection policy should be included in the overall company policy.

Age Discrimination -- The Age Discrimination in Employment Act states that people age 40 and over cannot be discriminated against in favor of younger people. The act borrows some strong features from Title VII and FLSA, and there are four statutory exemptions (tenured faculty, hiring/retiring laws for police/firefighters, bona fide executives, and policy-making officials) and one regulatory exemption (apprentice trainees). Disparate treatment is the most common charge in ADEA cases. Two cases regarding age discrimination are outlined below:

Landmark Case Regarding Age Discrimination -- The case of Mulvey vs. State of Connecticut involved an age discrimination claim brought under the Federal Claims Assistance Act of 1990 because plaintiff was denied promotions on the basis of age. The positions he applied for were assigned to younger, less qualified individuals. Plaintiff asked for the difference in pay between his present position and the director's position. The jury returned a verdict which doubled his request to $165,122. Under the terms of the Connecticut Anti-Discrimination Act for willful discrimination (Mulvey vs. State of Connecticut [1991], N. W. 2d).

Landmark Case Regarding Age Discrimination -- The case of Bagozzi vs. St. Joseph Hospital involved a 59-year-old assistant laboratory director who became the victim of staff reduction, allegedly for budgetary reasons. The plaintiff contended that the hospital had refused to follow its lay-off plan and had terminated him because he was the oldest employee in the laboratory. He also pointed out that defendant had violated its one-year recall policy, under which it promised to recall, by seniority, laid-off employees for positions requiring minimal retraining. Such a position had become available during the year of his termination, and he was not recalled. The job was given to a younger employee with less seniority. The jury awarded $347,000 (Bagozzi vs. St. Joseph Hospital [1991], Mich. N. W. 2d).

Disability Discrimination -- The Americans with Disabilities Act of 1990 protects people who suffer from a permanent impairment of a major life function such as walking, seeing, or breathing. Thus, ADA covers almost every type of disability specifically:

1)   Developmental disabilities, including retardation, Down's Syndrome, and such learning disorders as dyslexia;

2)   Medical conditions, including cancer, AIDS, diabetes, chronic fatigue syndrome, and disabling stress;

3)   Physical disabilities, including blindness, deafness, and being wheelchair bound;

4)   Mental illness, including schizophrenia, manic depression, and bipolar disease; and

5)   Rehabilitated drug and alcohol addiction.

Landmark Case Regarding Disability Discrimination -- The Connecticut Telephone and Electric Corporation, suspecting that poor eyesight on the part of some employees was causing defective work, set up a new vision-testing program, and many workers who could not pass the test were fired. However, an arbitrator reinstated the handicapped workers by ruling that workers could retain their job as long as they continued to meet the vision standards in effect at the time they were hired (Connecticut Telephone and Electric Corporation [1950] 22 Lab Atb.632).

Penalties for Discrimination -- The employment provisions of the American with Disabilities Act include the enforcement provisions of Title VII of the Civil Rights Act of 1964 and the Civil Rights Act of 1990. It provides that a person believed to have been discriminated against can file charges with the EEOC within 180 days of the incident. For some state agencies, the time limit is 300 days. The EEOC then investigates the charge and attempts to resolve the case in informal conference through mediation. If this process fails, the employee may be entitled to sue the employer in federal court within 90 days. A successful complainant who is entitled to a jury trial may recover:

1)   Whole or *equitable* relief;

2)   Back pay for lost wages;

3)   Attorney fees;

4)   Punitive damages; and

     5)   Retroactive seniority or other adjustment, including promotion.

Impact of Lawsuits

There is an increasing threat of employee lawsuits, and the trend has been set toward multi-million dollar verdicts. This section describes various specific ways that money damages are awarded to employees via lawsuits.

Actual Damages -- A denial of promotion or loss of job based on discrimination can net employees back pay or the amount they would have received if they had not been discriminated against, less what they earned in other positions, until the time of the trial date. Sometimes, employees also are awarded front pay -- the base salary including reasonable future pay increases and promotions they would have received from trial date to some future date. Older employees, especially those aged 55-plus, may even be awarded full salary for 10 to 15 years, because it often is difficult for them to obtain comparable jobs. Additionally, employees may be awarded actual damages as related to out-of-pocket expenses such as medical bills, costs due to forced sale of income property, and other reasonably foreseeable losses.

Compensatory Damages -- If an employee has been wrongfully terminated, or has experienced discrimination or invasion of privacy, compensatory damages may be awarded for emotional stress, pain and suffering, humiliation, and embarrassment.

Punitive Damages -- When a jury awards distress damages, punitive damages may be assessed which are designed to punish the company for intentional wrong doing. Usually, the amount is a percentage of the company's net worth, annual income, or some other financial measure determined by law or decided upon by a jury. In some instances of punitive damages, there have been no caps. However, in discrimination cases under the EEO, the following limits on compensatory and punitive damages have been established:

Exempt	Fewer than 15 employees
$50,000	15 to 100 employees
$100,000	101 to 200 employees
$200,000	201 to 500 employees
$300,000	More than 500 employees

Additionally, in some instances, the defaulting company is required to pay the employee's attorney fees.

Criminal Liability -- All companies are subject to random inspections by such government entities as OSHA, DOL, EEO, or state agencies and, if found in violation, are subject to fines, shutdowns, and even imprisonment of the officers. Also, managers of corporations can be found guilty under certain U.S. and state laws. For example, there is criminal liability for environmental crimes, federal contract fraud, and securities violations. Needless to say, fighting the government can be even more costly than defending a case filed by an employee. Such criminal penalties can range from $500,000 per offense to millions of dollars.

Negligent Hiring and Retention -- Negligent hiring is defined as the failure to exercise reasonable care in the selection of an applicant in view of the risk created by the position. Negligent retention occurs when an employer keeps an unfit employee on the job who later commits a crime involved with the job or indirectly related to the employment supervision. Employees who engage in criminal, violent, or other wrongful acts, during and/or after work hours, are among the greatest concerns in the current corporate arena. Under the negligent hiring doctrine, employers are obligated to conduct a *reasonable investigation* into a prospective employee's background to determine qualifications and trustworthiness for the particular position.

The duty to investigate each applicant's employment background, reference checks, and criminal record regarding a person's fitness for a position of trust or to work with other personnel, becomes more imperative than ever. To date, a court precedent has, at least, found no liability if an employer makes adequate inquiry or otherwise has a sufficient basis to rely on that an actual criminal record inquiry may not be necessary. However, negligent hiring and retention suits in which employers have been found liable have resulted in damages ranging from the hundreds of thousands of dollars to the millions.

Internal Lawsuit Costs -- A company must consider the tangible and intangible costs of internal law suits. Tangible costs include attorney fees, personnel department costs via payroll, benefits, and the time of accounting clerks and other involved employees as well as loss of productivity by the people involved. Some intangible costs can be realized in poor company morale and a tarnished reputation with investors, customers, vendors, competitors, business associates, current employees, and applicants for future employment.

Costs to Corporate Managers -- Corporate managers and human resource executives may experience costs such as: personal attorney fees; fines; stress-related medical bills; strain on marriage, family, and career; and loss of on-the-job time and productivity. A new legal precedent has been set regarding "individual personal liability" by a New Jersey federal district court. In this case, the court ruled that supervisors who discriminate against employees with disabilities may be personally liable for damages under the Americans with Disabilities Act (Bishop vs. Okidata, Inc., 1994). This decision has great significance in that it serves as a warning for all types of discrimination and all areas of employment law.

Avoidance of Lawsuits

The above descriptions of specific ways that money damages are awarded to employees via lawsuits were designed to be informative, not threatening. Nevertheless, when one considers the individual liability of employers and interviewers, as well as corporate liability, this information can become personally disturbing.

The primary purpose of this chapter is to offer prevention strategies to the practitioner to help avoid lawsuits. Seven points have been identified, followed by a discussion of each.

1) **Fair, Logical, and Defensible** -- Any and all methods of employment screening and interviewing and all decisions must be fair, logical, and defensible based on law;

2) **Consistency** -- All prospective employees must receive consistent consideration and treatment;

3) **Legitimate Business Reason** -- Every decision must be based on a legitimate business reason;

4) **Documentation** -- Every event must be thoroughly and consistently documented for every applicant;

5) **Multiple Screening Methods** -- The decision to hire must be based on a composite consideration and an analysis of multiple screening methods;

6) **Understanding a Human Process** -- An adequate understanding of the rights of employers and the rights of employees is a prerequisite to treating people fairly; and

7) **Expert Advice** -- When there is doubt in regard to any method, technique, interaction, or decision, call on an expert and document the advice received.

Fair, Logical, and Defensible

Any and all methods of employment screening and interviewing and all decisions must be fair, logical, and defensible based on law. The accomplishment of this feat calls for a clear corporate or business policy that considers all aspects of employment law, selection techniques, human relations, benefits, and a dynamic model for communication.

Affirmative Action Plan -- Initiated by Executive Order 11246, affirmative action actually applies only to federal government contractors and subcontractors and public agencies with at least 50 employees. These groups are required to write Affirmative Action Plans (AAP), recruit targeted groups, and hire the best. Protected or targeted groups are women and certain defined minorities. In 1973, Congress passed laws to include people with disabilities and, in 1974, Vietnam-era veterans. The AAP does not, however, apply to employees over age 40 or religious groups. Thus, employers who have Affirmative Action Plans are mandated to keep comprehensive data regarding race, sex, disability, and veteran status of all applicants. This means that questions, which are otherwise illegal, can be asked in order to comply with these data records. However, responses by the applicant are strictly voluntary. The data is monitored by the U.S. Office of Federal Contract Compliance Programs (OFCCP) to determine whether an employer is in compliance with the regulations of the AAP (*i.e.*, whether his quotas have been met).

It is advisable for all human resource departments, even those not required to have an AAP, to create a policy that will address all aspects of discrimination, negligent hiring, and a code of ethics to drive the preemployment hiring process.

Employee-Selection Techniques -- A fair, logical, and defensible policy on employee-selection techniques should be established. Because all aspects of the employee-selection process have possible legal ramifications, a comprehensive policy should be formed to cover all phases of the employment-selection process. The process is based on five elements.

1) **Job Analysis, Description, and Specifications** -- This phase involves a determination of the specific types of skills and attributes required of an applicant and a consistent plan of action for the entire employment selection process;

2) **Screening Techniques** -- This phase includes all screening techniques -- an examination of the application and resume; the initial screening interview; testing for honesty, personality, and skills and abilities;

3) **Interviewing** -- This phase includes all aspects of interviewing, especially question formulation and documentation;

4) **Reference Checking** -- Effective reference checking is meant to obtain verification of the applicant's information, but also can provide new insights into an applicant's suitability for the job; and

5) **Making the Offer** -- This phase includes the comparative evaluation of each applicant, making the final decision of selection, and, finally, offering the position to the most suitable candidate.

Consistency in Screening

Consistency is not so much the vital key to the selection process, as it is the key chain that holds all the keys together. Every aspect of the selection process must be consistent (*i.e.*, systematic and standardized) for every applicant. Essentially, this means the evaluation of all candidates for the same job with the same selection criteria and with no exceptions. Several reasons for the consistent evaluation policy are:

1)   To ensure that an applicant will not be hired on the basis
        of subjective, irrelevant values;

2)   To ensure that the selected applicant has the best set of
        critical attributes for the position; and

3)   To ensure that all phases of the selection process are
        within legal guidelines and compliance requirements.

Legitimate Business Reason

Everything a human resource executive does and says must be backed by a legitimate business reason. Presented below are some legal terms that should be in the working vocabulary of every successful practitioner:

BFBP -- Bona Fide Benefit Plan -- Hiring practices that permit the consideration of certain qualifications (*i.e.*, age, religion, or national origin) necessary to performance of the job.

BFOQ -- Bona Fide Occupational Qualification -- Specific qualifications required by the job description or considered as a business necessity. In regard to the Age Discrimination in Employment Act of 1967 (ADEA), an employer who defends a BFOQ has the burden of proving that:

1)   The age limit is reasonably necessary in the essence of
        the business; and either

2)   That all or substantially all individuals excluded from the
        job involved are, in fact, disqualified; or

3)   That some of the individuals so excluded possess a dis-
        qualifying trait that cannot be ascertained except by rele-
        vance to age.

Burden of Proof -- In evidentiary law, this is the necessity to prove the fact or facts in dispute in the mind of the trier of fact or the court.

Prima Facie Evidence -- Evidence that is good and sufficient in terms of face value. In the judgment of the law such evidence as is sufficient to establish a given fact, or the group or chain of facts that constitute the party's claim or defense, and which, if not rebutted or contradicted, will remain sufficient.

BFES -- Bona Fide Executive System -- Protects an executive position and allows special treatment as a condition of an executive position as opposed to lower level positions.

BFSS -- Bona Fide Seniority System -- Protects someone in a seniority position. EEOC regulations (Sec. 1625.8[a]) state:

though a seniority system may be qualified by such factors as merit capacity or ability, any bona fide seniority system must be based on length of service as the primary criterion for the equitable allocation of available employment opportunities and prerogatives among younger and older workers.

Business Necessity -- A qualification that is essential to fulfilling a position for a specific business need.

Defamation -- An intentionally false communication, either published or publicly spoken, that injures personal reputation or good name, such as holding up a person to ridicule, scorn, or contempt in a respectable and considerable part of the community. This may be criminal as well as civil.

Slander -- The speaking of base and defamatory words which tend to prejudice another in terms of personal reputation, community standing, office, trade, business, or means of livelihood.

4/5's Rule -- Adverse impact typically is evaluated by the 4/5's rule: That any protected group must pass a selection procedure at a rate of no less than 80% of the passing rate of the majority group. Example: The passing rate of a majority group is 50% on a selection procedure. Passing rate of a minority group must then be 50% x 80% = 40% to meet the condition of the 4/5's rule.

Essential Functions on the Job -- Covered by the Americans with Disabilities Act, essential functions are referenced under Title 1, Section 101 (8), which states:

The term "qualified individual with a disability" means an individual with a disability who, with or without reasonable accommodation, can perform the essential functions of the employment position that such an individual holds or desires. For the purposes of this Title, consideration shall be given to the employer's judgment as to what functions of a job are essential and, if an employer has prepared a written description before advertising or interviewing applicants for the job, this description shall be considered evidence of the essential functions of the job.

Major Life Activities -- ADA defines major life activities as those functions that involve care for one's self, performing manual tasks, walking, seeing, hearing, speaking, breathing, learning, and working.

Disability -- Disability is defined under ADA as a physical or mental impairment that:

1) Substantially limits one or more of the major life activities of an individual;

2) Is recorded as such an impairment; and

3) Causes the person to be regarded as having such an impairment.

Physical and Mental Impairments -- ADA defines *physical or mental impairment* as:

1) Any physiological disorder or condition, cosmetic disfigurement, or anatomical loss affecting one or more of the following body systems: neurological, special sense organs, muscular skeletal, respiratory including speech organs, cardiovascular, reproductive, digestive, genitourinary, hemic and lymphatic, skin and endocrine; or

2) Any mental or psychological disorder such as mental retardation, organic brain syndrome, emotional or mental illness, and specific learning disabilities.

Qualified Individual with a Disability -- As defined by ADA, a *qualified individual with a disability* is a person with a disability who satisfies the requisite skill, experience, and education requirements of the position, and who, with or without reasonable accommodation, can perform the essential functions of the position.

Reasonable Accommodation -- ADA describes the process of making *reasonable accommodation* as:

modifying devices, services, or facilities or changing standards, criteria, practices, or procedures for the purpose of providing to a particular person with a physical or mental impairment, and the equal opportunity to participate effectively in a particular program, activity, job, or other opportunity.

Documentation

Proper documentation is an imperative practice for human resource managers to develop. An organized, standardized, systematic documentation style must be adapted as a precautionary measure for proof of adherence to legal compliance requirements for employment screening and interviewing. Every aspect of the screening/interviewing process must be documented in exactly the same manner for each applicant and for each position. Standardized forms and charts should be adapted for an unbiased technique for final selection.

Multiple Screening Methods

The development of an appreciable knowledge and tactical skills level in the overall scope of interviewing and selection practices will increase the advantage for both the human resource manager or investigator and the company. It cannot be overemphasized that any and all methods of employment screening and interviewing, and all decisions, must be fairly, logically, and defensibly based on law. Employment screening techniques described here include the job analysis, the screening interview, preemployment testing, background checks, and polygraph testing. Each topic is explained and followed by specific protocol or sets of guidelines for the selection and application of these techniques.

Job Analysis -- The first step in the preemployment screening process or promotion of current employees should be a comprehensive, updated job analysis. The accurate and functional job description is dependent upon the diligence of the practitioner to define the parameters, the duties, the skills and abilities, and requisite characteristics of the ideal prototype to fill the position. This task especially is pertinent to meeting compliance standards of EEO law, as well as for ensuring against discriminatory selection practices. The following are considerations for completing a job analysis:

1) A content validity study must include an analysis of the important work behaviors required for successful job performance,

2) The analysis must include an assessment of the relative importance of work behaviors.

3) Relevant work products must be considered, and

4) If all work behaviors are not observable, the job analysis should include aspects of the behaviors that can be observed as well as work products.

The Preliminary Screening Interview -- The purpose of the preliminary screening interview is to determine if an applicant or employee warrants further consideration for hiring or advancement. It also is the precursor to the in-depth data gathering interview. Typically, the screening is very brief and can involve a visual appraisal of the applicant with a review of the application form. The interviewer usually conducts a stand-up screening interview by briefly describing the job to the applicant and asking some qualifying questions as a function of predetermining the applicant's qualifications for the general job requirements or specifications.

Application Review -- An applicant's resume or application may determine whether or not further consideration is merited. The application review will provide information in regard to the individual's educational and experiential background as well as a history of employment, including length of time in each position, gaps in employment, geographical or career moves, and salary history.

Qualifying Questions -- Straightforward, matter-of-fact questions may be asked to determine whether an applicant meets the most critical requirements or specifications of the job. For example, a position for an accountant may require an accounting degree and a specific number of years in practice, or an administrative assistant position may call for typing, computer, telephone, and people skills.

Telephone Screening -- The purpose of telephone screening is like the initial in-person screening process, and serves to determine whether the applicant merits further consideration. The interviewer should employ a prepared list of questions drawn from the job description and job specifications to conduct the structured, brief telephone interview.

Guidelines for the Screening Interview -- Whether the screening interview is conducted face-to-face or by telephone, it is essential that it be consistent in style and structure so as not to discriminate against applicants nor miss important criteria valuable in making a decision regarding further consideration.

Testing as a Screening Technique -- Despite current controversy regarding the usefulness and legality of some forms of testing, testing actually is a valid screening tool and can be one of the least discriminatory of all assessment techniques. Several types of commonly used preemployment testing techniques are described below:

Integrity Tests -- Preemployment integrity tests are an outgrowth of the elimination of preemployment polygraph testing and have been designed to measure honesty, drug avoidance, nonviolence, employee/customer relations, emotional stability, safety, and work values. Often, integrity tests are referred to as paper-and-pencil honesty tests. It is estimated that about 3.5 million written honesty tests are given annually in the United States, with 15 to 20% of Fortune 500 companies using them. The tests especially are used for preemployment screening in work settings where employees have access to cash or merchandise (*i.e.*, retailers, financial institutions, and warehouses, and for positions such as clerks, tellers, cashiers, and security guards).

Guidelines for the Selection of Integrity Tests -- Information on finding a testing consultant can be obtained from state psychological associations and from the American Psychological Association, 1200 Seventeenth Street, N.W., Washington, D.C. 20036. (202) 955-7600. Also, the Association of Personnel Test Publishers has published *Model Guidelines for Preemployment Integrity Testing Program*. A listing of these guidelines is presented below:

1)   What are the components of the test?

2)   What is the reliability rating?

3)   What is the extent of research from a validity standpoint?

4)   Was the test validated in accordance with APA guidelines?

5)   Can the validity studies withstand the scrutiny of the EEOC?

6)   Do the completed studies have applicability from one geographic area to another?

7)   What type of predictive studies have been completed?

8)   Who conducted the research?

9)   Does the test publisher provide legal counsel?

10)   Is there a history of any litigation and settlements?

11)   What are the prohibitions against using the test?

12)   Are there any state restrictions or prohibitions?

13)   How is the test scored?

14)   How is the test implemented?

15)   Are there problems associated with implementation?

16)   What is the length of time required to complete the test?

17)   Will the test publisher maintain a policy of confidentiality for test results?

18)   Is the test available in languages other than English?

19)   Is the test designed only for selected individuals or groups?

20)   How large a group can be tested at any one time?

21)   Are the following services available from the test publisher?

    a)   Test booklet and administration guide.
    b)   Scoring procedures and sample test reports.
    c)   Descriptions of norms of reference groups.
    d)   Psychological experts to discuss the validity of the test.
    e)   Retrospective studies.
    f)   Computerized analysis of test results.
    g)   Software availability.
    h)   Legal consultation.
    i)   Client service staff availability.
    j)   Training programs for test implementation.
    k)   Specialized pre-programmed computer availability.
    l)   Adverse impact studies.
    m)   Staff credentials and references.
    n)   Validity studies (*i.e.*, at what expense -- will the publisher indemnify the employer for any loss that results from a challenge to the test's validity?).

22)   Does the test account for cultural differences so that no one is wrongfully excluded?

23)   Can the test be given orally, and, if so, does this alter its predictive capabilities?

24)   What level of education is required to understand the test? What methods are available to ensure that applicants understand the questions? One risk in any written test of this nature is that less intelligent applicants are excluded merely because they do not comprehend the questions.

25)   What checks exist in the test to ensure that intelligent applicants cannot fake the examination by answering in the way that appears most honest?

Psychological Examinations -- Psychological examinations are another screening method utilized by employers to determine whether prospective employees can perform particular job-related tasks, especially those involving potential stress. Psychological examinations are designed to measure an individual's motivation, emotional adjustment, social relations, and interests. Sometimes referred to as personality tests, these examinations generally are conducted at the work site. Prospective employees are requested to respond to selected written questions. The scores produce a psychological portrait of a prospective employee. The two most prominent tests are the Myers-Briggs Type Indicator and the Minnesota Multiphasic Personality Inventory (MMPI).

Skills and Abilities Testing -- Skills and abilities tests are designed to determine a prospective employee's aptitude, strength, or physical agility when such are required to perform a particular job. As with all methods of preemployment screening, the employer is obligated to ensure that such tests are not applied in a discriminatory fashion. The following are guidelines for measuring knowledge and skill and ability tests:

1) The test should measure, and be a representative sample of, knowledge, skill, or ability;

2) The knowledge, skill, or ability should be used in, and be a necessary prerequisite to, performance of critical or important work behavior; and

3) The test should either closely approximate an observable work behavior, or its product should closely approximate an observable work product.

Guidelines -- The following are some guidelines for tests that purport to sample work behavior or work product.

1) The manner and setting of the test and its level and complexity should closely approximate the work situation;

2) The closer the content and the context of the test are to work samples or work behaviors, the stronger the basis for showing content validity; and

3) Paper-and-pencil tests intended to replicate a work behavior are most likely to be appropriate where work behaviors are performed in writing.

Additional Standards -- The following are some additional standards for tests of job knowledge:

1) There must be a defined, well organized body of information applicable to the job;

2) Knowledge of the information must be a prerequisite to the performance of the required work behaviors; and

3)   The test should fairly sample the information that is actually used by the employee on the job so that the level of difficulty of the test items should correspond to the level of difficulty of the knowledge required in the work behavior.

Additional Tests Related to Health/Medical Issues

Other things to keep in mind regarding health/medical issues, are:

Drug and Alcohol Testing -- Since drug and alcohol abuse is on the rise and has such adverse consequences for an employer who hires individuals with related problems, an increasing number of companies are adopting a drug and alcohol testing policy. On October 31, 1988, the Department of Defense (DOD) initiated the Drug Free Workplace rules, which specifically allowed contractors with the federal government to conduct preemployment drug tests on applicants. While currently there is not such a law covering the private sector, there is a considerable movement to administer drug and alcohol tests whenever feasible. Although the private sector must guard against invasion of privacy and defamation issues, there is a necessity and obligation to provide a safe workplace.

Genetic Screening -- Genetic testing may determine whether an individual is predisposed to occupational diseases associated with specific workplace hazards. Federal and state law may require genetic screening for prospective employees if the work involves access to toxic or hazardous materials. The issues of such screening become very controversial and pose a certain potential for misuse or abuse. In fact, several states have passed laws to specifically prohibit employers from obtaining and/or not discriminating on the basis of genetic information (Asquith & Feld, 1995). There is great public opposition to genetic screening. According to a 1994 Harris poll, 88% of employees and 93% of human resource managers oppose genetic testing by employers. The *National Law Journal* (1991) reported that less than 10% of Americans polled believed that employers or insurers should have the right to require genetic tests or access to tests results. Similar reports of national surveys state that three out of four Americans believed that only employees -- not employers -- should see the results of employer-provided genetic screening tests for cancer. The majority of these employees believed that employers should not be able to refuse to hire candidates whose tests showed genetic susceptibility to cancer, even for jobs that might expose the candidates to cancer-causing agents (*Wall Street Journal*, 1993). Nancy Asquith and Daniel Feld (1995) reported that, since legal, technological, and ethical issues continue to cast a shadow on genetic testing, it is not advisable for employers to conduct genetic screening.

Physical Examinations -- Because workplace productivity depends largely on the health of employees, many employers require prospective employees to undergo preemployment physicals to ensure that they are able to perform their duties. Employers must be aware of legal facts such as anti-discrimination laws that restrict preemployment physical examinations.

Background Checks -- Employers frequently conduct background investigations of prospective employees, especially for positions that involve a high level of interaction with children, the elderly, or the mentally and physically disabled and for those positions that involve money. A typical investigation will include a review of the applicant's work history, financial status, criminal record, driving record, and immigration status.

The Fair Credit Reporting Act allows an employer to obtain consumer reports on prospective employees, which will reveal a person's credit standing and credit history. However, if an employer decides not to hire someone on the basis of the credit report, he must notify the applicant of that decision. In regard to criminal records, federal and state laws regulate when and under what circumstances an employer may inquire about the conviction records of applicants. While the EEOC has determined that the use of criminal records has an adverse impact on African Americans and Hispanics Americans, Title VII and most state anti-discrimination laws limit such usage unless the employer can demonstrate the investigation as a *business necessity*.

As a whole, it should be considered that racial minorities may have higher conviction rates than their Anglo American counterparts. An example of this type of discrimination is the 1989 U.S. Supreme Court decision on Wards Cove Packing vs. Atonio, 109 S. Ct. 21115. Also, credit information may also be deemed to have adverse impact against African Americans, especially wage garnishment records. It is not legal to inquire into or make employment decisions based on an applicant's arrest record, since an arrest does not indicate that the person actually has committed a crime.

The Nature of Employment Ethics

Ethics, defined as the study of what constitutes right or wrong behavior, are the underlying principles of employment law. The nature and basis of ethics is that they are subjective and seem to be derived from philosophical postulates and religious belief structures that determine the nature of good and evil, right and wrong, fair and unfair, just and unjust. The reason for this comment here is that being governed by the law certainly has its limits in that the law cannot make all of these decisions. It must be recognized that personal ethical standards must guide the decision-making process and become the basis for policy and procedures within any business operation and within any business interaction with employees, potential employees, and all others within the business realm.

Employer Liability and Elements of the Law Summary

Based on the broad comprehensive historical perspective of employment law presented in Chapter One, this chapter presented an in-depth view of specific liabilities facing today's human resource managers and administrators. Issues included were the eight areas of potential discrimination, wrongful discharge, post-employment referencing, and other related dilemmas. These employment issues are explained in terms of employment law and exemplified by landmark cases. The primary purpose of this chapter was to offer strategies to the human resource manager for avoiding lawsuits. The seven elements of employment law designed to serve this purpose were presented:

1)   Fair, logical and defensible;
2)   Consistency;
3)   Legitimate business reason;
4)   Documentation;
5)   Multiple screening methods;
6)   Understanding a human process; and
7)   Expert advice

Also presented was the notion that personal ethical standards must guide the decision-making process and become the basis for policy and procedures within any business operation and within any business interaction with employees, potential employees, and all others within the business realm.

CHAPTER SIX

UNICOM_{SM}
UNIVERSAL INTERVIEWING AND COMMUNICATIONS

The cornerstone of workplace investigation is the interview. Interviewing is an art -- a skill that can be acquired through the development and refinement of knowledge about human behavior and communication and constant practice. By practicing Universal Interviewing and Communications, the investigator will be able to better interpret and understand more of the messages others send. He also will be better able to manage his own communication skills and the personal impression he imparts to others. In order to do this, the practitioner must develop, through practice and the use of proven techniques, the ability to discern behavior in others that may be indicative of deception.

Throughout time, different techniques have been utilized for the purpose of detecting deception. It is helpful to look at these various historical methods, because, while the customs themselves may have been cruel and unfair, many actually were based on sound physiological principles that still apply today. By understanding historical methods, the practitioner may more easily be able to apply these principles, though not the practices themselves, for today's interviewing and investigative needs.

Historical Methods of Deception Detection

"I am looking for an honest man." These words of Diogenes the Cynic, lamented over 2,000 years ago, are still on the tongues of every employer in the world. It is known that society, from the beginning of time, has consistently been concerned with identifying dishonest individuals in a universal attempt to search for truth and to determine falsehoods. Complex procedures founded on magic and mysticism were developed by primitive societies in an attempt to detect deception. As clinical psychologist Stanley Abrams (1977) wrote:

> *Divine creatures sent messages through their devices of fire, boiling waters, and torture to open the doors of truth, and faith in these powerful mechanisms miraculously, at least in some in-*

stances, allowed the innocent to go unscathed while the guilty bore the mark of guilt. Some of the rituals had a foundation based on sound physiological principles, probably learned by observation (p. 11).

For example, the Orientals' classic practice to distinguish truth from lying was to have the accused chew dry rice and spit it out. This method was based on a physiological observation that fear slows the digestive processes, including the natural production of saliva. Thus, the guilty persons would have an inadequate amount of saliva in their mouths and would be unable to spit out the dry rice, while the innocent supposedly would find it a simple task. Perhaps for the same physiological reasons, the Arabs applied a hot iron to the tongue of the accused, and the innocent were not burned (Neilson, 1890). The following were commonly used methods of determining truth, some of which continue to be used even today:

Trial by Ordeals -- Africa, for example, had suspects place their arm in boiling water. Only the guilty were expected to receive blisters or burns. Tibet followed a similar procedure in that the accused were told to withdraw a stone from a boiling cauldron of water. In India, suspects were forced to hold fire in their hands and were deemed innocent if they were not burned (Neilson, 1890).

Trial by Combat -- An early means of determining the innocent from the guilty, the accused were ordered to fight a duel. The defeated party was considered deceitful and, if still alive, was subjected to further punishment.

Trial by Torture -- This was considered in Medieval times to be one of the best confirmations of guilt. Perhaps the cruelest examples of torture were reported during the 16th and early 17th centuries throughout the European continent, especially in Germany, France, Italy, and Switzerland. Torture was used against accused witches to make them confess and name accomplices.

The Third Degree -- This replaced trial by torture in the less primitive societies. It employed sleep and food deprivation, bright lights, and general brutality to elicit admissions of guilt.

Hypnosis -- Also an early practice occasionally applied in uncovering deception, today it generally is agreed by experts in the field of hypnosis that people can lie as effectively in the hypnotic state as in the conscious state. For this reason, and also because hypnotists are unable to determine whether a subject is feigning the hypnotic state, hypnosis has not been accepted as a valid means for detecting deception.

Psychotherapy -- Some degree of validity in deception detection has been obtained from the use of psychotherapeutic techniques. Observation of expressive movements such as bodily movements, facial expressions, and voice inflection, has been an effective technique for determining what an individual thinks or feels at both the conscious and subconscious levels (Brengelmann, 1961).

The Polygraph -- The ability to consciously interpret behavioral cues sent out by others owes some credit to the research conducted during the development of the polygraph. The polygraph is not a concept that is the product of the 20th Century. It has its roots in the year 200 B.C., when Erisistratus used changes in pulse rates to determine deception. By 1895, the hydrophygmograph had been designed by an Italian physiologist, Cesare Lombroso, to identify deception by monitoring the blood pressure of criminal suspects as they were being questioned. With this method, the subject held a rod that was sealed in a rubber tank. The variations of the pulse raised and lowered the water level in a glass bulb which was transposed to a recording device. Since that time, research has continued, and a considerable number of research studies used blood pressure to differentiate between lying and honest responses during cross examination.

Measuring Honesty

In the early 1930s, industrial psychologist Hugo Munsterberg pioneered the development of two approaches measuring honesty. Using the term *lie detector* to describe his instruments and tests, Munsterberg considered four physiological measures (*i.e.*, blood pressure, breathing depth, breathing rate, and heart rate) and *three association* latency tests to determine dishonesty.

Some researchers believed that the conflict associated with the fear of being detected and the subject's expression can cause a change in blood pressure. Thus, fear and anger could cause physiological changes. These thoughts gave rise to two theories: the Arousal Theory and the Cognitive Theory.

The Arousal Theory -- Researchers have theorized that the act of lying in itself is enough to induce arousal and cause changes in blood pressure as well as cause other physiological responses. This observation gave birth to the *Arousal Theory*, an explanation of deceptive behavioral responses in psycho-physiological terms. During the period of 1960 to 1990, a considerable amount of research focused on the polygraph as a measurement of those physiological changes related to deceit, with a secondary focus on alternative sources of arousal, such as shyness, lack of confidence, and fear of punishment. It established the notion that these characteristics could result in nervous behavior that is not necessarily deceptive behavior.

The findings pointed to the necessity that deception detectors need to find out whether a subject is an aroused truth teller or is actually exhibiting behavior unique to deception-induced arousal.

The Cognitive Theory -- A second theory in explaining deceptive messages also was developed during that era. The *Cognitive Theory* maintained that effective deceptive messages require more cognitive effort to produce than do truthful messages. The increased cognitive effort associated with lying requires constant monitoring. Researchers discovered that the length of pauses, speech errors, and less specific responses occurred with greater frequency during deceptive responses than during those which were truthful. These theories also can be true for the interpretation of nonverbal behavioral cues.

Passage of Polygraph Legislation

While the polygraph has become more sophisticated and has earned a measure of respect from some quarters over the past half-century, it still has limited use because federal law prevents its utilization in many situations. Some employers routinely or periodically tested their workers. The purpose was exploratory in nature and primarily served for purposes of prevention. Repeated employee testing at six-month intervals served as a deterrent to employee theft and resulted in savings of millions of dollars a year. The Employee Polygraph Protection Act halted these practices when it took effect in 1988. Prior to the passage of the Employee Polygraph Protection Act, 70% of polygraph examinations given were conducted for preemployment purposes of screening and determining the overall acceptability of job candidates. Employers have gotten around this, to a certain extent, with the development of written integrity tests as industry struggled to develop other reliable methods for preemployment honesty testing.

Developing Deception Detection Skills

But even if it were legal for an employer to use polygraph testing in all situations, it would not always be desirable. It should be emphasized here that the polygraph is just one tool, and careful consideration should be given to its use. In many instances, its use may do more harm than good, and the results of a test can be impacted by outside factors. In many cases, the human resource practitioner/investigator can obtain results as valid or more valid through the utilization of effective interviewing techniques.

It is important for a human resource practitioner to develop an educated intuition. It is a given that human intuition, whether based on fact or an inarticulated hunch, cannot, and therefore will not, be legislated against. Learning deception detection and truth reading, whether from verbal or nonverbal communication cues, is by far the most important skill a practitioner can acquire.

A considerable amount of communication occurs at the nonverbal level and has meaning on an entirely different plane. Verbal communication is closely related to thinking, while nonverbal communication is intimately associated with feelings. In other words, nonverbal cues such as facial expressions, vocal tones, body movements and gestures are, essentially, a shift from cognition to emotion. The transmission of feelings is an important aspect of communication and social interaction, and scientists strive to understand the relationship between the neuropsychology, physiology, and sociology of nonverbal communications.

Development of Nonverbal Communication Research

Research on nonverbal communication is not new. The first treatise on physiognomy, the study of "the language of the face," was actually completed by Aristotle. It was written around 340 B.C. There are records that show the Chinese considered the face to be an indicator of personality as early as the 5th Century B.C.

Nonverbal communication was not studied scientifically, however, until about two centuries ago. Since then, it has been researched extensively. Among those who have contributed information to the field were French neurologist Gullaume Duchenne and Charles Darwin.

Nonverbal Communication Models -- There are two alternative models regarding the perception of nonverbal communication. The first claims that the work of perceiving nonverbal cues takes place entirely outside of awareness. The second hypothesis maintains that the work of perceiving nonverbal cues takes place partially inside awareness, but that it cannot be articulated.

Sometimes, it can be difficult to tell what others are feeling, especially when they don't want you to know what they are thinking. A person who is lying will attempt to disguise and censor facial expressions more than any other body movement. But researchers have found that behavioral clues to deceit cut across channels and are evident in the face, body, voice and speech. When knowledge of the expressions of the face and eyes are combined, people can obtain a very high accuracy rate in lie detection. It is human nature to try and maintain harmony, so even those who generally are honest practice some forms of deception, and sometimes we are not even consciously aware that we are doing it.

Leakage -- Whether or not a lie is intentional, the subconscious knows the truth, however, and cues will leak out through our nonverbal behavior. Although it is difficult for the untrained eye to observe, there are involuntary expressions of emotions that leak, despite a liar's best efforts to disguise them. When the language of the voice says one thing and the language of the body does not agree, that is the time that the communicator must question the truthfulness, accuracy, or completeness of a response.

The honest person has an open body posture, and often will lean intently toward the interviewer. This person's movement is not restrained and large gestures may be used to add emphasis. A person who has something to hide, however, acts completely different. He may express righteous indignation, but it will dissipate quickly. He may move his body away from the other in a closed, defensive posture. He'll display masking behavior, such as a blank expression on the face or a false smile. To mask his emotions, he may use nervous gestures such as smoothing his hair or picking imaginary lint from his clothing. Research also has found that, when people lie, their body movements decrease.

Thus, one of the keys to understanding Universal Interviewing and Communications is the development of skills enabling an investigator or human resource practitioner to interpret the nonverbal communication messages others send during the course of the interactive situation. The knowledge of the language of the eye and the face as a whole can provide a communicator with valuable insight into another's behavior. As UNICOM practitioners, we should apply this understanding in analyzing others and ourselves.

Behavioral Model for Verbal and Nonverbal Communication

All human behavior in an interactional situation has message value and is thus considered communication. The communication process or exchange of messages generally is accomplished by speaking, listening, reading, or writing. The complexity of communication is realized when one considers that it is an interactive process involving senders and receivers, the variety of ways in which we communicate, and the multiple possibilities for error in understanding human interaction. To provide a frame of reference, this chapter presents a Behavioral Model for Verbal and Nonverbal Communication, which demonstrates communication as an intricate, interactive process in relation to human life and social order.

UNICOM -- Universal Interviewing and Communications -- This chapter presents a Behavioral Model for Verbal and Nonverbal Communication drawn from a publication entitled UNICOM -- *Universal Interviewing and Communications: A Preemployment Application* (Slowik, 1995). The above-mentioned publication is the first in a UNICOM series for human resource development. The inherent strength of the Behavioral Model for Verbal and Nonverbal Communication is that it can be applied to a variety of tasks within the role of human resource managers and administrators, *i.e.* the same techniques and skills applied to a preemployment screening interview readily can be transferred to interviews involving all aspects of workplace investigations. The next three chapters are designed to provide the reader with foundational information to develop and build behavioral observation techniques and interactional and management skills based on the diagnostics and analysis of verbal and nonverbal communication. The component demonstrates how these factors specifically relate to a disciplined system for the three areas of workplace investigation. The UNICOM technique is demonstrated as a strategy designed to manage a trilogy of interactive activities, which include:

1)   Having a definitive understanding of the investigative objective,

2)   Discerning the dynamics and the interactive behavior from the interviewee's point of view, and

3)   Subsequently responding with the appropriate interactive behavior to facilitate investigation cooperation and disclosure.

The model provides an in-depth description of the cognitive interactive communication process as a way to illustrate and understand the dynamics of the ways humans send and receive messages.

The Cognitive Interactive Process

An in-depth view of the cognitive interactive communication process requires an understanding of the dynamics of the ways humans send and receive messages and, therefore, communicate. A number of variables are combined to make up the intrapersonal communication process, or that which takes place within a single person in relation to thoughts and feelings. Perhaps the most significant contributing variable is the self as a product of socialization. The "self-component" involves self-concept, the accepted sex role, personality, self-awareness, culture, socioeconomic status, and all other variables within the whole intrapersonal environment. Two other inherent variables have to do with cognitive processing and physiological processing. Each process is controlled by the brain and the central nervous system and involves emotions or the feeling state and physiological reactions to stimuli that occur at a preconscious level. Such reactions considered here are heart rate, brain activity, pupil dilation, muscle tension, skin conductance, blood pressure, and body temperature. The study of the interrelationship between these variables is termed psychophysiology.

Purpose of the Behavioral Model for Verbal and Nonverbal Communication -- As communicators, we consciously, and sometimes subconsciously, attempt to project the message and image we wish others to receive. We also seek messages which are informative and answer our questions. It is noted that humans communicate via a dual, interactive language: the language of words, and the language of the body.

Human communication is conveyed in many different ways -- by words; tone of voice; vocal inflections; facial expressions; body movements and gestures; clothing, color, and hairstyles; the use of physical space; touching; and psychophysiological reactions.

The Language of the Spoken Word

Since words are definitely formed by thinking and the use of the brain, the language of words briefly is discussed.

Words -- Vocabulary and choice of words send many messages. Besides their meanings, words can convey the level of someone's vocabulary, which implies educational level. Choice of words also can indicate a level of sophistication and, of course, ability to communicate effectively. Word selection and usage within the communication process can be isolated for discussion purposes only, but must be considered as only one vital interactive component in the communicative repertoire. The information exchanged verbally, of course, is imperative to the question/answer aspects of selection interviewing.

The ability to use language is genetically programmed for all normally functioning human beings. Scientists have identified certain areas in the brain where words, sentences, and verbal data are formulated, sent as messages, received, decoded, encoded, and stored into memory. Also, it has been determined that no matter how articulate a person may be, speech also is affected by the autonomic nervous system. Thus, when a person speaks under stress or tells a lie, the person may scramble words, use an inappropriate verb, stutter, or in some way utter something unintentionally. The ability to recognize and consider such cues is invaluable to an investigator when interviewing an accused/suspected employee or a witness who may have the inclination to be deceitful. Conversely, it is equally important for the investigator to have the skills and knowledge to recognize when an interviewee is telling the truth.

Vocalics -- The study of paralanguage, sometimes referred to as vocalics, includes all stimuli (other than words) produced by the human voice. These cues range from forceful articulation, screaming, deep resonance to whining, monotones, and vocalized pauses. Volume, pitch, and rate also convey messages. In fact, vocal data may be as important to the listener as verbal data, because the way words are said contributes to meaning and becomes an important part of the data one hears.

Tonality and Vocal Inflections -- The tone of voice and vocal inflections work interactively with words chosen to communicate messages. Vocalics, sometimes referred to as paralanguage, consists of all stimuli, other than words, that are produced by the human voice. These vocal or tonal cues range from forceful articulation, screaming, deep resonance to whining, monotones, and vocalized pauses as well as volume, pitch, and rate.

Vocalic accent is a contributor to communication and can provide clues as to the geographical origin of the speaker. Compare a New York accent to a Texan. Compare a Swedish accent to an English one. Thus, the way things are said may be just as important to the receiver as the words that are said, since all behavior contributes to the meanings. The most apparent attributes of sound that can convey messages and provide some measurable functions in interpersonal communication are noted:

1) **Loudness** -- The amplitude of sound is measured in decibels to indicate the acoustic energy reaching a receiver.

2) **Pitch** -- It is noted that emotion influences modal pitch (*i.e.*, someone who is sad or stunned is most likely to speak with a lower modal pitch, while excitement and gaiety are expressed by a higher modal pitch). Anger can be expressed in a quiet, low pitch or in a louder, high pitch.

3) **Rate** -- The number of sounds emitted during a given unit of time or the speed with which one speaks is referred to as rate. Rate of speech can convey how fluent or dysfluent a communicator is as well as the intensity of the message.

4) **Quality** -- Vocal quality allows us to distinguish one person's voice from another and can strongly impact the impression made by that person. To another person, a breathy voice may indicate shallowness and superficial meanings while a flat voice may indicate sluggishness, coolness, or withdrawal.

5) **Articulation** -- Careful articulation, necessary for effective communication, is defined by specific vowel or consonant sounds and by syllables that are emphasized and involve the use of moveable parts of the top of the vocal tract such as tongue, jaw, and lips to shape sounds.

6) **Pronunciation** -- Specific vowel or consonant sounds and emphasis of syllables in words are related to pronunciation. Correct and consistent pronunciation is necessary for effective communication.

7) **Silence** -- While silence is not an attribute of vocal cues, it serves a vital function in interpersonal communication, as it is considered an effective response in communicative interactions. Silence can express anxiety and can be used to convey such messages as defiance or annoyance.

The Unspoken Language

Nonverbal communication often is swift and subtle and can be referred to as nonverbal interaction since it represents the non-language aspects of social interaction. Kinesics is derived from the Greek word *kinein,* which means to move, and denotes the study of facial expressions; eye behavior; gestures and movements of the torso, head, legs and feet, arms and hands; and body postures -- sitting and standing, moving and static. These aspects of kinesics will be discussed individually with the caveat that communication, both verbal and nonverbal, always should be treated as a total and inseparable unit.

The Dimensions of Facial Expressions

The human face is made up of 22 major muscles which control thousands of expressions. Figure 6.1, Duchenne's Facial Muscles of Emotional Expression, illustrates the anterior view of the muscles of facial expression.

Physiognomy -- The study of the *language of the face* is known as physiognomy. It has been noted that the face is capable of thousands of different expressions that convey meaning without the necessity of a person speaking a word. In fact, it has been established that the face may well be the most expressive part of the body. For example, a smiling face radiates positive feelings via a curved mouth, bright eyes, raised eyebrows, and arching head movement, while a sad face expresses sorrow with the inner corners of the eyebrows raised, the inner corners of the upper eyelids drawn up, and the corners of the lips drawn down. A blushing face exhibits embarrassment or self-consciousness. Several of the emotions most commonly displayed in facial expressions are listed in Figure 6.2 in relation to their facial cues.

Figure 6.1
DUCHENNE'S FACIAL MUSCLES OF EMOTIONAL EXPRESSION

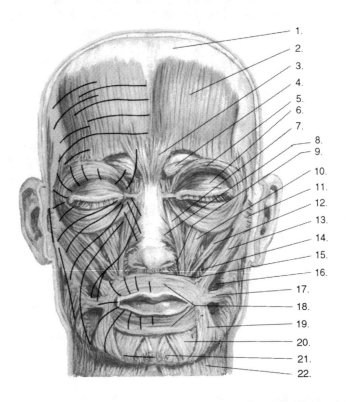

Facial Muscle   **Emotional Expression**

1. Galea aponeurotica...   (Not documented)
2. Frontal belly (frontalis) of epicranius muscle..   Attention
3. Procerus muscle...   Aggression
4. Corrugator supercilii muscle...........................   Pain
5. Orbital part   Reflection
6. Palpebral part } of orbicularis oculi muscle   Scorn/Crying
7. Levator labii superioris alaeque nasi muscle.......   Sniveling
8. Transverse part   Lasciviousness
9. Alar part } of nasalis muscle   Passion
10. Levator labii superioris muscle........................   Crying
11. Auricularis anterior muscle..............................   (Not documented)
12. Zygomaticus minor muscle.............................   Affliction/Crying
13. Zygomaticus major muscle.............................   Joy
14. Levator anguli oris muscle...............................   (Not documented)
15. Depressor septi nasi muscle...........................   Irony/Aggression
16. Buccinator muscle...   Irony/Aggression
17. Risorius muscle...   (Not documented)
18. Orbicularis oris muscle....................................   Sadness/Aggression
19. Depressor anguli oris muscle..........................   Sadness/Aggression
20. Depressor labii inferioris muscle.....................   Irony/Aggression
21. Mentalis muscle..   Pain
22. Platysma muscle..   Fear/Anger

Smiles -- Mouths are important communicators in that a smile can convey many meanings, even though no word is spoken. Research has distinguished at least 18 theoretically different types of smiles which are either voluntary or involuntary in nature. There are distinctive smiles of embarrassment and satisfaction. A broad smile with lips parted and teeth showing indicates that one is less guarded and open, while a partial smile with closed lips portrays shyness and uncertainty. Forced smiles indicate anxiety, hostility, or a rigid attitude. There is a sensuous smile that expresses love, caring, or seduction, and there is even a criminal smile (*i.e.*, that of a *sick smile* or *devilish grin*).

Figure 6.2
THE LANGUAGE OF THE FACE

1) *Happiness* is most visible in the lower face and the eye area.

2) *Sadness* most often is revealed in the eyes.

3) *Surprise* generally is shown in the eye area and the lower face.

4) *Disgust* most accurately is discerned in the lower face.

5) *Fear* predominantly is shown in the eye area.

6) *Anger* is visible in the overall facial composition.

7) *Contempt* is illustrated by narrowed eyes, flared nostrils, and a tight jawline.

Eye Behavior -- Eyes are fascinating and can be one of the most potent elements of body language. In fact, there are those who believe that the eyes may well have a language of their own with a specific syntax and grammar. Some believe that eye behaviors are the most reliable indicators of deception while it is recognized also that eye behaviors are important determinants of credibility. For example, direct eye contact is most apt to communicate competency and trustworthiness, just as averted eyes may be interpreted as less trustworthy.

Gaze -- The sign repertoire of the eye is another feature of study within the realm of physiognomy and nonverbal communication. It may be observed in social interaction that gazing or not gazing at another may be equally communicative. Generally, it has been noticed that an increase in gaze tends to produce reciprocal responses during communication. The eye offers additional information when viewed as the physiological eye, an extension of the brain, in that pupils dilate and contract to serve as gauges of likes and dislikes.

Functions of Eye Behavior -- Seven functions of eye behavior have been identified through research:

1)   *The Attention Function* -- necessary for social interaction and functions with eye contact.

2)   *The Persuasive Function* -- communicates competence and trustworthiness.

3)   *The Intimacy Function* -- conveys the *loving* or *caring* look.

4)   *The Regulatory Function* -- the ability of the eyes to effectively regulate turn taking, turn yielding, turn requesting, and turn maintaining generally essential to the management of conversation.

5)   *The Affective Function* -- expresses positive or negative emotions and reveals the intensity of emotion.

6)   *The Power Function* -- designates the power of one person over another.

7)   *The Impression Management Function* -- is the conscious control necessary to create a desired impression to deceive, ingratiate, dominate, or avoid others.

Language of the Eyes
The following behavioral labels are presented to define types of eye communication:

1)   **Eye Contact** -- eyes meeting while communicating.

2)   **Face Gaze** -- people focusing on each other's face.

3)   **Eye Gaze** -- a direct focus on someone's eyes.

4)   **Mutual Gaze** -- two people gazing at each other's face.

5)   **Mutual Eye Contact** -- two people establishing eye contact.

6)   **Gaze Avoidance** -- intentional avoidance of eye contact.

7)   **Gaze Omission** -- unintentional failure to establish eye contact.

8)   **Gaze Aversion** -- moving the eyes away from another's gaze.

9)   **Eye Shifts** -- movement of eyes from contact to noncontact.

10)   **Staring** -- a constant gaze at another.

11)   **Eye Blinking** -- number of times eyelids close per unit of time.

12)   **Eye Flutter** -- number of times the eyeballs move per unit of time.

13)   **Pupil Size** -- diameter of the pupils measures dilation.

The Language of Bodily Cues

Movement also communicates meaning and lasting impressions. Bodily cues communicate meanings and information that can be functional and dysfunctional. Gestures, for example, often accompany words to enhance their meaning or to clarify a message.

Paul Ekman, a recognized scholar of nonverbal communication, with his colleagues, has classified body movements on the basis of origins, functions, and coded behavior into five categories:

1)   *Emblems* -- behaviors that serve as word substitutes.

2)   *Illustrators* -- behaviors that accompany and illustrate spoken messages.

3)   *Affect Displays* -- behaviors that communicate emotions.

4)   *Regulators* -- behaviors that monitor and control verbal communication.

5)   *Adapters* -- include body movements that are not intended for communication.

The Language of Posture

Communicative functions of posture can be reflected in:

1)   Attitudinal information,
2)   Psychological state,
3)   Intensity of emotion experienced, and
4)   Relational information.

The Language of Proxemics

Proxemic research is concerned with the communicative function of space -- the way people use space and distance in interacting. Proxemic behaviors have a significant impact on the communicative functions of interviewing, especially in the areas of impression management, affiliation, and privacy and comfort of the communication environment. Violation of proxemic norms and expectations can have a negative impact on communication and effective interviewing. Five interrelated proxemic concepts have been identified:

1)   **Space** -- The use of visual space in communication can significantly impact the outcome of the interaction. For example, closeness can promote communicative interaction and a feeling of involvement, whereas distance tends to keep people from forming an understanding and promotes withdrawal.

2)   **Distance** -- Communication distance is considered as a relational concept which measures the physical distance between individuals. Four types of informal distance have been discerned:

   a)   **Intimate,** for close and intense communication;

   b)   **Personal,** the amount of space individuals prefer to place between others and themselves;

   c)   **Social-Consultative,** that space typically used in business or social interaction; and

   d)   **Public,** a distance that is interactive but has no close contact for communication.

3)   **Territory** -- Territorial behavior is defined by marking off boundaries. For example, many human resource personnel tend to protect their offices as personal territory by the use of desks and name plates, and the arrangement of furniture. This function also can regulate interaction with interviewees and others who visit the office.

4)   **Crowding** -- Crowding is said to exist when a person's personal space is violated by others. Crowding can be quite uncomfortable and can have a negative impact on the ability to establish and maintain effective relationships with others.

5)   **Privacy** -- The major dimensions of privacy are listed below:

    a)   **Physical Privacy** -- determined by closeness,

    b)   **Social Privacy** -- determined by social interaction,

    c)   **Psychological Privacy** -- determined by protection of feelings and emotions, and

    d)   **Informational Privacy** -- determined by personal information protection.

The Language of Touch

Tactile communication may have many meanings, and the practitioner should not underestimate the power and value of touch as an interactive component of communication. Touch can communicate reassurance, comfort, caring, and affection. It becomes extremely dynamic when combined with facial expressions and vocal cues.

The nature of touch and the realization that the skin is a sense organ of great value in interpersonal communication is noted here. The skin is capable of expressing many important messages that can be observed through skin color, muscular tension, skin temperature, and perspiration. Also, the skin is recognized as a receiver of emotions or messages expressed by touch. For example:

1)   **Positive-Affect Touches** communicate appreciation, inclusion, attraction, support, and affection;

2)   **Playful Touches** communicate playful affection and aggression;

3)   **Control Touches** communicate power or compliance; and

4)   **Ritualistic Touches** communicate the meanings associated with greetings and departures.

Explanation of Behavioral Model (Figure 6.3)
        The left and right sides of the model illustrate the manner in which messages are received. For example, verbal communication, including vocalics and what is known as paralanguage, generally is heard by the receiver and is therefore represented by the ear. Nonverbal communication most often is observed by the receiver. Thus, it graphically is represented by the eye.

The Verbal Component of Communication
        The left section of the UNICOM Behavioral Model presents the verbal component of communication and is denoted by an ear, which hears the spoken words of a communicator. Recognition, Analysis, and Diagnosis represents the three-part process experienced by the communication receiver.

The Nonverbal Component of Communication
        The right section of the behavioral model presents the nonverbal component of communication and is denoted by the degree of an eye, which observes nonverbal messages of communicative events. Recognition, Analysis, and Diagnosis represent the three-part process experienced by the communication receiver.

The UNICOM Behavioral Model
        The anatomical figure in the center (Figure 6.3) represents a human communicator who sends messages via a multitude of interactive modalities. The anatomy of the UNICOM model is presented by three separate study zones described below:

The Head and Face
        Zone A -- 1, 2, and 3, which contains the head and neck, is the control center for communication and therefore is the most communicative segment of this hypothetical behavioral model.

        The Brain -- All thought, reasoning, and reactions are processed in the brain. The brain and the spinal cord contain the **Central Nervous System (CNS),** which controls all basic functions, maintains internal integrity, and responds to external changes. The second aspect of the nervous system is the peripheral nervous system, which includes the nerves that enter and leave the spinal cord and those nerves that travel between the brain and organs without passing through the spinal cord, *i.e.,* the optic nerve between the eye and brain.
        Messages sent from the body to the brain are carried by sensory nerves. The nerves sending messages from the brain to the muscles and organs are called motor nerves. There are voluntary and involuntary pathways. A special division of the nervous system, the **Autonomic Nervous System (ANS),** contains the motor nerves which connect the brain and spinal cord to the heart muscle, glands, smooth muscles in the walls of hollow organs, and the smooth muscles in the walls of the blood vessels in the skin, skeletal muscles, and organs. For the most part, messages sent along those motor nerves are involuntary.

Figure 6.3
THE UNICOM BEHAVIORAL MODEL
FOR VERBAL AND NONVERBAL COMMUNICATION

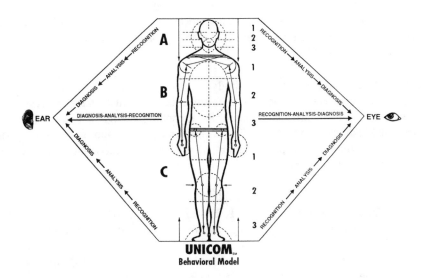

The Special Sense Organs -- The special sense organs of sight, hearing, smell, and taste are extensions of the brain. The eye and ear are the most highly specialized organs and serve as external receptors which report on the external world. The external aspect of these organs reveal nothing of the elaborate nerve apparatus within them. Only the openings through which stimuli reach the nerve receptors are visible, that is, the pupil of the eye, ear canal, nostrils, and mouth.

The Face -- The face is a great communicator, and the study of the *language of the face,* as previously introduced, is known as physiognomy. Research in the area of physiognomy has discovered that the face is capable of thousands of different expressions without a word being spoken. At least 18 distinctive smiles have been identified, all of which are somewhat subjectively distinguished (Ekman, 1972). However, the Duchenne smile (Figure 7.2), or the real smile, is most easily distinguished and is considered universal -- that is, everyone smiles the real, happy smile the same way. Also, there are frowns and other facial expressions of emotions to consider, such as fear, disgust, hate, and love.

The Eyes -- Eye behavior is perhaps one of the most potent elements of body language. The eyes are expressive and are sensitive to (and can broadcast) inner feelings. They can be intense, happy or sad, clear or glazed, light or heavy, or they can offer an icy stare, evil eye, fish eye, far away look, come hither look, and even an *if looks could kill* look. It has been noted that the eyebrows have 23 possible positions, each with an ability to communicate (Birdwhistell, 1970). Desmond Morris (1985) stated: *"The main function of the eyebrows is to signal the changing moods of their owner."*

Nonverbal Language of the Upper Body
The upper body, **Zone B -- 1, 2, and 3** in the UNICOM model, is the second greatest communicative component, for it contains the hands and arms, which gesture; the body trunk, which exhibits posture and tension; and, most importantly, the greatest portion of the spinal column, which serves as the conduit for all messages sent to and from the brain.

Nonverbal Language of the Lower Body
The lower body, **Zone C -- 1, 2, and 3** in the UNICOM model, contains the base of the spinal column. The legs and feet also contribute substantially to the communication process.

Based on the Behavioral Model for Verbal and Nonverbal Communication presented, the Anatomical Behavior Inventory, as illustrated in Figure 6.4, is designed to establish the source origin of the human behavior and a listing of the possible emissions generated, managed, or exhibited by that respective source origin. The following inventory will assist a practitioner in isolating, cataloging, and diagnosing an interviewee's verbal and nonverbal behavior.

Figure 6.4
The Anatomy of Communication

ZONE A -- HEAD AND NECK AREA

Hair
　hairline up/down
　style

Forehead
　perspiration
　furrowed
　smooth

Eyebrows
　up/down
　furrowed
　arched
　flashes

Ears
　exposed/covered
　listening attitude

Eyes
eyelid sag
squinting
closing
shifting
smiling
flutter
winking
openness
staring
rolling
blinking rate
pupil dilation/constriction
sharp movements
crying
tearing
clear or flat
type of contact
type of gaze
muscle tension around eye

Mouth
compressed
open
dry/clicky
chalky film
chewing
chewing fingernails
muscle tightness/twitching

Tongue
dryness
showing
licking
movement

Face
makeup (females)
shaven/beard (males)
frowning
flushed
discolored
blanched
tight
too much/little animation

Face (continued)
orientation to interviewer
jawline (relaxed/tense)
facial skin changes
complexion

Lips
smiling
unnatural smiles
forced smile
pursed
nonvocal movements
stiff upper lip
tremor
biting
thin lipped

Head
up/down
tilted
back/forward
movement jerky/abrupt
rolling
nodding
shaking yes/no

Neck/Throat
swallowing rate
posture
movement
larynx/Adam's apple quiver
clearing throat
throbbing carotid artery

Voice
clear
strong/weak
shaky
pitch (raised/lowered)
amplitude (loud/soft)
choking
hoarseness
breathy
loud
soft

Nose
  stuffy
  increased nasal discharge
  itching
  twitching
  red

Speech
  pauses
  errors
  slip of tongue
  rate (fast/slow)

Speech (continued)
  articulate
  floundering
  tirades
  indirect
  talking to self
  laughter (appropriate/not)
  sentences (complete/not)
  hesitation before response
  anxious to respond
  avoidance of words
  answers (clear, concise)

ZONE B -- UPPER BODY AREA

Hands
  temperature (warm/cold)
  dry or sweaty
  color (natural/blanched/reddened)
  fine motor coordination
    (exact or fumbling)
  hidden in pockets

Hands and Arms
Expressive gestures/movements
  wringing hands
  folded arms
  arms across body
  extended arms
  holding out hands or arms
  palms out/in
  clenching fists or hands
  hand shrugs
  hand to face
  hand covering eyes
  the "stop" sign

**Hands and Arms, Relief Movements
  and Gestures**
  sagging/slumping
  fidgeting
  waving
  self-touching
  trembling fingers
  circling hands/arms

**Hands and Arms, Relief
  Movements, Gestures, (cont.)**
  playing with hair
  scratching nose
  choppy movements
  putting pen in/out of pocket
  creating jobs
  inspecting nails/hands
  adjusting glasses
  stroking beard/chin
  tie preening
  smoothing
  sweeping
  arms across abdomen
  arms hugging body or loose
  playing with clothing
  rubbing eyes
  rubbing face
  rubbing anything
  playing with face
  grabbing neck
  patting/tapping
  scratching
  scratching shoulders
  scratching head

Body
  sitting wide/narrow
  mimicking/mirroring
  breathing (heavy/shallow)

Body (continued)
taking deep breath
(before or after speaking)
leaning toward door
leaning toward interviewer
turned away
perspiration
swaying
fidgeting
rocking
turning

Body (continued)
shaking
sagging/slumping

Shoulders
sagging
tilting
shrugging
nodding
bowing
shaking

ZONE C -- LOWER BODY AREA

Feet and Legs
crossed/crossing legs
crossed/crossing ankles
circling leg/foot
swinging leg/foot
jiggling leg/foot
extending leg/foot
bouncing leg/foot
tapping

Feet and Legs (continued)
shaking
spreading legs
feet flat on floor

Knees
raised
ankle on knee
arm or hand over knee

Universal Interviewing and Communications Summary

The UNICOM Behavioral Model for Verbal and Nonverbal Communication was presented. The chapter demonstrated the cognitive interactive process of human communication as an intricate, interactive set of activities related to human lives and social order. The model illustrated the dual human interactive language of words and body. Verbal language was explained in terms of words and vocalics. Nonverbal language was explained by all aspects of kinesics: the dimensions of facial expressions, bodily cues, posture, proxemics, and touch. The behavioral model illustrated the anatomy of communication as portrayed within three bodily zones. Zone A, which represents the head and face presented an in-depth discussion of the brain and the spinal cord and the interaction of the central nervous system and the autonomic nervous system as humans communicate. Zone B illustrated the communicative aspects of the upper body while Zone C represented the lower body. This Anatomical Behavior Inventory was designed to establish the source of origin of human behavior and listed the possible emissions generated, managed, or exhibited by each respective source origin. The inventory is meant to assist an investigator in isolating, cataloging, and diagnosing an interviewee's interactive verbal and nonverbal behavior.

CHAPTER SEVEN

UNIVERSAL COMPONENTS OF COMMUNICATION

The Dynamics of Communication

All behavior in an interactional situation has message value and is thus considered communication. It has been said that *"no matter how one may try, one cannot not communicate"* (Watzlawick, Helmick, & Jackson, 1967, p. 49). Humans communicate in many different ways: by words, by tone of voice, by vocal inflections, by facial expressions, by bodily movements, by clothing and color, by use of physical space between people, and even by psycho-physiological responses, such as blushing and speed or depth of breathing (Dittman, 1987). Generally, the communication process, or exchange of messages, is accomplished by speaking, listening, reading, and writing. The complexity of communication is realized when one considers the variety of ways in which we communicate, the multiple possibilities for error in understanding human interaction, and that it is an interactive process that involves both senders and receivers.

As communicators, consciously, and sometimes subconsciously, one attempts to gather all the information available to *read* or understand another's communication. Also, as communicators, we consciously, and sometimes subconsciously, attempt to project the message and image that we wish others to receive. As communicators, we also seek messages which are informative and which answer our questions. There is a science to effective communication, and we are all students in this regard. As with other sciences, there is a theoretical base and a rich history of past studies available to serve as stepping stones to future research and application of this interactive process of communication.

The Phenomenon of Universal Communication -- Since much of human communication has been recognized as universal, this chapter is a near replication of the theoretical base and historical perspective of communication described in the first of the UNICOM series: *Universal Interviewing and Communications: A Pre-employment Application* (Slowik, 1995). This informational background is a prerequisite to understanding how humans communicate and is applicable to all realms of human resource personnel whether interacting with employees on a daily basis or interviewing for preemployment screening purposes or for workplace investigations.

Comparisons of Cultural Communication

While it is recognized that several emotions, such as authentic happiness indicated by the Duchenne smile, are expressed in a universal manner, it also must be assumed that each culture has its own distinct nonverbal communication. Successful intercultural communication requires that one develop skills as impression managers.

Detecting Lies Across Cultures -- In a study of lie detection across cultures, Charles Bond Jr. and his associates Omar, Mahmoud, and Bonser (1990), compared Americans to Jordanians to test the *Universal-cue* hypothesis which theorizes that liars in all cultures exhibit the same behavior. They noted that, while the principles of human lie detection may be universal, the cues to deception are not. Americans could not detect lies told by Jordanians and Jordanians could not detect lies told by Americans.

Conversely, Bond, *et al.* (1990), reported that the cues to apparent honesty generalize across cultures, as the individual who looks honest to Americans also looks honest to Jordanians. A similar finding by McArthur and Berry (1987) was that Americans and Koreans showed a strong cross-cultural agreement in judgments of facial honesty. The studies by Ekman (1972) and Friesen (1972) determined that Japanese and Americans showed the same facial expressions when experiencing fear, disgust, and distress if they were alone. Quite different expressions were evident, however, in social situations (*i.e.*, Japanese covered the facial expressions of negative emotions with a smiling mask much more than Americans). The authors noted that there are measurable differences between felt and false smiles and other kinds of smiles.

Ekman (1985) stated that deceptions are common, and the detection of deception is vital in business, legal, and military settings. Bond and colleagues (1990) warn that *"Voters can be advised to choose honest-looking leaders, with assurance that their honesty will generalize overseas. But international negotiators should be warned that anatomically-based perceptions of honesty are often invalid"* (p. 203).

Gender Differences in Communication

There are noted differences in communication styles between sexes. For example, women tend to prefer higher levels of nonverbal involvement with one another than do males in that women prefer closer interaction distances and more frequent touching. Women also tend to be more facially expressive than men. Women smile more often and are more bodily expressive in head, hand, and body movements. Men, however, tend to be less verbally expressive and nondisclosing (Buck, Baron & Barrette, 1982; Buck, Baron, Goodman, & Shapiro, 1980; Leathers, 1992).

Cognitive Dissonance

Another element that contributes to the complexity of communication is the natural tendency of humans to strive for harmony, consistency, congruity, and balance. Essentially, the term cognitive dissonance, as it relates to language, is when a person verbally says one thing and portrays the opposite meaning by non-verbal behavior. An example would be a person stating, *"I love spinach,"* while showing a distorted facial expression indicating that spinach really is disliked (Festinger, 1957). Many times, these disparate expressions, when considered unimportant or inconsistent, are valid indicators of untruthfulness or serve as a cover-up tactic or a smoke screen to the truth.

Toward Universal Understanding

The art of communication translation requires rapid observation, knowledge of human behavior, and an awareness of such factors as cultural differences, cognitive dissonance, and possible alternative meanings. It is recognized that nonverbal cues are *implicit messages* embedded within the ongoing stream of real-time -- multi-channel communications that characterize even the simplest interaction. Decades of research have demonstrated that these cues have universal meaning. Judges shown sequences of nonverbal behavior are able to construct inferences with a surprising degree of accuracy. While accuracy in perception seems to be well established, the manner in which an inference is construed is still somewhat of a mystery. Research suggests that perceivers are conscious of the process of understanding nonverbal cues, but the interpretive process reflects inarticulation.

The Study of Communication and Deception

According to the literature, Mark L. Knapp (Knapp, Hart, & Dennis, 1974) and his colleagues, R.P. Hart and H.S. Dennis, were the first communication researchers to study deception and to emphasize the role of verbal and nonverbal behavior in deceptive transactions. Knapp stated: *"Deception is the other side of truth; any message has the potential to be deceptive depending upon the motives or intent of the communicator"* (Miller & Stiff, 1993, p. x).

Deception is difficult to detect. However, Mark A. deTurck and Gerald R. Miller (1990) reported that special skill training can create human lie detectors. These researchers (1985) suggested that deceivers exhibit a distinctly deception-induced type of arousal that most truthful communicators do not experience. Hale and Stiff (1990) concurred that nonverbal cues are the most important source of information for deception detection, especially when verbal and nonverbal portions of a communicator's message are contradictory or not consistent. An example of this incongruency was explained by Ekman (1985, p. 81):

> There are only clues that the person is poorly prepared and clues
> of emotions that don't fit the person's line. These are what provide
> leakage or deception clues. The lie catcher must learn how emo-
> tion is registered in speech, voice, body, and face; what traces
> may be left despite a liar's attempts to conceal feelings, and what
> gives away false emotional portrayals. Spotting deceit also re-

quires understanding how these behaviors may reveal that a liar is making up his line as he goes along.

What makes deception detection most difficult, however, is the fact that the untruthful face leaks least because it is most susceptible to the conscious control of the communicator. Myron Zuckerman and colleagues (1981) believed that *"Since the face is more controllable, it is less likely to give away deception. Stated differently, the channel that is the most informative when the communicator is truthful is most misleading when the communicator is deceptive"* (p. 5). They also stated that *"the extent to which deception fosters guilt, anxiety, and/or duping delight varies according to the purposes of the deception, its social context, and the characteristics of the deceiver"* (p. 9).

In the article *"Learning to Detect Deception From Three Communication Channels,"* Zuckerman, Coestner, and Colella (1985) note that an observer is not likely to distinguish between truth and lie telling on the basis of facial expression alone. They explained that, in studying speech plus facial expression, one can become a more accurate lie detector.

A person's demeanor can be considered an obstacle to lie detection since some people look honest even if they are lying while others look dishonest even if they are telling the truth. Zuckerman, DeFrank, Hall, Lawrence, and Rosenthal (1979) refer to this phenomenon as the *demeanor bias* and believe that deception judgments are stimulus-driven in that they depend more on the target's apparent honesty than on the perceiver's detection skills.

Bond and Robinson (1988) reported that the effectiveness of deception reflects its contribution to survival and adaptive principles and to inherited, honest looking anatomical characteristics or a dishonest-looking anatomy. Bond, Kahler, and Paolicelli (1985) suggested that people who inherit honest-looking demeanors succeed as liars and therefore are reinforced when practicing deception. Those who look dishonest fail as liars and are thereby discouraged in developing the ability to deceive.

Gerald R. Miller (1931-1993) and associates have contributed greatly to the understanding of deceptive communication. Miller, who was a distinguished professor at Michigan State University, became the founding editor of the journal, *Human Communications Research*. Other researchers who have examined the role of verbal content in deception and deception detection are Cody and associates (1984), Kraut (1978), Stiff and Miller (1986), and Wagner and Pease (1976).

Vocal Cues to Deception -- Vocal cues may be indicators of deceit. A number of studies have found that deceivers exhibit more speech errors than honest communicators (deTurck & Miller, 1985; Druckman, *et al.,* 1982; Knapp, *et al.,* 1974; Mehrabian, 1971). Researchers have found that deceivers tend to hesitate and pause more frequently and for longer periods of time than do truth tellers (Harrison, *et al.,* 1978; Kraut, 1978; O'Hair, *et al.,* 1990) but that liars also speak at a faster rate than truthful communicators (Hocking & Leathers, 1980; Zuckerman, *et al.,* 1981).

Vocal nervousness is another identified indicator of lying (deTurck, *et al.*, 1990; Hocking & Leathers, 1980; and Zuckerman, *et al.*, 1981). Another study found that voice pitch was higher in the deceptive than in the honest subjects (Ekman, Friesen, & Scherer, 1976). The following is a listing of the deceptive verbal cues as determined by these investigators:

- *Self-References:* The number of times a subject refers to himself or herself during a response.

- *Other-References:* The number of times a subject refers to others during a response.

- *Mutual References:* The number of times a subject mutually refers to himself or herself and others during a response.

- *Statements of Personal Responsibility:* The number of statements in which a subject assumes personal responsibility for an event or outcome during a response (e.g., "It was my idea," "I was the one in charge," "I guess it was my fault").

- *Statements of Mutual Responsibility:* The number of statements in which a subject indicates that responsibility for an event or outcome should be shared by himself or herself and at least one other person (e.g., "We all were a little to blame," "it was my fault as much as it was theirs," "we all should get the credit for this").

- *Factual Statements:* Statements about people, objects, or events that, in principle, are verifiable. These statements do not have to be true, only verifiable (e.g., "I studied five hours last night," "The size of the group has been steadily increasing").

- *Hypothetical Statements:* Statements that refer to a situation or event that has not occurred, but has some probability of occurring (e.g., "If I get the raise, then I will probably work harder," "People would have responded differently to another leader").

- *Opinion Statements:* Statements in which the subject indicates his or her own opinion about some person, object, or event (e.g., "I would prefer to do things differently," "I don't like situations like this") (p. 58).

The flow of speech during an investigative interview is at times as complicated to follow as the nonverbal interaction but must be considered concomitantly.

When one considers that a pianist can play as many as 16 notes a second, compared to the motor commands in the speech musculature which have been calculated to be as high as 1,400 per second (Lenneberg, 1967), it is perplexing to fathom the great abundance of spoken words and behavior co-occurring at such rapid speeds. Thus, the ability to coordinate and synchronize with a variety of other people under various circumstances has a significant impact on one's professional competence and effectiveness in the interviewing process (Bernieri & Rosenthal, 1991).

Verbal Correlates to Deception

In regard to verbal correlates to deception, Miller and Stiff (1993) reported that typically deceptive statements are shorter than truthful ones, tend to be more general, and contain fewer specific references to people, places, and temporal ordering of events. Also, deceptive statements have a tendency to over generalize through such terms as *all, never, none,* and *nobody.*

- *Audible Pauses: The number of times a pause is filled with sounds like "err," "umm," "aah," "ya know," etc., during the response.*

- *Silent Pauses: The amount of silent time that occurs once the subject has started to answer a question or make a statement.*

- *Sentence Repairs: The number of times a sentence or phrase is started, interrupted, and then repeated during a response.*

- *Response Latency: The amount of time between the end of an interviewer's question and the beginning of the subject's response.*

- *Response Length: The amount of total time (speaking and silent) from the beginning to the end of a response* (p. 57).

The Physiological Aspects of Deception

From the beginning of time, there has been a universal search for truth and an effort to determine falsehoods. Complex procedures founded on magic and mysticism were developed by primitive societies in an endeavor to detect deception. Perhaps that magic was based on that phenomenon of events that defy articulation. Most of those magical rituals and those intuitive realizations actually were based on sound physiological principles. Those pioneers who developed the polygraph instrument made substantial contributions to the fields of communication and deception detection because of their understanding of such physiological functions as pulse rate, blood pressure, respiration, galvanic skin response, and muscle activity. A brief review of the physiology and anatomy of the brain and nervous system will set the foundation for understanding physiological reactions to the anxiety and fear that tend to be associated with lying or deception.

The Central Nervous System

The Brain -- The brain is considered the master organ of life, the center of consciousness, self-awareness, and thought. It controls basic functions, including breathing and, to some degree, heart activity. Messages from all over the body are received by the brain, which decides how to respond to changing conditions both inside and outside of the body. The brain also sends messages to muscles to facilitate bodily movement and to vital organs so they will carry out their specific functions.

The Spinal Cord -- The spinal cord is a relay between most of the body and the brain. Messages are sent to and from the brain through the spinal cord.

Reflexes -- Reflexes allow quick reactions to take place without the brain having to send orders. The spinal cord is the center of reflex activity.

The Autonomic Nervous System (ANS) -- There is a special division in the nervous system called the Autonomic Nervous System (ANS). The nerves of the ANS connect the brain and spinal cord (*i.e.*, the central nervous system) to the heart muscle (myocardium), glands, smooth muscles in the walls of hollow organs, and the smooth muscles in the walls of the blood vessels in the skin, skeletal muscles, and organs. One may refer to the autonomic nervous system as the automatic nervous system because responses occur automatically. Several ANS responses are listed in Figure 7.1. Biofeedback training can teach limited control over the ANS, but, for the most part, all responses are involuntary or cannot be controlled.

Figure 7.1
FUNCTION OF THE AUTONOMIC NERVOUS SYSTEM

1) Slowing or increasing heart rate.
2) Increasing or decreasing the strength of heart contractions.
3) Constricting blood vessels in the skin.
4) Constricting or dilating blood vessels in skeletal muscles.
5) Dilating or constricting blood vessels in abdominal organs.
6) Slowing or increasing respiration.
7) Changing bronchial diameter.
8) Contracting or relaxing the urinary bladder.
9) Dilating or constricting the pupils of the eye.
10) Increasing or decreasing secretion of saliva.
11) Contracting or relaxing of the muscular system.

The Physiology of Emotions

It is recognized that the autonomic nervous system plays a vitally important role in controlling emotions experienced, whether displayed or hidden. Given this information, it seems feasible that one can carefully and somewhat accurately observe these bodily changes that result from the ANS response to such stimuli as anxiety and fear. For example:

1) A decrease in secretion of saliva will cause the mouth to be dry and clicky.

2) An increase in heart rate and strength of contractions may cause the face to be flushed, and one may notice beads of perspiration across the forehead.

3) A decrease in heart rate, and strength of contractions, associated with constricting blood vessels, may cause cold hands and feet and even a paleness of the face.

4) Changes in the respiratory pattern, as well as tension of the large upper chest muscles, may be the result of anxiety messages channeled through the ANS.

5) Muscular contractions also may be involuntary and send out cues of anxiety such as a shaky, weakened voice; arm and leg movements; and head and shoulder movements.

6) Perspiration also is monitored by the ANS and may tend to increase during anxious situations.

7) The eyes operate out of their own level of awareness, affecting pupil dilation, which is beyond our ability to consciously control and can reveal highly personal information that we would not chose to reveal if we could consciously control dilation.

8) As blood is diverted from the digestive tract and rerouted to the surface of the skin, a tingling sensation is felt and may cause itching.

9) Dramatic changes in the digestive system can cause nausea and even vomiting.

Universally Accepted Deception Cues

The practitioner who can become proficient at observing the physiological and psychological aspects of deception, and the ways in which bodily reactions send cues which communicate deception, has a greater advantage than through use of a polygraph device. Even though deception is difficult to detect, skill training can produce diagnosticians who are reasonably proficient in lie detection. The next section will discuss what some of these nonverbal cues are and how they function to protect the body from the stress and anxiety of lying.

Behavior Indicative of Deception

Research has determined that a liar will attempt to disguise and censor facial expressions more than other body movements. Perhaps that is because it is easier to disguise or control facial expressions. Nevertheless, behavioral cues to deceit are evident in face, body, voice, and speech. A word of warning here is that no one behavioral symptom should be relied upon singularly, but should be given in-depth collective consideration with all other verbal and nonverbal facets of communication. In fact, when combined, observation of the face and listening to the voice offer a very high accuracy rate in lie detection.

The astute practitioner must learn to detect emotion revealed in speech, voice, body, and face and use the information wisely to the full advantage of the interviewing objective. All persons must be reminded that the diagnostics of deception serve only as an interviewing aid and should not be used individually as the sole criteria to establish the truth and credibility of any job applicant or person being interviewed for another purpose. A responsible practitioner should independently corroborate any issues in a logical and defensible manner so as to avoid any employment litigation claims.

Nonverbal Cues to Deception -- Nonverbal cues to deception were separated by Miller and Stiff (1993) into visual cues and vocal cues, which are described below:

- *Adaptors: The amount of time either hand is moving while touching the body during the response.*

- *Hand Gestures: The amount of time either hand is moving while not touching the body during the response.*

- *Indirect Eye Gaze: The amount of time spent not meeting the interviewer's eyes while answering questions or making statements.*

- *Broken Eye Contact: The number of times eye contact is established and broken during a response.*

- *Eye Blinks: The number of eye blinks during the response.*

- *Smile Duration: The amount of time spent smiling during the response. A smile occurs when the corners of the mouth are turned upward.*

- *Posture Shifts: The number of times the trunk of the body is shifted during the response.*

- *Leg/Foot Movements: The amount of time either leg or foot is moving during the response (p. 57).*

Disguised and Censored Facial Expressions

The Universal Smile -- It has been known since 1862 that there is a type of involuntary smile implicit of all humans which involves the combined contraction of a muscle around the eye and a muscle that governs the lips. This particular smile was termed a *felt happiness smile* and later renamed the *enjoyment smile.* Since 1990, however, the smile has been referred to as the *Duchenne Smile* to honor the French neurologist, Gullaume Benjamin Amand Duchenne, who first reported this phenomenon. Duchenne also is credited as the first investigator of the anatomy of facial muscles because he identified over 100 facial muscles.

Universal Smile Characteristics -- Distinguishing characteristics of the Duchenne smile are the crow's feet wrinkles around the eyes and a subtle drop in the eye cover fold so that the skin above the eye moves down slightly toward the eyeball. Research is consistent with Duchenne's early findings that most people are unable to voluntarily contract the muscles that formulate the Duchenne or real smile. Photos illustrating the real smile are shown in Figure 7.2 with contrasting masked smiles in Figure 7.3.

Masking Smiles -- A smile can be produced on demand, and research shows that people have *display rules* which tend to modify the smile even when it is heartfelt. Therefore, the smile can be one of the most obvious nonverbal indicators of behavior since it is relatively easy to distinguish a *smile* from a *no-smile.* These produced smiles often are referred to as masking smiles or miserable smiles. They exhibit muscular traces of disgust, anger, fear, sadness, or contempt, which are thought to be the consequences of lying. These smiles tend to occur when people are concealing something, not when they are frankly showing their true feelings. Thus, smiles can be most informative when the communicator is telling the truth, but can be the most misleading when the communicator is lying. A photo illustrating a masked smile is shown in Figure 7.3.

Leakage -- Those deception cues discussed above can be seen by the trained eye as microexpressions or fragments of an expression that cross the face quickly, in less than half a second, and before most people notice them. They are much more readily discernible when filmed as a video and played back at slow speed. These deception clues are referred to as *leakage* since they tend to leak information to the observant person's trained eye even when the subject desperately attempts to control the response. Eye behaviors that have been deemed indicators of deception are excessive blinking and pupil dilation, as well as eye avoidance or limited eye contact.

Figure 7.2
DUCHENNE SMILE

Figure 7.3
MASKED SMILE

Deceitful Eye Indicators -- Eye behaviors that have been deemed indicators of deception are blinking and pupil dilation (O'Hair, *et al.,* 1990; Zuckerman, *et al.,* 1981), avoidance or limited eye contact (Exline, *et al.,* 1970; and Hocking & Leathers, 1980), and averted gazes (Druckman, *et al.,* 1982).

Vocal Cues Indicating Deception

Deceitful speakers tend to exhibit more speech errors than honest communicators. Deceivers also tend to hesitate and pause more frequently and for longer periods of time than do truth tellers. But, sometimes, liars also speak at a faster rate than truth tellers. Voice nervousness is another identified indicator of lying. Vocal pitch has been noted as being higher in the deceptive person than the honest one.

Emotions and feelings most noted in the voice are:

1)	Disgust	6)	Contempt
2)	Happiness	7)	Surprise
3)	Interest	8)	Anger
4)	Sadness	9)	Determination
5)	Bewilderment	10)	Fear

Other emotions and feelings to observe and listen for are:

1)	Indifference	6)	Despair
2)	Grief	7)	Impatience
3)	Anxiety	8)	Amusement
4)	Sympathy	9)	Satisfaction
5)	Pride	10)	Dislike

It is important to become aware of the deception process and the techniques and cues to discern truth from lying. As a successful communicator, this skill development can lend itself to becoming the effective human lie detector that is so necessary in the decision-making process of selecting friends and business associates, and in all daily transactions both private and public, including workplace investigations.

The Art of Discerning Truth and Deception
The art of discerning truth and deception during an investigation requires knowledge of interactive communication and the ability to simultaneously observe and listen while interacting with that interviewee. Society, from the beginning of time, consistently has been concerned with identifying dishonest individuals. This insatiable need has culminated in the development of a multitude of honesty assessment measures that can be categorized in the following five methods of preemployment screening:

1) Physiological measures,
2) Biographical data analysis,
3) Disguised purpose personality type tests,
4) Clear purpose honesty tests, and
5) Systematic selection interviews.

Other assessment methods of determining integrity prior to employment include reference checks, criminal background checks, and credit checks.

Diagnosis of Nonverbal Communication
The entire body can present a symphony of messages communicated by concerted, interactive dependency. The following section lists and photographically illustrates some universally accepted kinesic indicators of meanings. These behav-

ioral indicators are empirically based and have been fully described in *Universal Interviewing and Communications: A Preemployment Application* (Slowik, 1995).

Diagnosing Gestures

The modality of gestures as nonverbal communicators are considered to be visible bodily action by which meaning is given voluntary expression and is separate from emotional expression.

- **Openness gestures** (*i.e.*, open hands, unbuttoned coats, loosened neckties, relaxation of body) tend to stimulate interaction and appear to be a necessary precondition for individuals to reach an agreement.

- **Closed gestures** (*i.e.*, crossed arms, crossed legs, hunched shoulders, hugging body) in contrast tend to communicate defensiveness and inaccessibility.

Behavioral Indicators

During the first few seconds of an investigative interview, an investigator can discern a multitude of messages. Drawing from the UNICOM Behavioral Model presented in Chapter Six, the investigator must observe and discern the interviewee's verbal and nonverbal messages. The investigator should observe the behavior of an interviewee entering the room, approaching a chair, and sitting. Some behaviors to be noted are:

- Did the person project an image of confidence, fear, or anxiety?

- Did the person smile a natural smile or a forced smile?

- Was the person well groomed?

- Was the chair moved before sitting?

- Did the person sit straight or side saddle?

- Did the person perform grooming gestures, *i.e.*, arranging hair or picking imaginary lint?

Genuine Facial Expressions -- Genuine facial expressions are considered representational in that they truthfully represent a felt emotion. An example of a genuine felt emotion is shown above in Figure 7.2.

Indicators of Truthfulness -- The photos shown below in Figure 7.4 are indicative of truthfulness. Also listed are several universal indicators of truthfulness.

Deceptive Facial Expressions -- Deceptive facial expressions are considered presentational in that they are controlled by the communicator and represent a false face. An example of the deceptive facial expression is a masking smile, or a miserable smile, which are each described as smiles people display when concealing or not revealing their true feelings. An example of the masked smile is shown in Figure 7.3.

Indicators of Deception -- The photos shown in Figure 7.5 are indicative of deception. Also listed are several universal indicators of deception. Defensiveness cues that can alert the interviewer to the possibility that the interviewee is being deceptive are illustrated in Figure 7.6.

Opposing Indicators of Defensiveness -- Figure 7.7 presents illustrations of the ways various types of people might display defensiveness. For example, some people may erect barriers while others may become aggressive when responding to a line of questioning that may, for whatever reason, seem somewhat threatening to the interviewee. Also listed in Figure 7.7 are several indicators of defensive aggression and barrier behaviors.

Interest and Listening -- Figure 7.8 presents photos showing body language that illustrates interest and listening and includes a listing of indicators that denote these emotions. Among these cues are open body postures which include drawn back legs and leaning forward. The eyes and facial expression also play key roles in denoting these emotions.

Indicators of Interest or Liking -- A photo illustrating these emotions, along with a listing of cues, is presented in Figure 7.9. Among these cues are the Duchenne smile and open body posture.

Indicators of Disliking or Disinterest -- These cues are illustrated in Figure 7.10. Closed bodily stance, tension and rigidity are among the behaviors that illustrate the emotions of disliking and/or disinterest.

Indicators of Assertiveness/Nonassertiveness -- Assertiveness and nonassertiveness cues are illustrated and described in Figures 7.11 and 7.12. Many of these cues are in direct contrast to each other. For instance, the assertive person is more likely to make direct eye contact whereas the nonassertive person may keep his gaze averted or eye contact may be evasive. Vocal cues also are abundant here. The assertive person may speak in a strong, clear voice, whereas the nonassertive person may mumble, clear his throat a lot, or speak softly.

Concealment -- Concealment behavioral cues are illustrated in photos in Figure 7.13. People with something to conceal often will cover their mouths or faces with their hands while they speak.

Disinterest or Boredom -- Photos illustrating these cues, which show closed communication postures such as crossed arms and legs, are presented in Figure 7.14. Disinterested or bored persons often have non-enthusiastic facial expressions and do not show attention to the person speaking.

Figure 7.4
BEHAVIOR INDICATORS OF TRUTHFULNESS

- True "felt happy" smile
- Clear, confident eyes
- At ease
- Appropriate movements

- Direct eye contact
- Confidence
- Relaxed responses
- Erect posture

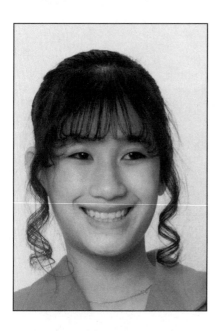 

Figure 7.5
BEHAVIOR INDICATORS OF DECEPTION

- Masked smile
- Blinking and pupil dilation
- Eager to please
- Extraneous gestures
- Controlled reactions

- Averted gaze, limited eye contact
- Slumped and protected body position
- Defensive gestures
- Bodily nervousness
- Changes in behavior

Figure 7.6
DEFENSIVENESS

Figure 7.7
OPPOSING INDICATORS OF DEFENSIVENESS

<u>**Defensive aggression**</u>
- Crossed arms
- Closed body
- Direct eye contact

<u>**Defensive barrier**</u>
- Closed arms
- Closed body
- Avoided eye contact

Aggressive Defensive

Protective Defensive

Figure 7.8
INTEREST AND LISTENING

The following photos illustrate body language that denotes interest and listening. Each leans forward, eyes are focused, and facial expression is attentive. Other indicators: hands are still and relaxed, leg drawn back, body and eyes are in the open receiving position.

Figure 7.9
INDICATORS OF INTEREST OR LIKING

- Smiling (genuine)
- Open-body position, gestures
- Leaning toward another
- Directly facing another
- Affirmative head nodding
- Closeness
- Touching or reaching out
- Limited gesturing or animation
- Direct eye contact
- Mirrored or matched positions
- Relaxed body
- Enthusiastic expression

Figure 7.10
INDICATORS OF DISLIKING/DISINTEREST

- Averted eyes/limited eye contact
- Furrowed eyebrows
- Rigid body
- Closed bodily stance
- Arms and legs crossed
- Body tension and rigidity
- Disinterested expression
- Unpleasant expression
- Resistant
- Tight lipped
- Tense jawline

Figure 7.11
INDICATORS OF ASSERTIVENESS

- Leaning forward
- Direct eye contact
- Congruent verbal/nonverbal
- Accentuating gestures
- Strong clear voice
- Vocal inflections

Figure 7.12
INDICATORS OF NONASSERTIVENESS

- Averted/evasive eye contact
- Hunched posture
- Inhibited or nervous gestures
- Hand wringing
- Smiling out of context or fake
- Clearing throat
- Mumbled speech
- Meek expression
- Arms hugging body
- Legs crossed
- Hand over mouth

Figure 7.13
CONCEALMENT

Sometimes when people lie or withhold information they cover the mouth with a hand or hide their face with a hand.

Genuine Facial Expressions

Genuine facial expressions are considered *representational* in that they truthfully represent a felt emotion. An example of a genuine facial expression is the *felt smile,* referred to as the Duchenne smile (Figure 7.2).

Deceptive Facial Expressions

Deceptive facial expressions are considered *presentational* in that they are controlled by the communicator and represent a false face. An example of the deceptive facial expression is a *masking smile* (Figure 7.3), or *miserable smile,* described as smiles people display when concealing or not revealing their true feelings.

Figure 7.14
DISINTEREST OR BOREDOM

The following photos illustrate body language that translates as disinterested or bored: Note that both have arms and legs crossed, indicating closed communication. Facial expressions are non-enthusiastic and eyes are averted and do not show attention.

Universal Components of Communication Summary

The theoretical base of the components of communication was presented as it has evolved during the past century. A brief literature review was presented here to provide a foundational basis for the workplace investigator to understand the universal, cultural, and gender dynamics of human communication and how they relate to our ability to discern truth and deception. This chapter described the universally accepted components of communication, as well as cultural and gender comparisons of differences and similarities. Secondly, the chapter explained verbal and nonverbal communicative cues that can be interpreted for detecting truth and deception.

CHAPTER EIGHT

UNICOM_{SM}
A TECHNIQUE FOR INVESTIGATIVE INTERVIEWING

UNICOM -- A Technique in Interviewing for Workplace Investigations

The following section defines and describes UNICOM as a technique in interviewing for workplace investigations. When one understands the attributes and qualifications of a skilled practitioner, a logical task would be a self-evaluation to determine personal strengths and weaknesses in order to assist the student in the selection of the most needed area of emphasis in the instructional process. While it is recognized that interviewing for workplace investigations is specialized and includes employee interviewees who are either suspects or witnesses, the skills for interviewing are very similar to the preemployment application.

Developing Effective Investigation Skills -- The importance of developing effective investigation skills cannot be overstated. It should be the goal of every employer to treat employees fairly. Furthermore, the law dictates that the entire employment process protect against discrimination in regard to race, national origin, ancestry, color, religion, sex, sexual orientation, marital status, medical condition, pregnancy, age, physical or mental disability, and veteran status. If there are violations within the realm of any of the above classes, the Human Resource Department must be prepared to conduct a professional, comprehensive, and objective investigation.

Conducting a professional investigation is an acquired skill. It involves special skill in interviewing and question formulation and the ability to gain cooperation and disclosure from an employee reluctant to reveal vital information. It requires the skill to sift the relevant from irrelevant details, and it takes integrity to make credible resolutions. Special skills also are mandatory for determining truthfulness during the investigation process. The professional investigation obligates the investigator to be secure in the knowledge of employment law and to develop techniques to ensure objectivity. The UNICOM Investigation Model considers all of these aspects and provides a step-by-step strategy to ensure a professional, comprehensive, objective formal workplace investigation.

Universal Interviewing and Communications

Universal Interviewing and Communications (UNICOM) is a multifaceted process of preparation, data collection, and quantitative and qualitative analysis essential for making internal investigation decisions. UNICOM also is a multidimensional process of procuring and deliberating both objective and subjective information. Conscientious attention to detail and a scrupulous regard for the entire demeanor of the employee is required as well as a full awareness of how the investigator's behavior and demeanor influences that interaction and the attending circumstances.

The UNICOM Investigator -- Imagine the measure of concentration required of a competent investigator who interacts conversationally with an employee while simultaneously focusing on the employee's nonverbal behavior. The investigator simultaneously asks designed questions, listens intently to the employee's answers, and scrutinizes the interaction for all types of psychological and physiological behavior. The types of psychological and physiological data an investigator gathers in this dynamic process are those basically communicated by body language (*i.e.*, posture, eye contact, gestures, and movements, facial expressions, breathing, or any nonverbal expression in reaction to a question or situational stimulus during the interaction).

Development of UNICOM

UNICOM offers a structured, organized approach to gathering a large variety and quantity of data about an employee or employment situation. This technique has been selectively created and based on the application and research of over two decades of personal and professional experiences in interviewing and interactive communication. The primary source for the UNICOM model's framework is the author's career experience as a human resource practitioner, security analyst, and psychometrician.

Investigator Skill Development

This section addresses the prerequisites and qualifications of all effective, proficient investigators and presents information pertinent to investigator skill development. The complexity of internal workplace investigations is acknowledged since it dictates the role of a competent human resource investigator. One false step can plunge employers into a wrongful termination suit. Even in the most clear-cut cases, conducting an investigation is a delicate venture because of the potential for charges of defamation, coercion, invasion of privacy, and even false imprisonment. Thus, quality is important at every step of the investigation.

Investigator Defined -- Proficient, astute investigators cultivate a quiet confidence, substantiated by a balance of discriminating sensitivity and technical knowledge, and a sense of warmth interwoven with technically proven tactics and techniques. Competent investigators project a genuine concern, warmth, and serenity toward interviewees while maintaining a neutral mien.

High-caliber investigators, as a distinct group of people, seem to be in the minority and are greatly valued for their skills and proven effectiveness. In contrast, less qualified investigators do not appreciate the relevance and potential of their skills and thus contribute to or compound their own inefficiency. They tend to become oblivious to the procedure and miss their mark. Thus, in understanding the difference between the expert investigator and the less-skilled investigator, it is not difficult to realize that skills and effectiveness must be learned, developed, and nurtured. It is the primary purpose of this instructional section to assist any dedicated investigator in becoming a proficient, high caliber, and valued interviewer.

Recognizing Levels of Competency

Someone who generally is competent in his or her skills, and who comprehends the dynamics of the interactive behavior involved in the investigative process, can readily recognize the inefficiency and incompetency of untrained investigators. Often, investigators in various capacities, whether professional, intermediate, or middle management, realize their own personal level of mastery. They privately and confidentially experience a sense of ecstasy, or even a sensational feeling of confidence, because of this mastery. Their peers recognize that as well.

Competent investigators are easily recognized within the work environment because their interviewing and screening efforts obtain much more adequate and accurate information than unskilled investigators. When one is competent, time engagement is minimized, hard-core objectives are accurately accomplished, and delicate issues are handled, not sidestepped, with unusual pervasiveness.

The magnitude of these personal skills cannot be understated. When the reader considers the multifarious essence of verbal and nonverbal behavior in conjunction with the required observation, comprehension, and interpretation of such interaction, it becomes apparent how the UNICOM practitioner must operate.

A Trilogy of Interactive Activities

An effective UNICOM practitioner conducting an investigation must be able to accurately interpret and meticulously catalog numerous covert and overt behaviors to meet the interview objectives. This process can become complex, because verbal and nonverbal behavior occurs simultaneously at a very rapid rate. To have this advantage, an investigator must employ a trilogy of interactive activities (Figure 8.1).

The ability to masterfully manage this trilogy of interactive activities will ensure a better performance, a refined efficiency, and increased productivity in the accomplishment of the overall investigation objective. Managing these interactive activities is a challenging process. In the section that follows, each component of this interactive trilogy is discussed separately with its individual elements and then addressed interactively.

The UNICOM Investigator as Multidimensional

The UNICOM investigator operates within an interrelated set of decision-making rules. These rules determine what the investigator says, how it is said, and when it is said. They also govern what is not said. Most importantly, the astute investigator must maintain ultimate control while subtly staging a convincing neutral, yet positive, impression to the employee. This particular skill, like most skills, is not innate but must be learned and practiced.

Figure 8.1
TRILOGY OF INTERACTIVE ACTIVITIES
FOR INVESTIGATORS

The Investigator Must:

1)   Have a definitive understanding of the investigative objective,

2)   Discern the dynamics and the interactive behavior from the point of view of the person being investigated, and

3)   Subsequently respond with the appropriate interactive behavior to facilitate investigation cooperation and disclosure.

The UNICOM investigator must be multitalented and multidimensional, and must serve as a superb diagnostician who clearly comprehends the objectives of eliciting and identifying information, data, and behavior, and of disclosing various facts that are not always obvious. In a sense, the effective UNICOM investigator develops the ability to accurately read physiological responses as related to verbal responses and the investigative objective. Simultaneously, the investigator must accommodate or adapt to the employee's verbal and nonverbal communication in such a manner that the employee perceives the situation to be safe for full disclosure.

Investigator's Knowledge and Experience

A broad knowledge, and informational-based prerequisite is essential for a successful investigator. This knowledge base not only involves a historical and theoretical perspective of preemployment selection tools and techniques and employer-employee interaction techniques but also requires a full understanding of current law and ethics in relation to internal workplace investigations. Thus, a successful investigator essentially is a historian, a researcher, a sociologist, and a behaviorist who understands employment law with regard to employee interviewing. The experienced UNICOM investigator draws from the development and personality theories of psychology, the social interaction theories of sociology, and from volumes of literature on both verbal and nonverbal communication.

Theatrics and the UNICOM Investigator

Generally speaking, *theatrics* can be defined as a convincing or even dramatic performance delivered to an individual or an audience. In regards to the UNICOM investigator's theatrics, it is intended to describe the overall behavioral dynamics for the purpose of developing an astute set of dramatic personal skills for a human resource application.

Effective and appropriate theatrics are employed by UNICOM investigators who, in a sense, become actors or actresses as they adapt or acclimate to situational events. Gestures, emphasized speech, certain emulations, and effective mirroring are common techniques used to bridge relationships and establish a common ground for effective communication. Thus, the UNICOM investigator can effectively adapt or acclimate to any interview situation that involves people of the opposite gender, other races or cultures, a different socioeconomic status, or varying social and regional differences in behavior.

The utilization of theatrics is not intended to be deceptive or unethical to the employee. The designed intent is to facilitate an interviewer/interviewee relationship that will minimize the apprehension or discomfort of the employee and simultaneously maximize the opportunity for employee truthfulness and disclosure of information that has a business necessity for legal inquiry.

Fundamental Interviewing Techniques

An effective UNICOM investigator's techniques are much more sophisticated and dynamic than easily can be explained. However, the next section is dedicated to an explanation of how these techniques work to gain favorable responses from the employee because investigators value the human interaction element to the utmost degree.

The Investigator's Impression Management -- Impression management is the investigator's conscious attempt to exercise control over communicative behaviors, particularly nonverbal cues, for purposes of making a desired impression. Not only must the investigator learn to exercise conscious control over the impression he or she makes on another person, but he or she will consciously control his or her emotional responses to what that person says or has done. An interrelated component to applying these skills is the idea of investigators associating themselves with desirable image traits while simultaneously disclaiming association with undesirable image traits. The latter includes the investigator's personal interactive process with the interviewee as well as the investigator's duty to ensure that the investigative interview environment presents the ideal image. The nature of impression management is divided into four dimensions:

1)   Credibility,
2)   Likability,
3)   Interpersonal attractiveness, and

4)   Dominance.

Each of these is defined below:

Credibility of Impression -- It is essential that the investigator present a believable image. The more believable the impression and communicative demeanor, the more likely he will achieve success with the interactive interview. Conversely, one can assume that the greater the facade, the less likely it is that the investigative interview will be successful.

Likability of Impression -- Common sense and a considerable amount of research denotes the importance of being likable in the interactive investigative interview process.

Interpersonal Attractiveness -- The dimension of interpersonal attractiveness is much more than the initial physical impression in that it involves the emotional psycho-social aspect of expression during the interactive activities.

Dominant Impression -- It is essential for the investigator to present a very positive image of dominance and to have the ability to manage power and assertiveness in an acceptable manner without the appearance of arrogance.

The Challenge of Impression Management -- The challenge that the investigator must meet is dependent upon learning the skills to accomplish the above dimensions of impression management and then to extend those skills to meet the objective of effectively managing interactive interviews with those of the opposite gender, those of other cultures and races, and those of other socioeconomic backgrounds.

Interactive Behavior with the Employee -- The UNICOM investigator must be careful not to noticeably mirror or imitate the behavior of the employee. Often, the inexperienced interviewer feels the quickest way to establish data is to try to harmonize by mimicking the individual's behavioral pattern. When an interviewer unsuccessfully emulates the employee's behavior, he or she will be perceived as manipulative. This action can gridlock and jeopardize the goals of the interview process.

The UNICOM investigator should selectively and carefully model behavior in a qualified way to ensure that the employee will feel comfortable. If the employee uses profanity or violates any common courtesy ethics, the investigator should not be drawn into the situation or become offended, but should remain casual and appear unaffected by such behavior. It is important to show warmth but maintain a certain degree of distance.

The perceptive investigator should not avoid eye contact even if uncomfortable with an employee's direct eye contact. Under an adverse circumstance, an effective management technique is to look away momentarily and re-establish eye contact. Effective investigators always are in control of their own behavior so as not to compromise themselves with the employee.

The UNICOM investigator, through accomplished subtlety and intimation with undisclosed communication, must manage to convey to the employee that it is safe to participate in the fact-gathering exercise. It is fundamental that the investigator develop the personality characteristics of warmth, acceptance, empathy, caring, and respect as well as the ability to interact in a non-judgmental fashion. The investigator must recognize that an attitude of condescension, contempt, and arrogance is counterproductive.

The Investigator's Demeanor -- Anytime an investigator voices a personal position or philosophy, a degree and advantage of neutrality is forfeited, and consequently, influences the quality of rapport with the employee. Therefore, the investigator must constantly monitor personal feelings, biases, and behavior in relation to the interactive process. The investigator must be fully cognizant of certain conditioning techniques and discriminating in regard to word selection and execution as well as gestures and movements. Simultaneously, the investigator mentally records pertinent verbal and nonverbal communication exhibited by the employee.

The investigator must continually process and analyze what the employee is saying in relation to what should be said or what is appropriate for the situation. This freshly retained data should, as soon as possible following the interview, be transferred to paper to be assimilated and considered in relation to all other data exhibited by the employee.

Maintaining Control of the Interview

The effective and confident UNICOM investigator maintains control and direction of the interview. Perceptions mean a great deal when an employee walks into an office. Regardless of age or station in life, a tremendous amount of information is communicated nonverbally during the first few moments of the initial interaction between the investigator and the employee. It is critical that the investigator carefully manage this episode, because initial encounters can be an influential variable in the early stages of this process. An investigator must feel exceptionally comfortable with the interactive process at all times. The integration of this behavior eventually will become second nature to the investigator following continuous practice and application. An investigator must be able to constructively adapt to any situation, and can either sit or stand while going through the interview process without in any way communicating to the employee that he might be on unfamiliar ground.

Dynamics of Control -- The competent investigator very tactfully and selectively sets the scene for a control advantage so as not to embarrass or ostracize himself. Sometimes, very eloquent, deceptively speaking interviewees attempt to take control or mandate the interview process. The investigator must be aware of the dynamics of interaction and possible power struggles and know how to strategically handle an employee's attempt to take advantage. An example is the employee who challenges the knowledge of the investigator. This type of behavior is used as a testing mechanism by a dominant, arrogant type of subject who attempts to strive for supremacy.

A challenging employee may aspire purposefully to upset the investigator to a point of anger. It is of utmost importance that the UNICOM investigator does not become visually upset and lose control either subtly or overtly. If the employee attempts to irritate the investigator, this discernible action can be observed and dismantled. This particular situation will no doubt cause the investigator to draw upon every bit of talent, skill, and knowledge of UNICOM techniques and methods possible to maintain control and manage the interview process.

The UNICOM investigator must have an undaunting quality and never lose personal control: *"Those who anger you conquer you!"* (Elizabeth Kenny). It has been said that if one loses control, that power also is lost. Maintaining control, as subtle as it may seem, is, in a sense, maintaining the power.

Investigator Perception and Reception -- The UNICOM investigator must be fully aware of perception and reception. It generally is inappropriate for the investigator to register surprise or shock at any statement made by the employee and should not become personally offended or vindictive if, or when, the employee lies. It is essential to learn how to manage such adversity. This skill requires careful observation and quick interpretation by the investigator to analyze particular events and respond in the appropriate and effective manner.

This adeptness is vital for the investigator, especially in situations where there are marked differences between the investigator and the employee. These differences are becoming especially apparent in the emergence of the present culturally diverse workforce. For example, it would be a challenge for a female investigator, interviewing a brawny male employee, to confront that individual since the man might feel somewhat uncomfortable. It is essential that she facilitate a comfort level for natural interaction and work to prevent potential feelings of alienation. Consequently, the investigator's demeanor determines the direction and outcome of the interview.

The Investigator's Self-Behavior -- An effective investigator is fully aware of self-behavior since it radiates verbal and nonverbal messages in response to the employee's behavior. In fact, the competent UNICOM investigator is sensitive of the entire surroundings and activity in that interactive process, especially all the behavioral and verbal dynamics that occur between the investigator and employee. By being perceptive and clear about all behavior, the investigator readily can recognize behavior which is inconsistent or incongruent during the interview and engineer the appropriate respondent behavior.

The Dynamics of the Employee's Spectrum

One of the most critical issues in constantly dealing with other people, of course, is to not create hostility in a situation where there is a bad rapport between people. Ideally, the UNICOM investigator creates an untroubled, relaxed setting and carefully manages the interaction to obtain adequate and accurate information. The accomplished investigator, for that matter even any successful interrogator, functions in such a competent manner that the employee is unaware of the hidden dynamics employed. If the employee recognizes this process, it may create an inverse negative relationship which indicates that the investigator is not performing adequately. Investigator competency is in jeopardy, if not compromised, at this point, because it provides an opportunity for the employee to control the interview process.

The Employee's Characteristics

As a person's likes and dislikes were formed in the past, so are a host of other employment-related traits that correlate to current and past work performance history. UNICOM can be an efficient method, and facilitating agent, for an investigator to use in the information discovery process. If used properly, the UNICOM method will assist, if not amplify, other screening aids used during the overall hiring and selection process. During the entire process, the investigator continuously observes and scrutinizes the employee for characteristics and behaviors which may or may not be consistent with any other pre-established data about the employee.

Every employee situation is unique, and the employee brings a set of personal characteristics which the investigator must recognize with dignity and professionalism. The delicate and inflexible adherence to this practice truly distinguishes the UNICOM investigator from any professional counterparts.

The investigator always must examine any peculiarities about each individual to accommodate and direct a sense of orderliness as well as create a comfortable and appropriate environment. For example, if the employee is noticeably disabled, impaired, pregnant, *etc.*, the investigator must manage the situation with ease and respect and not draw undue attention or create discomfort for that person. Additionally, the investigator must adhere to the letter and spirit of the Americans with Disabilities Act.

Employee Vulnerabilities

For analytical purposes, an employee is especially vulnerable during the early stage of an investigative interview. Thus, the investigator should be exceptionally vigilant and careful to read and absorb behavior so as not to be drawn into any situation upon which the employee can capitalize. While it is difficult to determine when one stage of the interview ends and another begins, the first stage is very critical. An astute investigator will recognize exceptional cooperation, pretenses, deception, and offensive, aggressive, or misdirected venting. A truthful person categorically responds in one manner while a deceptive person responds in another way.

The Investigator's Analysis of the Employee -- The UNICOM investigator must separate and analyze collective behaviors (*i.e.,* offensive vs. defensive behavior, initiated or not, under or over cooperation). Isolated blocks of behavior become very obvious to the investigator. Typically, an innocent person accused of some wrongdoing will offer a strong, antagonized, and consistent denial. Generally, an innocent person experiences fear in intensity and consistency, while a guilty person contrives an intensity that quickly dissipates during the course of an interview.

This information is vital to the decision-making process whether it involves hiring a new employee or determining other issues for veracity of content.

The Nature of Interviewing

Questioning is the main component of interviewing. Interview questions should be designed to obtain the maximum amount of pertinent, job-related information and to facilitate interviewee truthfulness. Depending on the interview purpose, the developer of a well-planned interview will consider multiple types of questions, the sequence and transition, and the formulation and execution of questions. A formal interviewing guide may be used or the interviewer may question informally. At any rate, questions need to be strategically formulated, sequenced, and executed to obtain the most accurate and necessary information to make decisions and selections.

The primary purpose of interview questions is to obtain the maximum truthful responses from the interviewee to gather reliable and valid data about the job applicant. This chapter describes the relationship between the UNICOM interview phases and how they operate within the task of managing the trilogy of interactive events. This approach to interviewing offers some specific techniques for formulating questions which will accumulate and assemble the data necessary for analysis and decision making.

The Interactive Interview

It is difficult to teach interactive behavior, because it is a skill that requires a cognizant process, a sociological inventory, a psychological application, and involves a lifetime of practice. The trilogy of interactive activities must be applied in a concurrent and sequential fashion. This instructional section is an explanation of how to manage those interactive activities to effectively gather adequate and accurate data during an interview.

Management Strategy for Self-Disclosure Explained

The first segment will explain the Six-Step Management Strategy for Self-Disclosure which is a technique that, if effectively applied at critical points during the main phase of the preemployment selection interview, will facilitate the human resource practitioner's goal of obtaining essential information that may be omitted, falsified, or distorted by the interviewee. The second segment will illustrate how these steps can be applied to the various phases of a systematic interview.

Impression Management

The first step, impression management, is one that is in continuous operation throughout every phase of the interview. Impression management is a practitioner's conscious effort to exercise control over selected communicational behaviors and cues for purposes of effectively managing interactive interviews with people who are similar, as well as those of the opposite gender, those of other cultures and races, and those of other socio-economic backgrounds. This step is not to be confused with the First Personal Impression Phase of interviewing in that impression management is a constant from the beginning to the end of the interview, and involves the necessity of balancing all aspects of impression, *i.e.*, dominance, likability, and credibility.

**Management Strategy for
Self-Disclosure**
1) Impression Management
2) Environment Management
3) Response Management
4) Critical Moment Management
5) Strategic Question Management
6) Disclosure Management

Perceived vs. Internal Confidence -- Personal confidence is perhaps the greatest attribute an effective investigator must develop. There actually are two levels of confidence:

1) **Perceived Confidence** -- that which is perceived as belonging to the position, *i.e.*, a human resource manager is genuinely confident because he or she has acquired the basic academic and experiential requisites to fulfill the position.

2) **Internal Confidence** -- that which is internally manifested and stems from a core self-belief. Internalized confidence is portrayed with exuberance and radiates into a poise that is unmistakably authentic.

Thus, a confident investigator genuinely is confident -- not merely because he or she has earned an MBA, but because confidence has been strategically built.

Investigator's Self-Disclosure -- Self-disclosure, or the manner in which an investigator presents himself or herself to the interviewee, is a vital component to creating a credible impression, a likable impression, and the essential dominant impression. The authentic investigator will have the confidence, knowledge, and poise to disclose that part of himself or herself that exudes the message: *"It is safe to tell me about yourself."* While it may be impossible to be all things to all people, it is essential that the UNICOM investigator aim for perfection in managing the interview and interview setting. It stands to reason that the more realistic the impression and communicative demeanor, the more likely the investigator will achieve success with the interactive interview, *i.e.*, the candidate's disclosure of relevant information. Properly managed self-disclosure also lends itself to create the three aspects of impression management (dominant, likable, and credible).

Environment Management

In addition to creating and managing impressions, the investigator must concurrently set a safe, psycho-social scenario by establishing the essential trust and rapport and a comfort level conducive to interviewee self-disclosure. It is essential that the interviewee feel confident and safe. Whether the investigative interview involves upper management, middle management, or lower management, the employee deserves the greatest respect. The investigator must create the opportunity for the interviewee to comfortably disclose all relevant information. The safer the interviewee feels, the less likely he or she will omit, distort, or falsify information to the investigator and the more likely it is that he or she will disclose accurate and relevant information.

Steps one and two are segmented only for instructional purposes, but within an interview situation they are inseparable and are the total responsibility of the practitioner. That perfected level of poise and confidence that the investigator brings to the interview as well as the physical interview environment must communicate warmth and safety in a friendly and ethical manner.

The interview setting, carefully planned by the investigator, will be private, free of outside stimuli, and comfortable. The investigator's demeanor will be friendly, nonaccusatory, nonabrasive, and genuinely sincere during all phases of the interview. It is essential to set the scene and manage the first impression and to maintain that theme of safety and comfort throughout the entire investigative interview.

Response Management

Opportunity for disclosure is strategically created and facilitated by the investigator who employs all the tools and skills within the repertoire of practice. The investigator realizes that the more an interviewee has the opportunity to express denial, the more difficult it will be for him or her to express honesty. Therefore, the investigator must manage the scene by subtly dominating the conversation and continuing to set an even more comfortable level of interaction before allowing the interviewee the opportunity to explain or disclose. If the investigator can effectively stop or manage objections before they occur, it will serve to prevent omission, distortion, and falsification by the candidate. The investigator must gently but firmly move the flow of the interview to the point that is exactly appropriate to ask for that withheld information or correct any distorted or falsified information.

Critical Moment Management

The critical moment is recognized by a brief, verbal/nonverbal cue that the interviewee is willing to disclose the withheld information. It is a signal of resignation or giving in to the investigator's gentle urgings to relieve the tensions by disclosing information within the safety of the practitioner's domain.

Strategic Question Management

The strategic question is one that always provides a welcomed or an attractive alternative response, *i.e.*, "yes" or "no," "good reason," or "bad reason." Its purpose is to offer the candidate a way out or a way to save face in a confrontational situation. It allows the candidate to disclose withheld information that may be considered detrimental to the interview process. An example question: *"You must have had a very good reason for coming in late for work several days this past week?"*

Disclosure Management

The candidate will only disclose the withheld information if the former five steps have been effectively initiated and he feels safe enough to divulge information that may harm his chances of getting the job.

Management Strategy for Self-Disclosure Applied

The six-step strategy for self-disclosure should become the investigator's constant consideration during each of the five phases of the interview process. These phases are discussed in the next section with some brief recommendations of how the strategy can be applied in a continuous, concurrent manner.

Interactive Components of the Interview

Universal Interviewing and Communications offers some strategic question formulation techniques based on the interrelated components of the interactive interview. These UNICOM interview components are viewed in five interrelated, essential phases, the:

1) Pre-Interview Analysis Phase,
2) First Personal Impression Phase,
3) Main Data Collection Phase,
4) Concluding Interview Phase, and
5) Interview Follow-Up Phase.

With the criteria of the trilogy of interactive activities in mind, the assurance of being in legal compliance of employment law, and the challenge of eliciting as much information as possible from the interviewee, a discussion of each of the five interview phases follows:

Pre-Interview Analysis Phase

The UNICOM investigative interview process actually begins prior to the personal interview. Comprehensive data gathering occurs during every phase of the UNICOM process, and a considerable amount of information can be obtained before the actual interview is set. The data-gathering techniques during this phase are determined by the interview objective and the expected interaction with the interviewee. For example, if the objective is a preemployment application, the UNICOM investigator will obtain the interviewee's resume and references. Analysis duties during this phase include extensive perusal of the resume and a telephone interview with the interviewee. If the interview objective is a workplace investigation, the investigator will obtain the subject's personnel file and all pertinent information regarding work history and performance. If the interview is related to a post-employment investigation, the investigator will review all claims related to the issue and gather as much information from the previous employee's work history and performance. Once the initial data is gathered, a secondary analysis is completed to determine exactly what additional information is required.

Thus, the pre-interview analysis phase includes all the preliminary tasks necessary for initiating a successful investigative interview by creating the desired impression and setting the safe scene for self-disclosure. This procedure will assist the investigator in formulating an interview plan which will include strategy for seeking any missing information and verifying the presented data.

The secondary aspect of the pre-interview analysis is to draft the investigative interview plan. The interview plan is framed by the trilogy of interactive activities as well as by the remaining four interview components. The interview plan includes details such as creating the ideal interview environment, the formulation and execution of specific questions, the sequence and transition of the questions and interactions, and a final checklist to ascertain whether all aspects of the interview and data-gathering process are complete. It is during the planning stage that the critical first personal impression phase is designed.

First Personal Impression Phase

The first personal impression phase is based on the entire investigative interview plan and strategically is set to prepare the interviewee for the safe scenario to follow. This phase involves the manner in which the investigator will greet the interviewee, and includes setting the room environment, determining the wardrobe of the investigator, and choosing the physical and emotional demeanor the investigator will present to the interviewee.

Establishing Rapport -- The first few minutes of the interview establishes the rapport and sets the structure for the entire interview. Again, depending upon the purpose of the interview, the interviewer should plan the greeting accordingly. If the purpose of the interview is to sell something, the technique of choice is to be as positive as possible during the introduction or first impression phase and ask the interviewee questions that elicit a "yes" response. The following example could be used in any of the three types of investigative interview settings.

- **Examples:** *"Isn't this a beautiful day?"* or *"Isn't this wonderful weather we are having?"*

Opening Questions

The primary objective of opening questions is to help the interviewee feel at ease and to provide an opportunity for him or her to talk as much as possible.

- **Preemployment Example** -- After the initial small talk, covering such topics as whether the applicant was able to find the office easily, the interviewer may begin the session by asking an introductory, open-ended question such as: *"Would you begin by telling me about your educational and experiential background and how you perceive your experience and skills in relation to the job description that we sent you?"*

- **Employment Example** -- After explaining to the interviewee the purpose of the interview, the introductory, open-ended question might be: *"Would you begin by telling me what happened?"*

Main Data Collection Phase

The main content or purpose of the interview is identified between the introduction and the conclusion. One may choose a direct or indirect approach to interaction, for each has a profound impact on the interview structure. A direct style is straightforward and covers specific topics in a specific manner, while the indirect method is more inductive in form and offers the interviewee more freedom of expression.

Multi-Purpose Agenda -- The main data collection phase has a multi-purpose agenda. It is during this phase that the majority of interview data is gathered. This phase offers the practitioner an opportunity to verify details with the interviewee and to request further information required to accumulate the desired data set. Most importantly, this phase becomes the interactive event between the practitioner and the interviewee, as both parties get to know each other in a face-to-face situation. The UNICOM practitioner must manage this interaction to gather as much information as possible, even that information which may not be anticipated when formulating the questions prior to the interview.

Opportunity for Disclosure -- These serendipitous findings do not occur by accident. Opportunity for disclosure is strategically created and facilitated by the practitioner, who employs all the tools and the skills within the repertoire of practice. Other sections of this chapter present a multitude of questioning tools and skills that are helpful to the practitioner during this interactive event. Finally, this phase sets the scene for potential future interaction with the interviewee and paves the way for the concluding phase.

The Initial Interview Questions -- The first set of interview questions strategically should be designed to elicit a sampling of the interviewee's verbal and nonverbal behavior. These questions condition the interviewee for the entire interview and should consist of a series of questions that have been carefully formulated to provide the practitioner with an indication of the interviewee's truth or deception status without being of an accusatory nature. Brief responsive answers will allow the practitioner to observe the demeanor and general attitude of the interviewee.

Observing the Interviewee -- Specifically, the UNICOM practitioner will observe any delay in answering, eye movements, body movements, and the combination of verbal and nonverbal reactions to the questions and the interview situation. It is during this questioning phase that an astute practitioner will draw on knowledge and skills required from a comprehensive understanding of the materials presented in Chapter Seven.

In-depth Questioning Period

It should be possible, during an interview, to get past the initial superficial dialogue and create an opportunity for an in-depth dialogue with an interviewee. It is at this time that the UNICOM practitioner may ask some open-ended, follow-up questions. This questioning strategy involves a series or at least a three-part linked question that asks a primary question and is followed by a simple secondary question *"why?"* and a tertiary question that asks *"what?"*

- **A preemployment example question would be:** *"If you were to establish a sales force in Billings, Montana, what would be your procedure?"* This could be followed by, *"Why would you chose that particular technique?"* A third question could be, *"What would you hope to accomplish by these methods?"*

- **An employment example question would be**: *"Can you explain in your own words why you think this incident happened and how you think similar occurrences may be averted in the future?"* This could be followed by a question such as, *"Why would you choose this technique over another?"*

An advantage to this line of questioning is that interviewees must actually think on their feet. There is no way they can anticipate and rehearse the answer to this type of question prior to the interview. The sequence of *why* and *what* also encourages them to pursue the topic at a deeper level and presents a chain reaction situation which challenges both the interviewee and the interviewer.

Questioning Techniques

Certain strategies are involved in effectively conducting an investigative interview. These strategies and examples will be presented within three categories:

1)   Controlling the interview,
2)   Motivating the interviewee, and
3)   Probing for complete information.

This section offers an overview of the types of questioning often used in investigative interviews. The first task in beginning an investigative interview is to make the interviewee feel important and to make the position and entire interview process important. The investigator should create an emotional climate of safety, as well as importance. The investigator also may wish to obtain permission from the interviewee to take notes, to record, or even to videotape the interview. Basic types of questions are defined and described below as are suggested ways to formulate questions to achieve a desired objective.

Open-Ended Questions -- Open-ended questions are used to gather broad information and offer the interviewee the chance to talk. Open questions assist in revealing the greatest amount data because they ask Who, Where, What, When, How, and Why. They cannot be answered "yes" or "no."

- **Example of Open-Ended Question** -- A question such as *"Tell me about yourself,"* will give the investigator an opportunity to listen and observe the interviewee's articulateness, emotional state, frame of reference, body movements, facial expressions, and possible subliminal messages.

Open questions have some distinct limitations in that they tend to consume time, and answers are more difficult to record and tabulate. Other disadvantages are that the applicant may provide ambiguous answers that lack standardization, and the interview may be more difficult to control. Therefore, the investigator needs to manage the flow of conversation by asking direct questions to either stop or steer the interviewee in a desired direction. This tactic generally minimizes the threat for the interviewee and provides an opportunity for the investigator to observe and listen to the verbal aspects of the candidate's communication.

The investigator should be reminded that, since there is a constant need to be aware of the legal compliance requirements throughout this entire investigative process, it may be possible to gather a considerable amount of pertinent information during open-ended questioning that could not be gained by direct questioning. Some specific modifications of open questioning are as follows:

1)   **Directive Questions,** which move toward areas of agreement;

2)   **Reflective Questions,** which require the interviewee to answer from a feeling level; and

3)   **Pointed Questions,** which stir the interviewee into action.

Direct Questions -- It is suggested that direct questioning can be softened a great deal by using an introductory phrase: The following example is applicable for preemployment, employment, and post-employment investigative interviewing.

- **Example of Direct Question** -- *"Is it possible that...?"* or using qualifying words such as *"might," "perhaps," "to some extent," "somewhat,"* and *"a little bit."*

Hypothetical Questions -- Utilizing hypothetical questions creates a *"what if"* situation with questions that are simply a variation of the open-ended type because they cannot be answered with a simple phrase of *"yes"* or *"no."*

- **Example of Hypothetical Question**: *"What would you do if you discovered an employee under your supervision was under-ringing sales at the cash register?"*

Reflecting Statements -- A powerful method for creating a positive communication climate is reflection, which can be described as a nondirective tactic in which the investigator attempts to understand what an interviewee has said and then mirrors back this understanding to the applicant.

- **Example of Reflecting Statement**: *"That's very interesting, let me see if I fully understand what you just told me. You would really like to work for our company because you have a considerable amount of experience in designing interactive computer networks, and you feel that you could creatively and effectively manage our new computer networking program?"*

Reinforcement Statements -- The core social skills a UNICOM investigator must develop is the ability to reinforce others with interactive verbal and nonverbal behavior. This reinforcement can be accomplished by a nod of the head, a simple utterance such as *"uh huh"* or an approving smile.

Conversely, an investigator can down play unfavorable information by withholding such approval. The primary purpose of this technique is to create a climate in which the interviewee feels self-assured enough to reveal shortcomings or concerns and to truthfully interact with the interviewer.

It is recognized that the ability to reflectively interact in a positive manner with the interviewee is one of the most powerful techniques used to give interviewees the feeling that their achievements are worthy of talking about.

- **Example of Reinforcement Statement**: Comments such as *"Very impressive!"* or *"You deserve a lot of credit for that!"* or *"Excellent!"* give interviewees the encouragement to respond more freely.

Closed Questions -- Closed questions may be administered orally or in written form and may require multiple choice, yes or no, or short one word or one sentence answers. This type of questioning is a quick method of obtaining specific information. Specific questions that require a "yes" answer allow the interviewer to observe the interviewee in a position of assumed truthful state and thus provide a frame of reference to compare to a potential change in verbal or nonverbal behavior as the interview proceeds.

- **Example of Closed Question:** *"Your resume states that you obtained your B.S. degree from Stanford University. Is that correct?"*

Closed questions have limitations in that it is easy for the interviewee to falsify information. Applicants can inhibit explanations or dialogue which may, in turn, limit the information that is obtained.

Double-Barreled Questions -- Questions that require two responses often are referred to as double-barreled questions.

- **Example of Double-Barreled Question:** *"What is your experience in managing information systems, and how is it related to this position?"*

In most cases, neither question is answered in full and, many times, only the last portion of the question elicits a response. This technique often is used to confuse an academic candidate in dissertation defense sessions, or to determine how well the candidate can respond to a multilevel question. It is most interesting to note which portion of the question an interviewee answers and whether any part of the question is neglected or ignored.

Bipolar Questions -- One of two choices are offered in bipolar questions, which are meant to achieve a general reaction from the interviewee. Cautions that should be considered are: There may be more than two choices of answers, qualification is limited, and it may over simplify a response.

- **Example of Bipolar Question:** *"Do you approve or disapprove of abortion?"*

As in the above situation regarding abortion, a respondent may be adamant and closed about his or her position and may respond with a resounding approval or disapproval. Other respondents may have qualified positions such as approval of abortion if pregnancy would endanger the mother's life. Or there may be any number of other responses.

Baiting Questions -- The UNICOM investigator may choose to use "baiting questions" in order to avoid a challenge or to appear neutral in the questioning process. It is nonaccusatory but allows the interviewee to consider changing or redefining previously presented information. Thus, this approach may reveal the truth as well as a deceptive communication, *i.e.*, falsification, distortion, or omission.

- **Example of Baiting Question:** *"Many times, people who serve as cashiers borrow money from time to time with the good intention of paying it back. What do you think of that practice?"*

Leading Questions -- Leading questions have expected responses, and they may cause the interviewee undue stress. This technique may be effective in a preemployment interview setting to test how directly or indirectly a respondent reacts.

- **Example of Leading Question**: *"Jim, regarding your past five years of employment, how many times have you been let go by an employer?"*

Leading questions allow the interviewee to answer in a particular manner. There are several ways an investigator can provide cues to the interviewee's expected answer:

1)   Providing a context to the question that gives cues on how the interviewee should answer,

2)   Loading a question with emotionally charged words, and

3)   Challenging the interviewee or implying that he or she responded inappropriately.

It should be understood that leading questions have an appropriate and meaningful application but, because of their nature, excessive use can be construed by the interviewee to be disconcerting, if not accusatory.

Confirming Questions -- These questions are designed to confirm against positive or negative traits. The technique involves the interviewer making a statement that ends in a question mark or at least with a pause intended to elicit the interviewee's response. An example of both positive and negative-related statements are shown below:

- **Positive Example of Confirming Question:** *"It is always best to arrive at the job at least 15 minutes early?"*

Response to that statement could indicate whether the applicant is committed to promptness or whether one may be tardy or arrive in a hurried state to begin each day.

- **Negative Example of Confirming Question**: *"If I feel that my manager is impeding my progress on a project, I will go around or above him/her to reach my goal?"*

Response will indicate negative aggressiveness or, perhaps, a more creative way that the applicant might handle that type of situation. The latter may even illustrate positive behavior. Thus, what was initially intended to elicit a response to negative behavior might involve a creative solution. Perhaps the investigator would not want to hire a person who would go around or above a supervisor or manager. However, if an applicant had devised a creative approach to handling a such a situation, the practitioner may be favorably impressed.

Self-Disclosure Strategy -- Another interaction tool designed to elicit more secretive information from an interviewee is for the investigator to actually disclose some interesting and pertinent personal information. This strategy may put the interviewee more at ease and facilitate the establishment of a more in-depth dialogue with the investigator.

- **Example of Self-Disclosure Statement:** *"I can certainly identify with your last statement about how difficult it is to work for a dominant supervisor. I have actually been a more effective worker when I worked for a supervisor who maintains a more equitable stance."*

Follow-Up Questions -- Follow-up questions may ask for clarification or encourage a natural flow in the conversation. It is suggested that the investigator make comments rather than ask questions. However, a style combining comment and questions may be effectively applied.

- **Example of Follow-up Question**: *"That's very interesting; I'd like to know more about that."*

To effectively manage an investigative interview, the investigator may consider a combination of questioning techniques to obtain the greatest amount of information in a limited time frame. The type of question selected may well depend on what the investigator wishes to accomplish during the introduction, the body, or the conclusion within the structure of the interview.

Probing for Complete Information
The paramount requirement of an investigator is successfully handling the problems of inadequate responses and recognizing their various forms. An interviewee's responses may be inadequate in several ways:

1) **No Response** -- either silence or refusal to answer.

2) **Incomplete Response** -- providing general/not specific information.

3) **Irrelevant Response** -- or maybe a digression or change of subject.

4) **Inaccurate or Contradictory Response** -- information might be provided that is not consistent with former information.

5)   **Poorly Organized Response** -- confusing responses may be difficult to follow.

6)   **Unfamiliar Response** -- contains unfamiliar/uncertain words or terms.

Managing the Interview

Described below are some effective examples of how a UNICOM investigator can manage the interview process by aligning or altering his or her own behavior to influence the interviewee:

Silence -- The intentional use of silence often is referred to as *electric silence* or a *pregnant pause*. It is a powerful means that can bring important verbal and nonverbal responses to the surface. Valuable clues to innermost thoughts and feelings, withheld information, guilty knowledge, or forgotten memories may surface due to the silence of the investigator. Silence most effectively is used when an interviewee has completed a statement that seems unfinished. Rather than asking a question, the investigator may choose to remain silent and wait for the interviewee to continue.

Appear Uncomfortable -- If the investigator wishes to test for guilty knowledge it often is effective to appear markedly uncomfortable to the interviewee. This can be accomplished nonverbally by fumbling with notes, pen, clothing, or furniture or verbally by raising the voice or changing the vocal tone. These actions tend to increase fear, anxiety, guilt, or anger and often can tap into concealed information.

Confrontation -- Confrontation can be delivered in a very threatening manner, or it can be a very gentle and subtle process. At times, the investigator may confront the interviewee with a mixture of those two extremes. The exact manner in which an investigator chooses to confront an interviewee can be determined carefully through an evaluation of the situation, the personality of the of interviewee, and the purpose of the confrontation.

Rephrasing the Question -- Asking a question in a different way may elicit a different, or more complete response. It may clarify a point.

Repetition -- It is noted that inconsistencies between the verbal, vocal, and visual behavioral channels may indicate deception, while the truthful generally only have one story to tell. It is for this reason that repetitive questioning is in order, for it provides the investigator the opportunity to observe consistencies and inconsistencies in the interviewee's verbal and nonverbal communication style.

Knowing When to Stop -- Concluding an interview is not necessarily based on time of day, but is, more specifically, to be done when the investigator deems it advantageous to end the process. There generally is a feeling of completeness that leads the experienced investigator to bring the interview to conclusion.

Closing the Interview -- The closing should be designed to draw closure to the interview and pave the way for future interaction.

- **Employment Investigation Example**: *"I have no further questions. Are there any questions that you might have regarding this incident? Is there anything else that you would like to tell me?"*

The investigative interview must be a dynamic tool for obtaining the maximum information about the interviewee and the incident being investigated while ensuring legal compliance with employment law. The questions asked and the way questions are formulated require some thoughtful strategy. The models presented in Chapters Nine and Ten each contain a question formulation matrix to serve as examples of a question formulation and delivery technique.

Concluding Interview Phase
The interview conclusion phase does what it suggests, in that it concludes the interview with an opportunity for both the practitioner and the interviewee to provide closing statements and interaction. Concluding the interview typically involves recapping the entire interview and a last opportunity to make final statements to cover anything that has been left unsaid.

Questions to Draw Closure -- Questions for this phase may be formulated to draw closure rather than be open-ended. At this time, the practitioner reviews the overall interview objective, the entire interactive event that has occurred, and information received during the main data collection phase. He also determines what is needed to continue the data analysis and make final decisions or selection. A continued interaction agreement between the practitioner and interviewee also may be established at this point, since it relates to the interview follow-up phase.

Interview Follow-Up Phase
The interview follow-up phase is the final stage of the UNICOM investigative interview procedure. At this point, the interview plan and the checklist are reviewed and evaluated relative to the accumulated data, and an analysis of the personal interaction with the interviewee is completed to determine what is needed for concluding the data-gathering event.

Often, a follow-up interview is desirable and may serve several purposes such as an opportunity to review any points that were not clear during the initial interview or it may offer the practitioner an additional opportunity to confront what may have been questionable behavior during the initial interview. The follow-up interview allows the investigator to explore in greater depths some aspects of the interviewee's earlier presentation, and it allows for a test of consistency for both verbal and nonverbal behavior presented by the interviewee.

Structuring Questions

Depending on the purpose of the investigation objective, it is important to structure questions to comfortably elicit positive and negative information from the employee. Structured questions accompanied with the UNICOM investigator's knowledge and skills about this information extraction process will ensure adequate qualitative and quantifiable data. The employee's objectives, listening skills, interpretative skills, and diagnostic skills all can be revealed by this procedure.

Interactive Communication

Communication dynamics involve a myriad of components and their interactions as well as mutual perceptions of the individuals who attempt to communicate. The following set of techniques are designed to accomplish this purpose:

1)   The investigator must learn the art of disengagement, which requires the listener (in this case the investigator) to disengage from self concerns and concentrate on the task of gathering accurate information;

2)   The investigator must master the uncommon art of listening for consequences to locate a possible hidden communication;

3)   The investigator must develop an awareness of personal emotional reactions by determining how he feels as he listens;

4)   The investigator must develop an ear for patterns as well as for single, sharp responses or behaviors;

5)   The investigator must learn to discriminate between pertinent information and any contrived or manufactured diversions; and

6)   The investigator must have an understanding of the overriding function of compromise.

These techniques are not applied step-by-step but are orchestrated in a synchronized fashion within any interaction process.

Cognitive Behavior Within the Interaction Process

Effective UNICOM interaction between the investigator and an employee reveals an incredible amount of information at many levels and at a rapid rate. The interview must be managed by skillful planning, meticulous observation, and intricate interaction and response recording techniques. These techniques are described below as related to the body movements of the interviewer and the observation of verbal and nonverbal behavior of the employee.

Recording Interview Responses -- Much of the interactive interview process cannot be trusted to memory, and one may tend to confuse the current interview with other interviews. Thus, it is necessary for the investigator to record comments on paper. Careful planning should be given to the means and methods of recording interview information and how it is coded for follow-up analysis, because this data should be considered a public document and is even subject to formal review or subpoena. Thus, recording requirements, systems, and techniques must satisfy Equal Employment Opportunity Commission requirements and must be controlled so as not to discriminate in regard to race, sex, age, or marital status.

Empathic Interaction -- In an effort to better understand the employee, it is advantageous for the investigator to periodically envision himself as the employee. This momentary transference of position can provide a multidimensional insight as to how the employee perceives the process. Such empathy can disclose issues or problems that the investigator may not have understood or observed. Likewise, the investigator, by means of this empathic exchange, may discern opportunities for appropriate inquisition and development that may not have been otherwise noted.

Reading Body Language -- It is interesting to note that people invoke the entire body when communicating with others and that body movements are known to be concurrently produced as patterns of speech are generated. But even more interesting is the astonishing finding that one's body tends to physically coordinate with the verbal utterances of others while listening.

The body's tendency to move synchronously with speech is not clearly understood, but it is considered to enhance the efficiency of communication in that, by coordinating to the speaker's movements, one can anticipate and more accurately predict the termination of the other's vocalizations and be prepared to respond without premature interruption. It is further acknowledged that such synchrony serves a function in communicating the degree of understanding, agreement, or support that the listener experiences.

Maintain Eye Contact -- It is essential to maintain casual eye contact with the employee in the event that a deceptive person may be watching for indications of insecurity or lack of confidence. It also is important to note that a truthful person will easily maintain eye contact with the interviewer, whereas, a liar may either avoid eye contact or overreact by staring at the interviewer in a challenging manner.

Exploring Deceptive Behavior -- The investigator generally is perceived by the employee as an authority figure, which may cause some anxiety during the interview process. A skillful investigator will recognize some of the more obvious signs of employee anxiety: rapid breathing, rapid heartbeat, a tightness in the stomach, sweaty hands, clearing of the throat, sudden itches which must be scratched, belching, and sudden feelings of weakness or fatigue. Upon noticing any or a number of these indicators, it is prudent for the investigator to allow the employee to be at ease as much a possible. It is important to determine the cause of the anxiety. Is it based on the authority figure syndrome? Is it because the employee is too anxious to please? Or some other reason?

Verbal Communication

The flow of speech during an interview is at times as complicated to follow as the nonverbal interaction, but must be considered concomitantly. When one considers that a pianist can play as many as 16 notes a second, compared to the motor commands in the speech musculature which have been calculated to be as high as 1,400 per second, it is perplexing to fathom the great abundance of spoken words and behavior that occurs at such rapid speeds. Thus, the ability to coordinate and synchronize with a variety of other people under various circumstances has a significant impact on one's professional competence and effectiveness in the interviewing process. It would seem advantageous to become a student of the UNICOM process to achieve such effectiveness as an investigative interviewer.

The Role of Listening -- Listening plays a vital role in communication. In fact, the communicator spends almost 50% of his time listening, compared to about 30% speaking, and the remaining time reading and writing. Failure to listen results in failure to communicate. In fact, one of the greatest obstacles to communication and understanding can be attributed to poor listening behavior. It is important here to recognize that listening skills are not inherent, but must be acquired and practiced. It requires hearing (which is a physical activity) as well as an active attempt to understand another's viewpoint which may or may not differ from the listener's. A prerequisite to good listening is the ability to be genuinely interested in others and to monitor the tendency of self-preoccupation.

Acquisition of Effective Listening Skills -- To become an effective listener, one must learn to actively analyze and weigh what the speaker is saying, as well as what the speaker is not saying, and carefully observe and record the data received. It is only by this technique that the hidden meaning of words can be discerned (*i.e.*, the meanings others do not say or attempt to conceal). As investigators, one must always keep in mind the need to be *people pleasers*. One strategically plans to say the right thing at the right time in order to manage the interaction during interviewing. Often, the investigator compliments the employee, because it is necessary for the employee to like and trust the investigator. A natural consequence in this endeavor to please others is the tendency to conceal the *real* self and to present a *false front* or an image that will be liked by others. The investigator should be cautioned that a false presentation will be recognized by the employee. Therefore, it is a challenge to be as *real* as possible without any compromise of credibility during the interview process. It is a critical part of impression management to create a likable and credible impression, while remembering that the employee may not be that sincere.

Listening for Paralanguage -- Paralanguage, sometimes referred to as vocalics, includes all stimuli produced by the human voice, other than words. These cues range from forceful articulation, screaming, deep resonance to whining, monotones, and vocalized pauses that convey messages. Also, volume, pitch, and rate should be considered. Remember, vocal data sometimes is as important to the listener as verbal data because the way words are said contributes to their meaning and becomes an important part of what is heard.

Investigator as Observant Listener -- An observant listener must not only be aware of spoken words and gestures that serve as word substitutes, but also of timing, tone, voice inflections, directness, and total speaking demeanor. Thus, the attentive UNICOM investigator listens and watches in critical fashion what the employee says and how he respectively behaves.

The first indicator of truthfulness may be noted in the time period between questions and the verbal response. A delayed response may indicate deception, whereas a prompt answer often is considered a sign of truthfulness. Also, evasive answers typically are deceptive as is repetition of the question or a request to clarify the question. This tactic allows the responder to stall for time or formulate a defensible response. Often, a liar will speak in fragmented or incomplete sentences, mumble, perspire, laugh inappropriately, exhibit mental blocks, and be overly polite. On the other hand, a normal truthful person typically will give complete, direct, rational answers in a distinct, serious, confident, and clear voice.

Interpretation of Nonverbal Communication

Understanding the acumen of a skillful interrogator may be useful for limited application in any interviewing situation but especially for investigative interviewing. It is obvious that it is advantageous for the investigator to acquire the diagnostic skills and gain experience in the *language of the body*. In regard to eye messages: A normal truthful person's eyes generally appear clear, bright, wide awake, warm, direct, easy, soft, and nonprobing, but lying eyes will appear foggy, puzzled, probing, pleading, evasive or shifty, cold, hard, strained, or sneaky. The old adage, *"The eyes are the window of the mind,"* speaks well of the comparative behaviors.

In an extremely serious situation, a lying person may exhibit labored breathing and sigh uncontrollably. This stress may even cause stomach growls or an upset digestive system. Untruthfulness also can be marked by a variation of facial expressions, posture changes, grooming gestures and cosmetic adjustments, and supporting gestures, such as hiding hands or feet, crossing arms or legs, or holding the forehead with hands.

Management of the Employee's Behavior

The act of managing the employee fundamentally is linked to interpersonal coordination or rapport. The three distinct components of rapport:

1) Interpersonal coordination,
2) Intended emotional positivity, and
3) Attentional focus.

These components have been determined to make up the total experience of rapport. In managing the employee, an investigator may tend to control personal dynamics by masking nonverbal behavior as an attempt to appear neutral or inconspicuous. It should be remembered, however, that such passivity can be perceived as indicative of dullness, withdrawal, uneasiness, snobbish aloofness, or even deceptiveness. It also should be noted that if an investigator appears to be insincere or exhibits any deceptive verbal or nonverbal behavior, it likely will be noticed by the employee.

Perhaps it is better to achieve a more natural, high degree of confidence, an active element in a cycle of increasingly sophisticated self-presentational strategies and skills. The more practice and refinement of these skills, the more confident and the more likely investigator is to experience greater interpersonal success.

Interactive Management

Anything that occurs during the interview, whether positive, negative, or neutral, is felt by the employee. It is the investigator's responsibility to maintain harmony within this interactive process. The investigator must never take dignity away from anyone, because it can never be returned. Loss of dignity creates irreparable damage which can become personalized at that time and may never be repaired. The investigator should never lose sight or stray from the mutual interview objective.

The Employee's Listening Skills -- Sincere, attentive people typically are indicative of the innocent. They tend to listen one way while deceptive persons listen in another. Typically, deceptive people listen in a way that indicates they are seeking an opportunity to manipulate the circumstances. Innocent listeners have an intense agenda to exonerate themselves and fully cooperate by volunteering information. By observing the employee's listening skills, the investigator can gather a considerable amount of information about the employee and the employee's overall statement.

The Employee's Diagnostic Skills -- In any investigation situation, interviewees tend to put their best foot forward. An investigator understands that interviewees will offer their best set of attributes and, subsequently, carefully must distinguish between what is purported, what is theatrical, and what is real. It is the investigator's responsibility to discern between an employee's preposterous or contrived claims, which may be inconsequential, and what is pertinent to the interview objective and situation.

In an internal investigation situation, the investigator may question the employee about possible circumstances not reported during the interaction. Withheld information may have a direct consequence on the decision-making process. A competent investigator will have developed operative conditioning techniques and fundamental preformulation techniques to determine credibility and essentially separate the relevant from the irrelevant.

The Dynamics of Employee Arrogance -- At times, incontrovertible indicators of arrogance are associated with particular levels of professional people who, by their mere credentials or presumed position of supremacy, feel that an interview situation is not applicable or appropriate. They may become indignant about the interactive process. These individuals may radiate a presupposed immunity as a means of masking types of behavior.

The Dynamics of Investigator Arrogance -- Occasionally, interviewers, including investigators, after years of dedicated practice and commitment, will reach an apex of expertise. Regrettably, this author has observed an enamored few who clearly violate a sense of ethics and professionalism. This extremely small, select group develop a condition of egomania because of some maladjusted brilliance which demands an insatiable need to fixate and abuse its skills on completely innocent people. Often times, these professionals' acquired deviant behavior is exhibited by *toying* with people by means of mental manipulation. Others *push people* to test their tolerance levels about general self-disclosure issues of undetected criminality or other issues of suspected or unresolved impropriety.

This dysfunctional condition is not recorded in the research and communication literature. Typically, this Interviewer Abuse Syndrome (IAS) is consistent with practitioners and investigators who have been extensively interviewing large numbers of persons over a long period of time, and who reach an unusually high level of proficiency associated with boredom and lack of sufficient supervision. Such investigators view themselves and fellow abusers with a sense of unmatched superiority and bravado. Recipients of IAS abuse have recourse with civil and legal remedies under due process.

A Technique for Workplace Investigations Summary

This chapter has defined and described UNICOM as a technique for investigative interviewing for all aspects of workplace investigations. The importance of developing the multidimensional skills was explained as these skills relate to the dynamics of human communication and acting within the realm of employment law. This chapter stressed the importance of understanding the interviewee's frame of reference and the interviewee's goals and objectives through empathic interaction. It also addressed the complexity of the interviewing process and focused on the intricate role played by the investigator in establishing and maintaining the ideal setting for accomplishing the interview objective. The primary purpose of this chapter was to explain how these technical skills and tactics can be applied to manage a trilogy of interactive activities. The trilogy includes:

1) Understanding the investigative interview objective,

2) Discernment of behavioral dynamics from the interviewee's point of view, and

3) Subsequently responding with the appropriate interactive behavior to facilitate investigation cooperation and disclosure.

PART III

UNICOM_SM INVESTIGATIVE MODELS
APPLICATION COMPONENT

The Application Component introduces three UNICOM investigation models for instructional purposes, the:

1)   Model for Preemployment Investigations,
2)   Model for Employment Investigations; and
3)   Model for Post-Employment Investigations.

These models contain strategy and general guidelines but do not address specific factual situations. The human resource manager and administrator should carefully evaluate the facts and determine whether the suggestions apply before following any of these recommendations. Consultation with legal council is recommended in certain situations, especially those involving competing interests of the company and any employee. Before implementing any employment practice, make certain that it will not cause a disparate impact on the basis of race, color, religion, sex, national origin, or any other protected category. Also make sure that any employment practice is job-related for the position in question, that it is consistent with business necessity, and that it is lawful under Section 105 of the Civil Rights Act of 1991 as well as comparable state and local fair employment practice laws.

Chapter Nine -- UNICOM Model For Preemployment Investigations

This chapter presents UNICOM -- Universal Interviewing and Communication as an application for the preemployment interviewing and selection process. The UNICOM model is a multifaceted process of preparation, data collection, and quantitative and qualitative analysis. The model is designed for managing preemployment selection in an efficient, professional manner which considers requirements for legal compliance, the components of communication and human behavior, and the analysis and diagnosis of verbal and nonverbal behavior.

Chapter Ten -- UNICOM Model For Employment Investigations

Chapter Ten presents a model for employment investigation which applies the UNICOM philosophy. The model considers the components of verbal and non-verbal communication for effective interviewing, legal requirements for compliance with employment law, and the dynamics of managing a trilogy of interactive events throughout the entire workplace investigation process.

Chapter Eleven -- UNICOM Model For Post-Employment Investigations

Chapter Eleven presents a proactive approach for avoiding the threat of post-employment workplace investigations. Negligent investigation is presented as a new legal theory emerging among employment doctrine which can be brought into action as a result of haphazard or incomplete investigations leading to employee termination. The prevention of wrongful discharge is presented as a proactive technique to avoid negligent termination. The chapter discusses such caveats as management malpractice, invasion of privacy, false imprisonment, discrimination, and deviant behavior in the workplace. Specific suggestions are offered on handling post-employment references to avoid defamation suits. To guard against post-employment charges, companies must follow a prescribed technique for preemployment selection, hiring new employees, and advancing employees to another level of employment.

CHAPTER NINE

UNICOM_{SM}
MODEL FOR PREEMPLOYMENT INVESTIGATIONS

Preemployment Selection as Investigation

The more comprehensive the preemployment selection process, the more likely that the best employees will be selected for employment. This fact alone may be the greatest preventive measure against discrimination and negligent hiring an employer can take. This model, called UNICOM -- Universal Interviewing and Communication -- is a preemployment application drawn from the text *Universal Interviewing and Communications: A Preemployment Application* (Slowik, 1995).

While the text addresses the fundamental knowledge of theory and interviewing techniques, this chapter addresses strategic methodology for the preemployment interviewing and selection process. The UNICOM method is a multifaceted process of preparation, data collection, and quantitative and qualitative analysis. The method presents strategy for managing preemployment selection in an efficient professional manner which includes requirements for legal compliance, the components of communication and human behavior, and the analysis and diagnosis of verbal and nonverbal behavior.

Introduction of the UNICOM Preemployment Model

The dynamics of investigative interviewing are addressed here in their complexity as intricate interactive processes. This chapter describes the multiphase processes of Universal Interviewing and Communications. This stepwise strategy will guide the reader, in a structured, organized manner, through the five phases of the investigative interview process by explaining the dynamics of each vital component of successful interviewing. Comprehensive data gathering occurs during every phase of the UNICOM process in order to accomplish the most successful investigative interview.

Specific Instructional Objectives

The following is a listing of specific instruction objectives for the practitioner who wants to master the UNICOM model for preemployment application:

1)   The practitioner/investigator will recognize the importance and interrelatedness of each of the five phases of interviewing.

2)   The practitioner/investigator will understand the necessity of planning and preparation for the entire interview and screening process.

3)   The practitioner/investigator will have a structured procedure to utilize during each of the five interview phases of employee selection.

4)   The practitioner/investigator will have a checklist to ensure that all pertinent information has been gathered for each applicant.

Managing Within a Trilogy of Interactive Activities

An effective UNICOM investigator must learn to manage within a trilogy of interactive events as introduced in the previous chapter. This management style includes the ability to effectively interpret and meticulously catalog numerous covert and overt behaviors for the investigator's full advantage. This process becomes a challenge because behavior, verbal and nonverbal, occurs simultaneously at a very rapid rate, beginning at the second phase and becoming increasingly more dynamic throughout each phase to the conclusion of the interview. To have this advantage, an investigator must acquire and manage the following trilogy of skills and knowledge:

1)   Have a definite understanding of the investigation objective,

2)   Discern the dynamics and the interactive behavior from the interviewee's point of view, and

3)   Subsequently respond with appropriate interactive behavior to facilitate interview and investigation cooperation and disclosure.

Being able to masterfully manage that trilogy of interactive events will ensure a greater performance, a greater efficiency, and a greater productivity in the accomplishment of the overall interview objective. Directing these interactive events is a complex but manageable process.

The Interactive Components of UNICOM

A stepwise strategy is presented here to describe the multiphase processes of Universal Interviewing and Communications. These phases include the:

1)   Pre-interview Analysis Phase,
2)   First Personal Impression Phase,
3)   Main Data Collection Phase,
4)   Concluding Interview Phase, and
5)   Interview Follow-Up Phase

Pre-Interview Analysis Phase

The UNICOM interview process actually begins prior to the personal interview. The pre-interview analysis phase includes all the preliminary tasks necessary for initiating a successful interview. These essential tasks include:

1)   Determining the interview objective

2)   Performing a job analysis
         a) Purpose of a job analysis
         b) Strategy for performing a job analysis

3)   Developing a job description
         a) Identification, *i.e.*, job title and department
         b) Job summary, *i.e.*, overview and descriptive statement
         c) Specific duties and responsibilities

4)   Job specifications
         a) Skills, knowledge, and abilities

5)   Developing a profile of the ideal prototype for position

6)   Reviewing the applicants' paper credentials
         a) Cover letter
         b) Resumes and/or applications
         c) Letters of reference
         d) Transcripts, diplomas/certificates
         e) Test scores

7)   Reference checking
         a) Documentation

8)   Developing the interview plan
         a) Interview checklist

The Interview Objective

It is imperative for the UNICOM practitioner to have a clear and complete understanding of the interview or investigative objective in order to plan and execute a productive interview. The interview goal or objective could range from quite simple, as in purchasing a car, to very complex, as in a multi-million dollar business acquisition.

The interview objective, by its degree of complexity, essentially will determine the complexity of the data collection and analysis process. It also determines the exact extent of legal compliance requirements. For example, an understanding of the interview objective will assist in making decisions regarding policy and legal protocol for advertising and for recruiting applicants for the interview process. Then, the interview goal will require some specific decisions regarding the selected ideal environment, the decor and room arrangement, the prescribed manner of the practitioner/interviewer interaction, the question formulation, and selection execution techniques. This interactive plan specifically will spell out what the practitioner will wear, and when and how he will smile, frown, gesture, walk, talk, touch, and respond while interacting with the interviewee. The interview objective additionally will determine how the critical *first impression* scene will be conducted, *i.e.*, regarding the degree of friendliness, handshake, and eye contact.

The Preemployment Interviewing Objective

The preemployment interview or selection interview is designed to gather information in a systematic manner and evaluate the qualifications of an applicant for employment. The ideal objective would be to select the best-suited person for the position. More specifically stated, selecting the person whose skills, needs, and aspirations are best suited to the requirements of the job. Thus, the objective successfully met would create a two-fold benefit:

1)   The new employee will be fulfilled personally, and
2)   The hiring company will have successfully filled its position.

A complete job analysis and job description will, of course, be vital considerations for the UNICOM practitioner to determine a specific preemployment interview objective. Even though a company may have a preexisting job description, it is essential that it be updated each time a position-filling campaign is initiated to reflect the current position requirements.

The Purpose of a Job Analysis

A job analysis is defined as a detailed statement of work behaviors and other information relevant to a job. A review of the current job analysis is the essential first step. It goes without saying that, if the current analysis is up-to-date, the practitioner is ready to move to the next stage of preparation. An adequate job analysis is a prerequisite to a working job description, and is defined for UNICOM purposes as a systematic process for gathering information about a specific job. In simple terms, a job analysis states and describes what an employee does in a specific job. The importance of developing a proper job analysis is recognized for several reasons:

1) A job analysis is a requirement for workforce planning.

2) A job analysis is essential for an adequate job description.

3) A job analysis is important for legal requirements.

4) A job analysis assists with salary computation.

5) A job analysis creates a more accurate employer-employee understanding.

6) A job analysis helps to set the standards for employee evaluation.

7) A job analysis may identify the need to adjust the description, *i.e.*, certain tasks may have been added or deleted from the preexisting job description.

The relevance of a complete and accurate job analysis cannot be overstated. A job analysis may be the primary evidence for an employer who is faced with the *burden of proof* for selection decisions.

Strategy for Performing a Job Analysis

The UNICOM strategy for performing an adequate job analysis includes a composite rating drawn from the following evaluation techniques:

1) Observation of on-the-job activities and performance,
2) Employee description of activities,
3) Supervisor analysis and reports,
4) Interviewing workers about the specific position,
5) Questionnaires completed by workers in a specific position,
6) Analysis of critical incidents, and
7) Examination/comparison of previous job analyses.

Observing Activities and Performance -- The task of observing on-the-job activities and performance of employees who currently hold the position targeted for being filled is one essential element of the job-analysis process. The UNICOM observation strategy requires close attention from the job analyst, because he must ensure that all aspects of the job are observed and recorded over a period of time. The UNICOM job analyst can avoid bias by observing several employees as they perform on the job at various times of the day, week, and year. This technique allows the analyst to consider the way each employee does his job as well as aspects of the job that are performed daily and periodically. It also helps the analyst become familiar with work conditions, equipment used, and abilities and skills required in performing various tasks.

It is recognized that unskilled and semiskilled jobs are easier to analyze, while highly skilled jobs may be more difficult to observe. Thus, the composite function of the other job analysis strategies essentially are viewed in conjunction with the observation method.

Employee Descriptions of Activities -- It can be extremely helpful to obtain employee perceptions of the position because, ideally, the person performing the job should have the best knowledge of the job tasks and requirements. This UNICOM strategy suggests that current employees provide detailed descriptions of each task they perform on the job. The UNICOM analyst must then carefully consider these descriptions and, to avoid a distorted view, compare them with the previously recorded observations and the supervisor's analysis.

Supervisor Analysis and Reports -- Supervisors should have a good understanding of the positions they supervise and may have even performed these jobs themselves prior to becoming supervisors. Again, to avoid supervisor bias, the analysis should compare employee reports to supervisor reports for similarities and differences that may be recorded.

Interview Current Employees -- The UNICOM practitioner should interview the supervisor and employees related to the position to be filled. The interview should be structured and designed for the position and include open-ended questions so as not to limit the information provided by the employee. The practitioner must, as mentioned above, manage the trilogy of interactive events in these interviews as well as the preemployment selection interview with job applicants. The interviewer must obtain the required information and listen and watch carefully to ensure accurate interpretation of the interviewee's description and perceptions of the job in question.

Questionnaires Completed by Workers -- A job analysis questionnaire may be developed by the analyst, or a standardized questionnaire may be selected for the purpose of employee assessment of a position. Some standard questionnaires that have shown to be reliable and valid instruments are described below:

- **PAQ Position Analysis Questionnaire** -- Developed by the Purdue Research Foundation, the PAQ employs a checklist designed to identify what a worker does. It has been used for more than 25 years for a wide range of jobs.

- **MPDQ Management Position Description Questionnaire** -- This is a structured checklist of 208 items which include marketing, financial planning, productive scheduling, coordinating workers and divisions, and public and customer relations. It also measures one's level of financial responsibility, supervisory responsibilities, degree of stress and complexity, and/or responsibility for strategic direction of the organization.

- Listed below are additional job analysis questionnaires:
  TAS Task Abilities Scale
  Ability Requirement Scales
  Professional and Managerial Position Questionnaire
  Executive Position Description Questionnaire
  Managerial/Professional Job Functions Inventory
  Threshold Traits Analysis System

It is recommended that the employee and supervisor compare the results of the questionnaire to work toward an agreement on the tasks, qualifications, and skills required for the position before starting the job description.

Critical Incident Technique (CIT) -- The critical incident technique is a method of analysis that views certain past events as critical incidents that an employee has had to deal with and overcome. It was developed during World War II in an effort to determine why some fighter pilots crashed during critical flying maneuvers while others did not. It was discovered that pilots with smaller bodies were more successful than larger pilots, because the smaller pilots could move more easily to accomplish flying tasks within the small cockpits of the planes. Thus, the CIT applied to other jobs may reveal some unique characteristics and skills of successful employees vs. unsuccessful employees. It also may identify creativity in problem solving and specific mental and physical requirements for the job.

Review of Previous Job Analyses -- A review of previous job analyses will assist the UNICOM practitioner in determining how the position has changed and/or remained the same as well as identify a prototype of past employees who were most successful in the position.

Developing a Job Description

A job description may be described as a written, detailed summary of the basic tasks, duties, and responsibilities for a specific position. The job description includes three interrelated sections:

1) Identification,
2) Job summary, and
3) Specific duties and responsibilities.

The Identification Section -- The identification section of a job description essentially contains the job title, the department where the job will be headquartered, and the supervisor's title. In some cases, a job number may be assigned, and a range of pay may be listed.

The Job Summary -- The summary of the job should be a concise, descriptive statement which provides an overview of the job duties.

Specific Duties and Responsibilities -- It should accurately and completely cover all specific duties and responsibilities of the position.

Job Specifications

As an outcome of the job analysis and job description, a job-specifications summary can be developed to include the skills, background, and specific qualifications necessary for an employee to satisfactorily perform the job. Such specifications will include, but are not necessarily limited to:

1)   Education,
2)   Experience,
3)   Complexity of decision,
4)   Supervision, and
5)   Interaction with others

The Ideal Prototype

The ideal prototype describes a person who may be ideal for a position. It can be drawn from the job description and the job-specification constructs. It is, in fact, a profile that considers the tasks and role of the job performer and the range of specifications and qualifications necessary to adequately perform the job. Determining the ideal prototype may be a complex and interesting process, as it involves agreement on the potentially differing mental pictures drawn by other employers, supervisors, the head of the department, the corporate executive officer, and, last but not least, the human resource department interviewers. Another factor contributing to the complexity of drawing an ideal prototype is EEO law and the danger of discrimination.

The entire process of performing a job analysis to the end of writing an accurate job description is vital to the practitioner's concern for compliance of EEO law. When faced with the *burden of proof,* it becomes necessary to establish an accurate version of facts for selection decisions. It is just as important to select the best person for the position as it is to avoid looking for something in a candidate that is not needed to accomplish the job requirements.

Review Paper Credentials

Paper credentials (*i.e.*, cover letter, applicant resume, and letters of reference) often are the basis of early impressions formed by the interviewer.

Cover Letter -- The purpose of including a cover letter with a resume or application is that it provides an opportunity for the applicant to present specific aspects of his educational and experiential background in relation to the position under consideration. By examining the content and clarity of the cover letter, the practitioner can discern such information as the applicant's ability to communicate in a written form. The cover letter also may provide clues as to the applicant's attention to detail such as spelling, grammar, neatness, and style.

Applicant Resume and/or Application -- The resume traditionally presents educational and work experiences in chronological sequence. In examining an applicant's resume, the UNICOM practitioner should keep in mind that the resume is simply a representation of the candidate and that he may have both negative and positive aspects that the resume does not reveal. Some techniques to apply to the resume-evaluation process are:

- Write notes directly on the resume.

- Highlight possible gaps in employment history.

- Highlight points that are vague and need clarification.

- Note aspects of the resume that relate specifically to the position.

- Note aspects that may be contradictory to the position.

- Prepare questions to clarify or expand the resume information.

- Compare educational and experiential aspects to the job description.

- Compare educational and experiential aspects to the ideal prototype.

Some facets to scrutinize on an applicant's resume are noted as follows:

Educational Background -- The applicant may imply that he has a degree by stating that he attended a specific college or university. It is wise to verify college attendance and degree awarded. This can be accomplished by requesting a transcript of grades or letter from the college or university stating the dates the applicant attended as well as the degree earned.

Experience -- An applicant may state, for example, that he worked for a company from 1992 to 1993. Ask the applicant to be specific about month and year since those dates could represent a wide range of time, *i.e.*, 24 months if the applicant worked from January, 1992, through December, 1993, to less than two months if the applicant worked from December, 1992, to January, 1993. The applicant may state that he increased production by 100% or some other claim of increased productivity. Ask him what that means, and how he did it. Learn to question applicants on resume statements in a non-threatening manner but with the objective of discerning the truth about experience and education.

The Employee Application -- A typical employee application should request the following information:

- Applicant's full name, address, and telephone number;

- A list of prior employers, including the type of employment, the length of employment, the reasons for leaving, and the addresses and telephone numbers of prior employers;

- The names of references including their relationships to the applicant and the length of time they have known the applicant;

- Whether the applicant has been convicted of a criminal offense and, if so, the type of offense and the date of conviction; and

- The position for which the applicant is applying and facts or statements indicating that the applicant possesses the personal characteristics required by the position's job description.

Also included in the application should be an authorization from the applicant enabling any former employer to give the prospective employer any information it has regarding the applicant.

Letters of Reference -- Letters of reference often are submitted by the applicant's former employers, supervisors, teachers, business associates, and friends. Typically, these letters are so unduly positive and stereotypic that they convey little useful information.

Official Transcripts and Certifications -- An official transcript received from the applicant's college or university will provide proof and date of a degree earned, as well as the course work and grade point average earned by the candidate. Similarly, any reported or required certification should be verified as a means of ensuring against negligent hiring. A transcript received from an applicant should not be considered official and may have been tampered with to provide erroneous data, whereas a transcript received directly from a college or university can be considered official.

Test Scores -- Applicant ability test scores often are considered prior to an interview. For example, if a job specification calls for certain math skills or work attitudes, a written standardized test could appropriately measure these characteristics. Research has determined that, used properly, tests based on scientific principles can positively contribute to selection procedures.

Reference Checks

In addition to letters of reference, the practitioner also may want to contact other references listed by the candidate to obtain specific information regarding the applicant's past work performance and desirability as a worker. Reference checks should be considered a vital function of the diligent employer's preemployment screening protocol. It is suggested that the interviewer call former immediate supervisors for a more accurate and candid report on an employee's work history.

Documentation -- This information should be documented in a prescribed manner to ensure against negligent hiring charges. This reference contact list should include:

- The date and time of contact,

- The name and title of the person contacted, and

- The responses to the practitioner's questions.

It also is advisable to request that the person contacted record the inquiry as a way to substantiate the employer's inquiry.

The Interview Plan

The interview plan includes details such as creating the ideal interview environment, the formulation and execution of specific questions, the sequence and transition of the questions and interactions, and a final checklist to ascertain whether all aspects of the interview and data-gathering process are complete. It is during the planning stage that the critical first personal impression phase is designed.

Interview preparation is a critical component to the UNICOM Interviewing Model. Interviewers may make presumptions or omissions regarding an appropriate inquiry that may create a state of legal negligence. For example, one would not want a medical doctor to make an assumption about a health problem without going through some sort of diagnostic process or definitive testing procedure. Likewise, it is ideal to approach interviewing with a proactive attitude. One can anticipate possible problems and prevent them if one knows exactly what is needed and what one expects to be utilized when drawing conclusions or making the final decision. This preliminary data collection method should be as detailed and inclusive as possible so as not to overlook any aspect. Thus, the interviewer should operate from a well-planned protocol.

The Interview Checklist -- If the UNICOM practitioner develops a comprehensive checklist which details all the information required for the entire interview process, it will guard against the failure to gain the quality and quantity of information needed for the selection decision.

Interview Follow-Up Phase

The interview follow-up phase is the final stage of the UNICOM interview procedure. At this point, the interview plan and the checklist are reviewed and evaluated relative to the accumulated data, and an analysis of the personal interaction with the interviewee is completed to determine what is needed for concluding the data-gathering event. During this phase, reference and credit checks may be completed, and all unfinished business is handled.

Often, a follow-up interview is desirable and may serve several purposes, such as an opportunity to review any points that were not clear during the initial interview. It may offer the practitioner an additional opportunity to confront what may have been questionable behavior during the initial interview. The follow-up interview allows the practitioner to explore in greater depths some aspects of the interviewee's earlier presentation, and it allows for a test of consistency for both verbal and nonverbal behavior presented by the interviewee.

Background Checks

Prior to the Follow-Up Interview Phase, background checks for the final candidates generally are completed. As emphasized in Chapter Five, and again in Chapter Eight, there are a multitude of reasons for conducting background checks on potential employees. Applicants may present exaggerated credentials, the threat of negligent hiring lawsuits is increasing, and the practitioner is caught in the middle of the double dilemma of hiring the best applicant for the job and protecting himself and his company from today's litigious business environment.

A comprehensive background check usually will reveal information regarding prior work history, and a credit check, social security number trace, criminal record search, and motor vehicle report will provide other useful information. The following section describes techniques and question formulation methods for conducting reference checks regarding work experiences.

Past Work History -- Prior to the final selection interview, or at least before offering a position to the chosen candidate, it is good practice to conduct a standardized reference check with past employers, past supervisors, and, if possible, some past co-workers. Many past employers only disclose the name, dates of employment, and, perhaps, whether they would rehire the said employee. They typically refuse to release any other information regarding job performance. However, there are a number of ways to minimize this closed attitude:

1) **Applicant's Authorization to Release Reference Information** -- If you have the job applicant sign a release consent form, you could achieve a double gain:

    a) The former employer may be more willing to discuss the applicant's past performance, strengths, weaknesses, and even reasons for termination; plus

b)   It is recognized that, when applicants sign consent to release forms, they tend to be more truthful during an interview.

2)   **Organize or Plan Interview** -- As with any interview, the reference checking process should be strategically planned, and questions should be formulated to ensure a successful check:

a)   Review resume and interview data for verification,

b)   Develop questions to target new information, and

c)   Identify the names and positions of the former employer, supervisors, and peers.

3)   **Record Reference Information** -- Have a pre-designed, standardized form to record the name, address, phone number, and title of the person providing the reference. Be sure that all information is recorded as completely as possible and date the document. Also, ask the person giving the reference to document the exchange of information as well so that you have a double record of such communication.

There are a number of ways to obtain the reference check: in person, by telephone, by letter, by fax, or by e-mail. Each of these is discussed below with some recommended questioning techniques.

Checking References in Person -- For a senior level or executive position, it perhaps is best to obtain a personal reference check interview with former employers and supervisors. While this approach perhaps is an exception to typical protocol, advantages for checking references in person are:

1)   It is easier to interact face-to-face than by telephone or letter.

2)   The interview may be more candid and revealing.

3)   An appreciation of the former workplace environment may be helpful to the practitioner.

4)   Both verbal and nonverbal communication can be considered when meeting the reference person face-to-face.

Checking References by Telephone -- The telephone interview is the second best method of reference checking. While conducting the telephone interview, listen for tone of voice, vocal inflection, and word choice of the reference provider. Establish a telephone rapport to allow the conversation to last as long as possible or as long as necessary.

Reference Checking Techniques -- Whether interviewing in person or by telephone, it is recommended that the interviewer assume a neutral stance. Rather than use the phrase *reference check* in your introduction, it is best to ask the person to verify some information with you. Arrange a time when it is convenient and private. Ask open-ended questions. As described above, open-ended questions cannot be answered by a "yes" or "no" but require a phrase or more lengthy description.

- **Examples** -- *"How would you describe the applicant's work style? Would you give me some examples of his or her best performances? Would you give me some examples of his or her worst performances?"*

Checking References by Mail or by Fax -- The mail or fax method of reference checking probably is the least productive and the most time consuming. Employers seem more reluctant to be candid with the written word. Mail may be slow or lost on someone's desk. A letter can be ignored, while a face-to-face contact or telephone call must receive instant response.

In summarizing the UNICOM interview procedure, the interrelated components have been presented for tandem consideration with the UNICOM trilogy of interactive events. The following section of this chapter is devoted to actual question formulation as the UNICOM questioning techniques relate to the above interview phases.

First Personal Impression Phase

Two primary sources of applicant first impressions are the initial paper credentials the applicant submits (*i.e.*, cover letter and resume) and the applicant's overall presentation. This initial impression often mistakably is the only basis on which a practitioner decides whether or not to interview.

Sources of First Impressions -- The applicant also has several sources of first impressions of the company offering the position:

- The initial job description and job specification document,

- The first phone call requesting an interview,

- The reception area and receptionist who greets the applicant,

- The interview environment, and

- The physical appearance of the interviewer.

It is noted here that physical appearance factors that can influence the interviewer's impression during this phase include superficial physical features of the applicant such as gait, facial attractiveness, and dress. Thus, the two aspects of the first personal impression phase, collectively considered in the following section on *impression management,* are not only for the first impression but for controlling the ongoing impressionable countenance of the entire interview and selection process. See Figure 9.1.

Figure 9.1
FIRST PERSONAL IMPRESSION PHASE

1)   Impression management
2)   Credibility of impression
3)   Likability of impression
4)   Interpersonal attractiveness
5)   Dominant impression
6)   Challenge of impression management

Impression Management -- As defined by Dale Leathers (1992), *"Impression management is an individual's conscious attempt to exercise conscious control over selected communicative behaviors and cues -- particularly nonverbal cues -- for purposes of making a desired impression."*
       The UNICOM practitioner will learn the presentational function and the affect-management function to become an effective impression manager. Not only will the UNICOM practitioner learn to exercise conscious control over the impression he makes on another person, but he will consciously control his emotional responses to what that person says or has done.
       An interrelated component to applying these skills is the idea of UNICOM investigators associating themselves with desirable image traits while simultaneously disclaiming association with undesirable image traits. The latter includes the practitioner's personal interactive process with an applicant as well as the practitioner's duty to ensure that the interview environment provides that ideal image. The nature of impression management is divided into four dimensions *(i.e.,* credibility, likability, interpersonal attractiveness, and dominance). A few principle statements about each of these dimensions are reviewed below:

       Credibility of Impression -- It is essential that the UNICOM practitioner present a believable image. The more believable the impression and communicative demeanor, the more likely he will achieve success with the interactive interview.

Conversely, one can assume that the greater the facade, the less likely the interview will be successful.

Likability of Impression -- Common sense and a considerable amount of research denotes the importance of being likable in the interactive interview process.

Interpersonal Attractiveness -- The dimension of interpersonal attractiveness is much more than the initial physical impression in that it involves the emotional, psycho-social aspect of expression during the interactive events.

Dominant Impression -- It is essential for the UNICOM practitioner to present a very positive image of dominance and to have the ability to manage power and assertiveness in an acceptable manner without the appearance of arrogance.

Challenge of Impression Management -- The challenge that the UNICOM practitioner must meet is dependent upon learning the skills to accomplish the above dimensions of impression management and then to extend those skills to meet the objective of effectively managing interactive interviews with those of the opposite gender, those of other cultures and races, and those of other socio-economic backgrounds. One might think that it is impossible to be all things to all people, but it is essential that the UNICOM practitioner aim for perfection in managing the interview and interview setting.

Main Data Collection Phase
       The main data collection phase has a multipurpose agenda. It is during this phase that the majority of the interview data is gathered. This phase offers the practitioner an opportunity to verify resume details with the interviewee and to request further information required to accumulate the desired data set. Most importantly, this phase becomes the interactive event between the practitioner and the interviewee since both parties get to know each other in a face-to-face situation. The UNICOM practitioner must manage this interaction to gather as much information as possible, even that information which may not be anticipated during questioning.
       These serendipitous finds do not occur by accident. Opportunity for disclosure is strategically created and facilitated by the practitioner who employs all the tools and the skills within the repertoire of practice. The following section will demonstrate some key impression management techniques that may be applied throughout the interview.

Mirroring the Candidate -- While blatant imitation will negatively impact the interview interaction, subtle mirroring may allow the candidate to feel comfortable and more at ease to disclose information.

Managing Attention -- If the candidate is withholding information or avoiding eye contact, the practitioner may wish to hold her pen up to draw the candidate's attention to a focal point, and closer to establishing eye contact. She may also move the pen up or down or from side to side, again to draw the candidate's attention.

Minimize or Maximize Importance -- The practitioner can maximize or minimize the importance of interaction with subtle hand positions that are congruent with her words. The practitioner may illustrate that she is *highly impressed*, or cause the candidate to see the situation as rating very high by holding a hand high above the head. Conversely, the practitioner may minimize the importance of an incident to allow the candidate to feel safe to disclose information by holding a hand low. While a hand held toward the center of the body can illustrate that something is of medium value or importance. These three *illustrators* again become stronger than words and thus are helpful impression management techniques.

Managing Disclosure -- The practitioner must manage that critical moment when the candidate may reveal the withheld information. She must be open to receive the information, and she must provide psychological safety so that the candidate will feel comfortable enough to make any disclosures.

The Interview Paperwork

Besides impression management techniques, the practitioner may wish to consider some more standardized paper tools. These tools are interview instruments and recording interview information.

Interview Instruments -- It is imperative that the UNICOM practitioner ask the right questions effectively. The questions should be developed well in advance of the interview and should relate to the job descriptions and job specifications.

Recording Interview Information -- A standardized recording system should be developed to ensure accurate tracking of each applicant. The system should allow the UNICOM practitioner to document the candidate's responses for future reference and comparison. This recording system should include a quantifiable rating system to support the practitioner's decision.

Concluding Interview Phase

The interview conclusion phase does what it suggests in that it concludes the interview with an opportunity for the practitioner and interviewee to provide concluding statements and interaction. At this time, the practitioner reviews the overall interview objective, the entire interaction event that has occurred, and information received during the main data collection phase. He also determines what is needed to continue the data analysis and make final decisions or selections. A continued interaction agreement between the practitioner and the interviewee also may be established at this point as it relates to the interview follow-up phase.

Final Impressions -- The final impression phase is when the interviewer considers the applicant's interview performance as well as the qualifications.

Interview Follow-Up Phase

    The interview follow-up phase is the final stage of the UNICOM interview procedure. At this point, the interview plan and checklist are reviewed and evaluated relative to the accumulated data and an analysis of the personal interaction with the interviewee to determine what is needed for completing the data-gathering event. During this phase, reference or credit checks may be completed and all unfinished business is handled.

    Post-Interview Issues -- The interview follow-up phase instruction is to assist the UNICOM Practitioner with the decision-making process of selecting the *best* applicant for the job. The post-interview phase has the potential to put the practitioner in a state of confusion. The UNICOM techniques described here are designed to allay that confusion and allow the practitioner to approach this systematic selection phase with confidence. The following points are presented for the interview follow-up phase (Figure 9.2).

Figure 9.2
INTERVIEW FOLLOW-UP PHASE

1) Uniform documentation system
    a) Uniform profile checklist
    b) Uniform organizational forms
2) Factors for final consideration
    a) Review objectives
    b) Review and compare applicants
    c) Evaluate test scores
    d) Consider intangible factors
    e) Evaluate reactions
3) Consider nonverbal behavior
4) Compare references
5) Consider background checks
6) UNICOM composite profile
7) Defense for discrimination claims

    Uniform Documentation System -- Before the preemployment selection process begins, the practitioner should develop a step-by-step procedure, in writing, for selecting employees. A separate file should be kept for each applicant, which includes a checklist to ensure that all pertinent information is gathered.

    Profile Checklist -- The profile checklist (Figure 9.3) is presented as a tool to assure the practitioner that he has gathered all the vital information, segmented as it may be, into an accurate profile of each applicant. This checklist is designed to be attached to each applicant's file to be used when considering all data obtained for each individual.

Figure 9.3
PROFILE CHECKLIST

1) Resume and/or application
2) Letters of reference
3) Documentation of pre-interview
4) Documentation of interview
5) Reference check
6) Background check
   a) Work history
   b) Driver's record
   c) Social Security Number
   d) Criminal record check
7) Education verification
8) Employment eligibility -- I-9

Figure 9.4
PERSONNEL FORMS

1) Application for employment forms
2) Interview evaluation forms
3) Candidate evaluation forms
4) Consent forms for:
   a) Reference check
   b) Background check
   c) Credit check
   d) Credential verification
5) Reference check forms
6) Test score report form
7) Education verification
8) Certification -- diploma verification form
9) Motor vehicle report form
10) Employment eligibility form -- I-9

Organizational Forms -- The practitioner is advised to adopt a set of uniform standardized forms designed to contain those vital informational segments that are gathered throughout the job applicant interviewing and screening process. Specific instruction on how they can be used most effectively also should be developed. The practitioner may choose to create the set of forms to meet the unique needs of the company. Forms also may be ordered from companies that provide such paperwork. See Figure 9.4.

Factors for Final Consideration

The post-interview phase of the selection process is a time to reflect on the entire activity that has occurred for each applicant. It is a time to consolidate a profile on each applicant and to compare those profiles. Listed below are a set of activities for a UNICOM practitioner to consider during this final phase.

Review Objectives -- By reviewing the job description, job specifications, and the goals and objectives of filling the position, a practitioner can gain an overall feeling of completion or lack thereof.

Review and Compare -- A comprehensive review of each applicant's work history and relevant educational credentials in comparison to the job requirements and specifications is recommended as an exercise to determine which candidate is the best match. Following this process, the practitioner may wish to rank the applicants according to this best fit.

Evaluate Test Scores -- An evaluation and comparison of the candidates' test scores are an important part of creating the composite profile for each applicant.

Consider Intangible Factors -- There are, no doubt, intangible requirements to the position to consider. The practitioner must consider these in relationship to those unique characteristics that each candidate brought to the interview or evaluation process.

Evaluate Reactions -- It is essential to interpret each candidate's reaction to the work environment and the interactive interview process. Step two of this exercise is the comparison of candidates to determine who had the most favorable reaction.

Consider Nonverbal Behavior -- A critical consideration is the candidate's nonverbal behavior throughout the interactive evaluation process. A comparison of each candidate's behavior should reveal the most ideal behavior to match the position profile.

Compare References -- A determination of whether references matched each individual portfolio is one comparison required by the practitioner. This is followed by a comparison of each applicant. During this exercise, it is important to consider each applicant's reasons offered for leaving previous employers and compare to reasons listed to those provided by the referent. Salary requirements noted by each candidate also should be considered with regard to the salary range for the position.

Consider Background Checks -- In evaluating and comparing applicant background checks, it is important to rank or score each person's report before entering it as a component of each individual's personal profile.

The Employment Offer

Once the finalists have been chosen and ranked, it is appropriate to prepare an offer. However, there are a number of issues that accompany the act of making the employment offer.

Salary Determination -- Legal ramifications of determining a starting salary are numerous. Especially important for consideration are:

- The Fair Labor Standards Act,
- The Equal Pay Act of 1963,
- Title VII of the Civil Rights Act,
- The Age Discrimination in Employment Act,
- The Rehabilitation Act of 1973, and
- The Americans with Disabilities Act of 1990.

In addition to federal statutes, each state has a supplemental set of laws and guidelines that govern salary determination.

Defense for Discrimination

Discrimination is defined as the relationship between the use of selection procedures for reasons that have no relevance to the position. Six Congressional acts have set the pace for legislating a nondiscriminatory workplace:

1) **The Civil Rights Act of 1964** prohibits on-the-job discrimination on the basis of race, color, religion, sex, or national origin. It established the Equal Employment Opportunity Commission to enforce the law.

2) **The Age Discrimination in Employment Act of 1967** prohibits discrimination against employees and job applicants who are aged 40 to 70.

3) **The Vietnam Era Veterans' Readjustment Act of 1972** enacted the requirements for government contractors to hire and promote qualified disabled and Vietnam-era veterans.

4) **The Rehabilitation Act of 1973** requires government contractors to accommodate the physical and mental needs of qualified handicapped employees and job applicants.

5)   **The Pregnancy Disability Amendment to Title VII** (1978) prohibits the disparate treatment of pregnant women in the workforce.

6)   **The Americans with Disabilities Act of 1990** extended protections of the Civil Rights Act of 1964 to all handicapped individuals.

Adverse Impact -- Any selection procedure that has an adverse impact regarding selection due to race, sex, or ethnicity is considered discrimination. It is imperative that the entire interviewing and screening process be monitored to make sure it is in compliance with EEO law, and especially any company Affirmative Action Plan.

Defensive Record Keeping -- A complete file should be kept on every applicant regarding the information on impact applicable to race, sex, and ethnicity.

Evaluation of Selection Rates -- It is advisable during the follow-up process to review the total selection process to determine if there is the possibility of adverse impact. The selection rate for any race, sex, or ethnic group which is less than the four-fifths (4/5) or 80% of the race for the group with the highest rate could be considered evidence of adverse impact, whereas a greater than four-fifths rate generally will not be questioned.

Question Formulation Matrix

The reader is reminded that a general section on question formulation has been presented in Chapter Eight. The following section presents a question formulation matrix to serve as an example of a question formulation and delivery technique. This matrix format is designed to direct a line of questioning with the six-step management strategy for self-disclosure.

Truthful vs. Suspect Answers -- The delivery technique distinguishes between a *truthful* and a *suspect* answer for a series of typical preemployment interview questions. *Truthful* answers and *suspect* answers are qualified with explanatory delivery and nonverbal cues. The question-delivery format then moves from a suspect answer with the assistance of selected *suspect answer, response-management* statements, to a *revised, question follow-up* technique.

Response Management Statements -- The suspect answer and response management statements are preparatory to conditioning the candidate to feel safe enough to disclose information. These responses tend to minimize the importance of a question, or at least provide a rationalization to allow the candidate to disclose information.

Revised Question Follow-Up -- The revised question is a re-phrased question which reflects the response management statement. The question is rephrased so that it is less threatening and safer to answer. Thus, the matrix can be applied within the framework of the six-step management strategy for self-disclosure. This question-delivery technique employs the *suspect answer responses* to assist the practitioner in reaching the *critical moment*, while the revised question follow-up actually can be selected as the *strategic question*, to elicit the omitted or falsified information from the candidate. While a complete set of question guide-lines can be developed for application to an entire interview, only select topics are presented here as a representative instructional sample.

Question Formulation Matrix Design

The following question formulation matrix series is intended to illustrate the basic framework design for the entire preemployment interview. Each individual matrix is graphically divided to progressively demonstrate the following:

1) (Q) Opening question styles and inquiry variations,

2) (TA) Truthful answer illustrations,
   (SA) Suspect answer illustrations,

3) (RM) Response Management Styles and prequestion conditioning statements, and

4) (RQ) Revised follow-up question variations.

A question formulation matrix is included for each of the following interview topics.

1) Employment History
   a) Disclosure -- completion
   b) Termination issues
   c) Disciplinary actions
   d) Job skills
   e) Job experience

2) Education
   a) Verification

3) Military History
   a) Discharge status

QUESTION FORMULATION MATRIX

INQUIRY AREA	1	EMPLOYMENT HISTORY
Focus area	A	Disclosure -- Completion

Opening Question

Q 1   Did you include all jobs you had during the last (...) years?

Q 2   Did you list all jobs in your employment application?

Q 3   Did you list all employment in your resume?

Q 4   Is this a fair accounting of all the jobs you've had?

Truthful Answer Illustration

TA 1   Yes! (Immediate response -- without hesitation.)

TA 2   Yes, I did! (Direct response.)

TA 3   Yes, except for summer jobs during school.

Suspect Answer Illustration

SA 1   (Slight pause) ... yes.

SA 2   (Elongated response) y..e..s..

SA 3   Yes...to the best of my recollection. (Qualified yes answer.)

SA 4   Well...yes.

Suspect Answer Response Management

RM 1   Certainly, (name), its difficult to remember every past job. Most people today have to work several jobs at one time to make ends meet.

RM 2   As you can easily see, (name), most application forms can't provide enough space to list every job.

RM 3   Your cooperation is most appreciated, but as you know most people just don't have a fair amount of time to fill out long applications completely.

Revised Question Follow-Up

RQ 1   Having given yourself more time to remember, what other jobs have you worked in the past (...) years?

RQ 2   What other jobs have you worked, even if you were laid off or let go?

RQ 3   Besides what you told me, what other jobs did you have in the last (...) years?

QUESTION FORMULATION MATRIX

INQUIRY AREA	1	EMPLOYMENT HISTORY
Focus area	B	Termination Issues

Opening Question

Q 1   Were you ever laid off from any of your past jobs?

Q 2   Were you ever let go from any of your past jobs?

Q 3   Were you terminated or fired from any of your past jobs?

Truthful Answer Illustration

TA 1   Yes, because the plant closed down. (Direct, to the point.)

TA 2   Just once.

TA 3   Never.

Suspect Answer Illustration

SA 1   No. (Soft withdrawn answer.)

SA 2   No. (Slight pause.)

SA 3   No. Not for cause. (Qualified answer.)

Suspect Answer Response Management

RM 1   Everyone has an opinion of what really takes place when someone is fired or let go. That's certainly their right and yours, too.

RM 2   No one is perfect, and all of us make our fair share of mistakes in life. I certainly have made (smile) my fair share.

RM 3   The world is certainly not a perfect place. Everyone makes a mistake or two. That's why we are just human beings.

Revised Question Follow-Up

RQ 1   (Name), with all circumstances considered, what jobs were you ever let go from?

RQ 2   (Name), based on all the information, what jobs were you unfairly let go from?

RQ 3   Besides what you told me so far, (name), what other jobs were you let go from -- regardless of the reason?

QUESTION FORMULATION MATRIX

INQUIRY AREA	**1**	**EMPLOYMENT HISTORY**
Focus area	**C**	**Disciplinary Actions**

Opening Question

Q 1   Were you ever given any "oral warnings" in the last (...) years?

Q 2   Were you ever given any "written warnings" in the last (...) years?

Q 3   Were you ever "suspended" for any work "infractions?"

Truthful Answer Illustration

TA 1   Never.

TA 2   No. I have a perfect record.

TA 3   No. (Very direct response and direct eye contact.)

Suspect Answer Illustration

SA 1   (Slight pause) ...No.

SA 2   No. (Briefly breaks eye contact.)

SA 3   No. Not really. I quit first. (Qualified answer.)

Suspect Answer Response Management

RM 1   You know, (name), warnings are not intended to condemn people -- but really are meant to help them.

RM 2   As you know, (name), there simply is no such thing as a *perfect* employee. We're all human, and we all make mistakes.

RM 3   Often overlooked are the companies who make mistakes, too. Employees make their fair share of them. That's why were human.

Revised Question Follow-Up

RQ 1   Perhaps you unknowingly violated an important rule and later learned you innocently made a mistake. Was that the case?

RQ 2   Momentarily looking back, (name), what types of infractions were you accused of even if you didn't do it?

RQ 3   (Name), could you have simply made only one mistake as opposed to many?

Summary Points of UNICOM Model for Preemployment Investigations

The Model for Preemployment Investigations presented in this chapter was drawn from the first of the UNICOM series for human resource development: *Universal Interviewing and Communications: A Preemployment Application* (Slowik, 1994). This model was designed to be employed as a proactive preventive measure against all forms of discrimination and negligent hiring and to increase the possibility that the best employees will be selected for employment. This interviewing model includes a stepwise strategy to describe the multiphase process of effective interviewing. Interviewer impression management was stressed for each of the five phases of the UNICOM interview to be combined with the management of the trilogy of interactive activities as a basis for selecting the best possible applicant.

CHAPTER TEN

UNICOM_{SM}
MODEL FOR EMPLOYMENT INVESTIGATIONS

This chapter presents a model for employment investigation which applies the UNICOM philosophy. The model, as explained in Chapter Six -- Part II, considers the components of verbal and nonverbal communication for effective interviewing, legal requirements for compliance with employment law, and the dynamics of managing a trilogy of interactive activities throughout the entire workplace investigation process (See Figure 10.1). The UNICOM technique presented below is demonstrated throughout the chapter as a strategy to manage that trilogy of interactive activities:

Figure 10.1
TRILOGY OF INTERACTIVE ACTIVITIES
FOR INVESTIGATORS

1) Have a clear and definitive understanding of the investigation objective,

2) Discern the dynamics and interactive behavior from the point of view of the person/s being investigated, and

3) Subsequently respond with the appropriate interactive response to facilitate investigation cooperation and disclosure.

The Investigation Objective

Human resource managers and administrators have multiple reasons for conducting workplace investigations. The primary objective of any investigation is to determine a factual basis for decision making. The purpose of an investigation may determine the interaction necessary to accomplish complete and accurate fact finding, to be in compliance with the laws governing the workplace, and to subsequently make the appropriate decision at the completion of the investigation. Three major categories of objectives or general reasons for investigations are listed below:

1)   Employee competence and performance,

2)   Employee deviance or misconduct (See Appendix B and Chapter Three), and

3)   Employee violation of corporate policy or employment law (See Chapter One).

The Dynamics of Interactive Behavior

The UNICOM Model for interactive communication is based on the dynamics of the ways humans send and receive messages. It has been determined that humans communicate via a dual, interactive language: the language of words and the language of the body. The astute practitioner must develop the multidimensional skills of interpreting this interactive behavior and learning to discern between truthful and deceitful communication. This process involves effective listening, attentive observation, interpreting the combined verbal and nonverbal communication, managing interaction, and appropriately responding to facilitate investigation cooperation and information disclosure with everyone involved in the entire investigative practice. These skills, once attained, require a lifetime of practice. Chapters Six, Seven, and Eight in Part II present a comprehensive description of the components and interactive dynamics of human communication and techniques for interpreting and interviewing which can be applied to all aspects of workplace investigations.

Appropriate Interactive Response

The workplace investigator must interpret and manage each phase of the investigative process. An essential component to this management strategy is to respond in an interactive manner, using verbal and nonverbal communication techniques designed to gain full cooperation and informational disclosure from all people involved in the entire investigation. Response management is a skill that can be developed only after attaining a cognitive grasp of the interactive dynamics of human communication. Those chapters in Part II are prerequisites for learning and applying these skills.

Strategy Outline for Workplace Investigations

A chronological format should be established for each workplace investigation so that interviews are scheduled and conducted in an impartial and standardized manner. It is important for the practitioner to have a working knowledge of the underlying political and social network of relationships between and among those being interviewed. Company policies and guidelines may also be a determining factor regarding the ordering of interviews and the step-by-step strategy to be followed for an internal investigation. Once the investigation plan is in place, it should be reviewed periodically to check for any loopholes or oversights that may exist. Timing may be of the essence to protect against the possible destruction of physical evidence, loss of key witnesses, or personnel security or safety considerations, including the general welfare of employees. A step-by-step strategy for conducting formal and informal workplace investigations is presented below. This outline is followed by specific instruction for managing and conducting each stage of a workplace investigation. The information presented throughout is intended to provide the practitioner or administrator with a list of generic steps, not requirements, to follow when conducting such investigations. Each investigative situation has different requirements, and this should be taken into consideration when developing an investigation plan.

STRATEGY OUTLINE FOR EMPLOYMENT INVESTIGATIONS

I. Determine the need or requirement to investigate
    a) Preliminary investigations
    b) Advantages of investigating
    c) Disadvantages of investigating
    d) Reasons for investigating
    e) Issues of immediacy

II. Initiating a formal investigation
    a) The nature of the issue
    b) Supplemental information
    c) Special expertise
        1) Legal expertise
        2) Security expertise
        3) Risk management
        4) Internal audit

III. Selecting the investigator
    a) Attributes of a professional investigator

IV. Developing the investigation plan
    a) Legal compliance
    b) Identifying potential witnesses
    c) Determining documents to be reviewed
        1)   Company documents
        2)   Employee-related documents

V.   Documentation design
        a) Scope of documentation
        b) Employee-generated documentation
            1) Description of issues
            2) Relevant facts and dates
            3) Names of persons involved
            4) Supplemental information
            5) Employee's signature and date

        c) Employer-generated documentation
            1) Description of issues
            2) Relevant facts and dates
            3) Names of persons involved
            4) Confirmation of issues
            5) Description of investigation plan
            6) Outline of company's expectations

VI.   The investigative interview design
        a) Who?
        b) What?
        c) When?
        d) Where?
        e) Why?

VII.   Question formulation

VIII.   Interactive interviewing

IX.   Interim action decisions

X.   Interviewing witnesses
        a) The cooperative witness
        b) The adverse witness
        c) The neutral witness
        d) Questions for witnesses

XI.   Closing the interview

XII.   Assessing the interviewee's credibility
        a) Corroborating evidence
        b) Circumstantial evidence

XIII.   The investigation summary

XIV.   Drawing conclusions
        a) Objective facts

       b) Subjective facts
       c) Compare and contrast all interactions

XV.   Recommending action

XVI.   Implementing the recommended action
       a) Consulting management
       b) Notification of subject
       c) Notification of complainant

XVII.   Final investigation file

XVIII. Allowing for an appeal

XIX.   Final appeal file

Determine the Need to Investigate

Internal workplace investigations are a matter of discretion, diligence, and legal responsibility. The decision to formally or informally investigate is based on the reason or potential investigation objective and its degree of seriousness. The need to investigate may be recognized by the human resource manager in a number of ways:

- Issues/events effecting personnel security or safety,
- Notification of a lawsuit,
- Report of suspicious employee misconduct or deviance,
- An administrative or employee complaint, and
- Loss of company assets/inventory shrinkage.

Preliminary Investigation -- It is recognized that any complaint or legal notification is serious. The degree of seriousness will be the human resource manager's first determination. However, before a full-fledged investigation is conducted, a preliminary or informal investigation must be utilized to determine whether or not to actually conduct a formal investigation. During the preliminary phase, the investigator should:

    1)   Identify all issues or problems:

           a) Have the company's policies, guidelines, or philosophy been violated?

           b) Have any federal, state, or local employment laws or general ethics been violated?

           c) Is the violation a serious offense?

  d) Review company policy of past similar situa-
     tions and decisions.

  e) Consider adverse impact on company.

  f) What can be done to avoid the costs of litiga-
     tion and its disruptive effect on the company?

  g) Does the issue/event require immediate inter-
     vention?

2)   Gather all material facts regarding the accused/suspected
      party:

  a) What is the accused's/suspect's performance
     history with the company?

  b) How long has the accused/suspect worked for
     the company?

  c) Has the accused/suspect had past violations? If
     so, what were they and what action was
     taken?

3)   Make the decision as to whether a formal or informal in-
      vestigation is required:

  a) Can the issue easily be resolved without a
     formal investigation?

  b) Does the situation demand a formal investi-
     gation?

4)   Instill confidence in the system and the investigator.

The ideal situation would be for the company to resolve complaints or
problems in-house to avoid potential lawsuits and expenses. A preliminary investigation is designed to carefully weigh the advantages and disadvantages of an in-
depth investigation. Listed below are the advantages (Figure 10.2) and disadvantages (Figure 10.3) a human resource manager must consider while making the
decision of whether or not to investigate.

Figure 10.2
ADVANTAGES OF INVESTIGATIONS

- Determine a factual basis for decision making
- Create a record for legal opinion/action
- Reveal deviant employee behavior/misconduct
- Halt deviant employee behavior or misconduct
- Avoid litigation
- Preclude or avoid a government investigation
- Limit employer liability
- Prevent adverse publicity

Figure 10.3
DISADVANTAGES OF INVESTIGATIONS

- Cost of time, money, and resources
- Uncertainty of investigation results
- Adverse publicity
- Inability to control scope of investigation
- Disruption of workplace relationships
- Potential civil litigation
- Revelation of evidence against employer
- Admission of problem

The Reason for Investigation -- The reason for making an investigation will set the purpose and objective of the investigation and will determine the procedure for conducting it. The following (Figure 10.4) is a broad illustrative listing of personnel incidents, criminal activities, business issues, circumstances, or events commonly experienced by administrators and human resource managers. Corporate management has a compelling obligation and ethical responsibility to initiate an inquiry, notification, or workplace investigation in these cases.

Figure 10.4
TYPES OF ISSUES REQUIRING INVESTIGATIONS

---

absenteeism (abusive)
abuse (verbal)
accidents (traffic/industrial/other)
acquisitions (corporate/business)
affirmative action complaints
arson
assault
background, preemployment
battery
bribery (commercial, kickbacks)
business, unfair practices
charitable contributions
competitor intelligence
computer security violations
conduct, reckless
conspiracy, criminal
contract analysis
copyright infringement
counterfeit merchandise
coupon fraud
crime, organized
customer claims
customer complaints
damage, criminal
deceptive practices
defamation
discrimination complaints
     age
     ancestry
     color
     gender
     marital
     medical condition
     mental condition
     military status
     nationality
     political
     pregnancy
     physical disability
     race
     reverse

     salary
     sexual orientation
     union
dress code violations
drug usage, sales, trafficking
eavesdropping, electronic
EEOC complaints
employee complaints
environmental complaints
espionage
ethics violations, complaints
extortion
family leave
forgery
fraud (internal, external)
gambling
garnishment
harassment
     sexual
     ethnic
     racial
health violations
information disclosure
injury, employee, customer
insubordination
insurance, claims
intellectual property violations
intimidation
license verification
misappropriations
misconduct on duty
misconduct off duty
negligence
     hiring
     training
     retention
     supervision
     investigation
OSHA complaints
pandering
parental notification

Types of Issues Requiring Investigations (continued)

patent infringement

performance

policy violations

pornography

privacy, invasion

prostitution

regulatory violations

robbery

sabotage

safety violations

security, clearance

security violations

service background

sexual offenses

slander

subcontractor background

substance abuse

supplier background

surveillance, unauthorized

stress-related claims

tardiness

theft, general

threatening/communications

time abuse

trust, antitrust

union-related

vandalism

vendor background

workers' compensation claims

work slowdowns/stoppages

whistle blowing complaints

Initiating a Formal Investigation

Certain problems may be resolved easily without a full-scale investigation. It may be in the best interest of the employee, the company, and the human resource manager to resolve issues quickly and efficiently. Initial considerations might be:

- Does the incident require the involvement or notification of law enforcement authorities?

- Does the incident require the involvement of mental health professionals/authorities?

- Does the allegation require immediate suspension of an employee or other measures to curtail the misconduct?

- Consider the presence of the accused/suspect in the workplace. Is there risk of injury, bother, or intimidation to other persons? Could the accused/suspect destroy records or computer files? Is there risk of a negative public image or media attention?

- If the accused/suspected employee is to be suspended, double check that the suspension does not have a discriminatory effect on protected classes, based upon historical treatment, company policy, and employment law.

Perhaps one of the most important tasks of HR is to consider the issues that are raised to obtain the information required to make the decision to investigate or to not investigate. It is recognized that a company has a legal duty to provide a safe workplace for all employees. Companies also have a right to protect against fraud and theft by employees. In fact, business entities are increasingly exercising their right to conduct self-policing in the prevention and detection of criminal conduct. A company may be scrutinized to prove that "due diligence" was exercised by such programs. Some specific guidelines are recommended:

- The company must have compliance standards and procedures to be followed by employees which reasonably can be expected to reduce the prospect of criminal conduct.

- The overall responsibility to oversee compliance of these standards and procedures must be vested in specific employees of high-level management.

- The company must exercise care not to delegate authority to any employee who may have the propensity to engage in illegal or improper behavior.

- Company standards and procedures must effectively be communicated to all employees.

- The company must take steps to achieve compliance with policy, *i.e.*, monitoring and auditing systems and utilizing reporting system whereby employees can report deviant behavior by others without fear of retribution.

In determining when a formal internal investigation is necessary, an HR manager may take a step-by-step analysis of the following outline.

1)   **The Nature of the Issue** -- It is important to fully understand the nature of the issue and any specific guidelines or obligations the company may have regarding the issue. Before calling for an investigation, it is imperative to first specifically identify the complaint or issue (see Figure 10.4). Secondly, it is necessary to determine what the company's obligation is to the issue, and, thirdly, identify who else within the company is required to assist in resolving the issue.

        a) Is the issue a complex problem that needs to be solved?

        b) Is the issue a simple situation that has a simple answer?

    c) Does the issue involve one employee or several?

    d) Does the issue evolve from a single incident or a pattern of behavior?

    e) Can the issue be ranked as minor, moderate, or of major significance?

2) **Supplemental Information** -- Are additional facts required that the employee can provide in order for the investigator to reach a resolution.

    a) If adequate information has been obtained, perhaps the issue easily can be resolved.

    b) If more information is required, or it is necessary to speak to other people, it is likely that it will require a formal internal investigation.

3) **Special Expertise** -- Is special expertise from other sources necessary in order to make a decision?

    a) **Legal** -- is a local, state, or federal law involved?

    b) **Security** -- is the issue related to theft?

    c) **Risk Management** -- does the issue involve a valid or potential workers' compensation case?

    d) **Internal Audit** -- are financial irregularities involved?

If an investigation is called for, the preliminary investigation will set the scene for how the investigation will be conducted and who will be the principal investigator. If it is appropriate or necessary to call in law enforcement support, the investigator should be aware that law enforcement officers are subject to stricter constitutional standards than are private employers. The employer loses control of the investigation once law enforcement is involved. If the case involves potential workplace violence, the investigator may wish to consult a psychiatrist or psychologist for guidelines on conducting the investigation and for evaluating the testimony and mindset of either a witness or the targeted employee of the investigation. The investigator also may consider consulting with an employment law attorney for risk assessment or a security specialist for ensuring company and public safety. Thus, the preliminary investigation can set a strategic investigation plan suitable for the reason or purpose of investigation.

Attorney-Client Privilege

The attorney-client privilege protects all communication between the client and the attorney from disclosure demands from a third party. It is the client's privilege, and it cannot unilaterally be waived by an attorney. The rationale for this privilege is that it encourages full and frank communication between a client and an attorney. Investigators need to understand a technical aspect of attorney-client privilege -- that the privilege belongs to the investigating company which is considered the client, and not to individuals within the company who speak to the attorney. Thus, attorney-client privilege is one of the major benefits of having an attorney involved.

Guidelines for Using Attorney-Client Privilege -- The decision to use attorney-client privilege for a workplace investigation generally is dependent upon the degree of seriousness of the investigation objective. For informal investigations related to employee absenteeism or tardiness, the attorney-client privilege may not be appropriate. However, attorney-client privilege would be used for formal investigations of a more serious nature, *i.e.*, a complaint that may evolve into a lawsuit, criminal claims, or any issue that may involve a large number of employees, have safety hazard concerns, have significant monetary risk, or have negative public-relations impact. If in doubt about the use of attorney-client privilege, it is suggested that the investigator consult legal council for advice on when to apply the privilege and how to protect the investigation information under such immunity. A few general instructions for its use that an attorney might suggest are:

- Have all written communication addressed to the attorney;

- Stamp or label the top of each communication: *"Privileged and Confidential -- Not Subject to Discovery;"*

- Permit only a few people who have a legitimate business need to know to have access to the information -- if documentation is shared with others, the privilege may be lost; and

- Do not disclose any confidential information without first consulting the attorney and obtaining his or her agreement or permission that the information may be shared.

Attorney-Client Privilege Exceptions -- Exceptions to the attorney-client privilege stem from a 1981 U.S. Supreme Court ruling that communications between an employee and the employer's attorney may be privileged if it meets three requirements:

1)   It is information not known by the managing group,

2) It is information that an employee knows from his or her scope of duty, and

3) The attorney is gathering the information to give legal advice to the corporate entity.

It is important to consider that the facts related to an event or complaint may not be protected by the attorney-client privilege. For example, the communication may not be revealed, but the employee may have to retell, in a subsequent lawsuit, the events he or she witnessed. In other words, while communication between attorney and client is protected, the privilege does not protect the underlying facts.

The Attorney Work Product -- The "attorney work product" doctrine protects work undertaken by an attorney in the form of documents and theories prepared by that attorney in the process of an investigation. The information may be obtained from the same witness but cannot be drawn from the attorney's documentation.

The Self-Critical Analysis Privilege -- Another emergent doctrine designed to protect types of information gathered in investigations is the "self-critical analysis privilege," which includes investigators who are not attorneys. This privilege calls for a comprehensive emphasis on employer self-auditing and self-policing. While this privilege does not apply to criminal enforcement proceedings, it successfully has been applied to discrimination investigation matters.

Selecting the Appropriate Investigator

The general integrity of the investigation must be protected at all times so that it cannot be attacked or discredited later in any court proceeding. The choice of an appropriate investigator is a major concern in this regard. There are instances where an attorney is the prudent choice as a comprehensive and impartial investigator, while there are other instances that the HR staff member or an appropriate employee may be the most effective investigator. At any rate, the investigator should have the full support of senior management and full cooperation of company employees. The investigator, while making recommendations for management action, should have the authority to decide what issues to pursue, which personnel to interview, and when and where to conduct the investigation.

The investigator should determine if the person or complainant raising the issue is comfortable that the investigator will be fair and objective. The investigator may ask:

"Do you believe that I can be fair and objective in this situation?"

If the statement is affirmed, the investigator may proceed. If not, the investigator should ask for a recommendation as to who would be fair and objective.

Attributes of a Professional Investigator -- Whether the investigator is an outside professional or a corporate employee, 13 personal attributes are required of that person. These attributes are listed in Figure 10.5.

Figure 10.5
ATTRIBUTES OF AN EFFECTIVE INVESTIGATOR

- Understanding investigation objectives
- Personal credibility and respect
- Knowledge of law, policy, procedures
- Perceptive listening and observation skills
- Ability to develop rapport
- Ability to be impartial and objective
- Ability to analyze complex problems/data
- Ability to develop and document evidence
- Ability to interactively communicate
- Ability to diagnose interviewee verbal and nonverbal behavior
- Ability to tactically formulate questions
- Ability to compose and write reports
- Ability to maintain confidentiality

Developing the Workplace Investigation Plan

A strategic investigation plan is mandatory for a comprehensive and effective workplace investigation. The planning stage should involve considerations such as legal compliance of federal, state, or local employment law; compliance with corporate policy and philosophy; the identification of potential witnesses to be interviewed; specific documents to be reviewed; the strategy for investigation; design of questioning techniques; documentation strategy for recording all interaction; drawing conclusions; recommending a plan of action; and reporting the final results. An in-depth discussion of these issues will be presented in the following section:

Legal Compliance -- Employee rights are primary considerations and must be viewed within laws governing employee/employer relationships. A review of the laws and landmark cases presented in Chapter One and Chapter Two should be an initial assignment for the diligent human resource manager. A simultaneous review of the company's policies and procedures also is in order. During this phase, the investigator also should consider the need for legal council as well as consultation with appropriate members of upper management.

Identification of Potential Witnesses -- Those employees who are most apt to provide valuable evidence or information regarding the investigative incident should be interviewed. Perhaps the initial interviews should be planned for the complainant and the accused. From these interviews, a list of co-workers who may have information or have witnessed the incident can be obtained from employees. Witnesses also may include customers, suppliers, and others who may have pertinent knowledge regarding the alleged incident. The investigator should list:

- Name, title, division, and department of the employee(s) raising the issue.

- Name/s, title, division, and department of person/s accused/suspected of violation/s.

- All information received should be listed and dated with the source identified.

Determination of Documents to be Reviewed -- Documents most commonly considered by human resource managers during a workplace investigation are the corporate rules, policies, and procedures. Those policies that are designed to be in compliance with employment law are imperative to review. Other documents may consist of employees' personnel files, manager's notes, confidential files, samples of employee work, special related communications to employees, memos or notes regarding the investigative incident, time cards, expense reports, logs, receipts, and complaints filed by other employees or management.

Company Documents -- A specific list of policies, guidelines, or practices related to the company is shown below:

- Company personnel policy and procedures manual,

- Company ethics statement,

- Company finance manual,

- Company security guidelines or policy, and

- Company benefits book.

Employee-Related Documents -- A specific list of relevant documents for an employee are listed below:

- Employees' master personnel files,

- Employees' performance appraisals,

- Employees' expense accounts,

- Documents of internal interviews, and

- Information regarding prior investigations/complaints.

Documentation Design

It is a fundamental function of any investigator to establish a standardized form for documentation of all interviews, interaction, document reviews, communiqués, and all the steps and procedures followed during the entire investigative process. The investigator should establish special, secure files and records to ensure safety and confidentiality of all documents related to the investigation. Such practices will further ensure the integrity of the overall investigation.

Documenting By Notes -- Comprehensive notes should be taken of all meetings, interviews, phone conversations, and planning sessions. Notes should include only the relevant facts and should be objective and concise. Note taking should avoid interpretations, beliefs, "feelings," frustrations, or assumptions but rather should be based on factual accounts of interactions, conversations with others, and direct observations of behavior and actions. Thus, an employee's behavior or demeanor should be observed and recorded without conclusions about why this behavior is occurring. It is suggested that notes be kept in a separate file from notes regarding other employee or business issues. In the event that an investigator's notes are needed for litigation, notes should be recorded on separate pieces of paper and should not be bound or attached to information that may not be relevant to the case.

Plan to take detailed notes during the interview. Comprehensive documentation should be accomplished for all interactions throughout the investigation process. For each interview, it is necessary to list the names of those present, the date, time, and place of the interview. Notes should be objective and factual. Writing should be legible, accurate, and free from misspellings or grammatical errors so that the interviewer is not discredited in the event of litigation. If the information falls within the realm of "attorney-client privilege," all notes, memos, letters, documents, and files should be stamped accordingly and filed in a secure place.

Two critical documents that must be generated following the initial interviews are employee-generated documentation and employer-generated documentation. This is done to encourage the employee and employer to write down his or her viewpoints and to avoid misunderstandings.

Employee-Generated Documentation -- Any employee who raises an issue or files a complaint should be encouraged to provide a summary in writing explaining the incident. The summary should include:

- A description of the employee's issues or complaints,

- All relevant facts and dates related to the issue or incident,

- Names of witnesses/persons who may have relevant information regarding the incident,

- Any suggestions the employee may have for obtaining further relevant information, and

- The employee's signature and the date the document was written.

Employer-Generated Documentation -- The employer or investigator should prepare an "issue-confirmation memo" for the employee raising the issue to ensure that all issues are clearly understood before beginning an investigation. The information included in the issue-confirmation memo should be:

- The identified issue/complaint,

- A listing of facts provided by the employee or complainant,

- A confirmation of all issues raised,

- The name of the person investigating the issue or incident,

- A description of the investigation plan, and

- A description of the company's expectations for the employee filing the complaint.

Scope of Documentation -- Prior to and during interviews, the investigator should identify and collect all documents relevant to the investigation. The initial documents gathered, depending on the type of investigation, could be employee files, performance review documents, timecards, sales reports, expense reports, telephone logs, and any other pertinent files. Additional documents may be collected during interviews such as memos, inter-office communiqués, and such items that may be called to the investigator's attention by interviewees. For legal and fairness purposes, these documents can be separated into two categories: Documentation provided in confidence, and information to be shared with others. Each category is described more fully below:

Documentation Provided in Confidence -- Of primary importance in any investigation is the individuals' right to privacy. It is the investigator's discretion to weigh and balance the information received with the purpose of the investigation and the rights and obligations of those being investigated. Thus, determining what an individual's "reasonable expectation" of privacy is may be dependent upon the circumstances under which the interviewee shared the information and exactly what information is necessary to share with others during the investigatory process. Complete and unconditional confidentiality may be ideal for the interviewee, but it may not be in the best interest of the company for the investigator to promise that confidentiality. Perhaps it is preferable for the interviewer to promise to keep the disclosed information as confidential as possible but revealed only on a business "need-to-know" basis.

Business Need-To-Know Criterion -- To assist the investigator in the interviewee confidentiality issue, it is important to recognize what information should be shared with others who have a legitimate business need to know. These criterion may include:

- Any information necessary for decision-makers to draw conclusions,

- Any information necessary for conducting the investigation,

- Any information based on action taken as a result of the investigation, and

- Any information necessary to be shared in order to obtain additional relevant information.

It is recommended that, if a person has a legitimate business need to know any segment of information in a document, the investigator should only share that information rather than disclose of the whole document. It also is recognized that, since additional requirements are necessary for handling medical information and documentation, legal counsel be obtained in these circumstances.

Request Employee's Confidentiality -- An investigator should stress that confidentiality and the employee's privacy will be maintained as much as possible. The employee also should be informed that he or she has a strict duty to keep all investigation information confidential and that information should be provided to others only on a business need-to-know basis.

Documenting for Reporting the Final Results -- By carefully documenting all interviews and gathering all pertinent information, the investigator will be in a good position to compare and contrast interview results and to make an objective final report.

The Investigative Interview
        The investigative interview should open with a statement making it clear that the employee can leave or terminate the interview at any time. Be prepared to allow the interviewee to terminate the interview, and/or consult an attorney. The investigator's second statement should tactfully illustrate the seriousness of the allegations or purpose of the interview and the consequences that the interviewee may face. Generally, the investigation should gather information regarding the specific events that occurred during the relevant time frame, in chronological blocks of time

in terms of the basic five W's (*i.e.*, Who? What? When? Where? and Why?). Throughout each time span, the investigator should ask the following 10 questions:

1) Who is involved in the incident?

2) What occurred?

3) When did it occur?

4) Where did it occur?

5) Who was present during the incident?

6) Who else may have related information?

7) How did the event happen?

8) In order of occurrence -- who said or did what?

9) Why did it occur, and could it have been avoided?

10) Is there any other evidence?

Interview Question Formulation Techniques -- Developing "question sets" is one of the most important tasks for a successful investigator. To ensure a thorough, objective, legal, and consistent line of questioning, it is recommended that the investigator/s prepare an outline of questions for all interviews with the accused/suspect, the accuser, and key witnesses. A secondary advantage to the preparation of an outline of questions is that the interviews will be somewhat standardized and more convenient for comparing and contrasting the results. This standardization process is critical especially when an investigation could encompass scores of interviews conducted by multiple investigators. The interview design should allow for new or unexpected facts that may be revealed and designed with contingency plans to compensate for these unanticipated events.

Honest Disclosure -- Each interview should begin with appropriate disclosures of what the investigation is about. The investigator should be honest about the purpose of the interview and not have a hidden agenda. The investigator should strive to maintain a comfortable interview with a balance of amiable conversational style and a focus on the issues of the investigation. The investigator must always maintain control of the interview to ensure obtaining adequate information and to keep the interview on track. Specific questions will net specific answers. It is suggested that open-ended questions will allow the interviewee the opportunity to open up and disclose more information than the use of "yes" or "no" questions.

Guidelines for Conducting Interviews -- Listed below are a set of guidelines that should be considered during any workplace investigation interview:

- Always have another person present as a witness.

- Avoid making threats of adverse action.

- Avoid making promises of benefit.

- Do not promise confidentiality as testimony is public record.

- Do not use threats, coercion, or intimidation.

- Avoid making accusatory statements.

- Attempt to put the interviewee at ease.

- Be prepared to be questioned by the interviewee.

- If the interviewee becomes emotional or confrontational, it is best to take a break -- or postpone the interview.

- Avoid disclosing more information than is necessary to an interviewee.

- Conduct the interview in a professional and non-custodial setting.

- During all portions of the interview, avoid allowing the interviewee to see uniformed security persons.

- Avoid having law-enforcement authorities present during interviews on company premises.

- Clearly state that the interview is voluntary and that the interviewee can leave at any time.

- Always seek written permission to audiotape or videotape any interview.

Interim Action Decisions

Immediately following the initial interview with the person raising the issue or complaint, it is critical to determine if any interim actions may be necessary to be taken before the actual investigation begins. It may be necessary to protect the safety and welfare of other employees, to protect the integrity of the company's policies and procedures, or to protect company property. For example, the issue may involve allegations of violence or sexual harassment involving physical touching, battery, or rape. Another incident could be in regard to criminal misconduct such as theft of company equipment, assets, or trade secrets. Or the issues may involve whistle-blowing claims or other serious incidents. Some major points for an investigator to consider regarding interim action are:

- Will the accused/suspect be suspended?

- Will the suspension occur before or after the confrontation?

- Will the suspension make the investigation easier or more difficult?

- Is a risk assessment required before suspension?

- Who should be consulted before suspension? HR? Security? Legal?

- What should be the response if the accused/suspect questions the suspension?

- Should other employees, customers, or vendors be told of the accused's/suspect's suspension? If so, what should they be told?

- What are the terms of the suspension? Is it with or without pay? What should the employee do during the time of investigation?

- Is any person's physical safety or security at risk?

- Should the security or loss prevention department be notified and be continuously informed regarding the nature of the event?

Interviewing the Complainant

While the initial interview with the complainant most often cannot be planned, company policy can dictate guidelines for conducting such interviews. The goal should be to determine the full details of the incident. The complainant may be reluctant or unwilling to divulge names and details and must be assured that such cooperation is necessary and that she or he will be protected from reprisals. Some specific techniques for handling complainant interviews are listed below:

- Hold the interview in an environment that allows for privacy and security.

- Ask open-ended questions to allow the complainant to disclose as much information as necessary.

- Explain the company's commitment to neutrality and impartiality in investigations.

- Do not promise confidentiality, but ensure that information will be shared only on a business "need-to-know" basis.

- Ask for names of witnesses.

- Carefully observe nonverbal communication, especially eye contact, gestures, and overall body language.

- Repeat the story and ask for affirmation to confirm understanding.

- Document the facts.

- Start a confidential investigation file. Do not store reports or notes in any personnel file.

Interviewing the Accused

The interview with the accused/suspected employee should be carefully planned to allow for fair treatment and with the presumption of innocence. The investigator should be reminded that, at all times during the investigation, the accused/suspect has rights to due process and should never forfeit those rights while the investigation is being conducted. The investigator should inform the accused/suspect:

- The purpose of the investigation with the allegations described in enough detail to enable a full response,

- That the investigation will be conducted discreetly and fairly,

- That truthfulness and cooperation are required,

- That no conclusions have been reached regarding the allegations, and

- That retaliation against any complainant or witness will lead to disciplinary action.

First Personal Impression Phase -- The first few moments of an interview with an accused/suspected employee should be spent asking nonthreatening questions. Such questions might focus on the individual's employment history, how long the person has worked for the company, his or her present duties, and the names of subordinates. This format is designed to allow the interviewer to establish control and to evaluate the employee's normal behavior in a non-threatening setting. The investigator should be acutely aware of the interviewee's eye contact, response latency, and the directness of answers. A significant deviation from the interviewee's normal behavior when the investigation issue is discussed may be a cue that the employee is withholding information or is being deceptive.

The Main Data Collection Phase -- Some guidelines for conducting interviews with accused/suspected employees follow:

- Open with the statement that this is an internal investigation, and describe the purpose of the investigation.

- State what initial action will be taken, *i.e.*, will the accused/suspect be suspended?

- Advise that no judgments have been made and that the accused/suspect is presumed innocent.

- Give the interviewee full opportunity to respond to the accusation or purpose of the investigation.

- If the accused/suspect expresses anger, let time pass before encouraging a response. Give the accused/suspect empathic attention.

- Ask for the names of any witnesses who may know about the situation.

- Carefully observe nonverbal communication, especially eye contact, gestures, and overall body language.

- Explain that any retaliation against the complainant or any other person(s) is prohibited.

- Review the company's policy with the accused/suspect.

Interviewing Witnesses

The investigator should interview all persons who are identified as having knowledge of the alleged incident or of related incidents. Often, the written or recorded statements of witnesses will be more helpful in an investigation than those from the complainant and the accused/suspect. While it is only natural that anyone who is not being investigated will feel less anxious than one who is under investigation, he or she may not give full cooperation. These types of witnesses may be grouped into three separate categories:

1)   Those who are cooperative,
2)   Those who are adverse, and
3)   Those who are neutral

Each of these prototypes are discussed briefly below:

The Cooperative Witness -- The cooperative witness is more than willing to be interviewed and fully cooperates with an investigation. The major disadvantage of interviewing the cooperative or overly friendly witness is that he or she may be friends with the victim and tend to combine fact and opinion or even furnish irrelevant information in an attempt to be helpful. There are a number of other reasons a witness might be too cooperative or overly friendly:

1)   The witness may be naturally friendly and cooperative.

2)   The witness may wish personal gain as a result of testimony.

3)   The witness may gain ego satisfaction by being involved.

4)   The witness may enjoy "playing detective."

The investigator may specifically need to identify the facts from the overly cooperative witness who, in a zealous attempt to be helpful, may provide prejudicial information. In the early stages of the investigation, interviewing this type of witness is quite credible, but it becomes less credible during the later stages of the investigations.

The Adverse Witness -- Perhaps the greatest challenge for an investigator is to interview an adverse witness. To meet that challenge, an investigator must attempt to gain cooperation and truthfulness during the investigative interview. This can be accomplished by talking, by asking neutral or innocuous questions, and even by providing a reason for the witness to cooperate with the investigation. The investigator should conduct an interview with an adverse witness on a formal basis and should question the person in a non-predictable manner to avoid the possibility that the witness may anticipate the questions and be prepared in advance to answer them. The investigator must manage the interview to avoid deception and gain cooperation as explained by the UNICOM strategy and techniques.

The Neutral Witness -- The neutral witness may prove to be the best witness and provide the most reliable information. The neutral witness seemingly has nothing to gain or lose as a result of testifying, and thus is cooperative. Establishing the true neutrality of this caliber of witness should not be taken casually by the investigator.

Questions for Witnesses -- Prior to the interview, the investigator must plan the questioning tactics to strategically meet the objective of the interview and to enhance the probability of a successful interview. When interviewing witnesses, the following questions and guidelines are suggested:

- What knowledge do you have of the event?

- What is the source of your knowledge?

- Were you present at the time of the event?

- Did you hear about the event from someone else?

- Did you see the information in writing?

- Carefully observe nonverbal communication, especially eye contact, gestures, and overall body language.

- Ask open-ended questions.

- Tell the witness not to discuss the interview with others.

Chronology of Questions -- It is recommended that the witness be questioned about the particulars of the investigation in the order in which they occurred. However, if the events have little chronological significance, the questions may be organized according to the specific event or transaction.

The Investigator's Demeanor -- The investigator's overall demeanor and personal style of interaction has much to do with the success of any investigation. It is suggested that the investigator be somewhat friendly rather than show a tough or indifferent demeanor. Some suggested guidelines are:

- Never be condescending or disrespectful to an interviewee.

- Never talk down to the person or assume that the person is less intelligent.

- Always be sensitive to the personal concerns of the witness, victim, or complainant especially in regard to the eight protected areas of discrimination.

- Always be professional and business-like.

- Never lose your temper with an interviewee.

- Always be respectful and sympathetic with the victim, and do not place blame.

- Plan each interview carefully to be consistent in giving careful thought to language and interaction.

- End each interview by thanking the interviewee for his or her time and cooperation.

Managing the Interviewee's Behavior -- The act of managing the interviewee is fundamentally linked to interpersonal coordination of rapport. The three distance components of rapport: interpersonal coordination, intended emotional positivity, and attentional focus, have been determined to make up the total experience of rapport. In managing the interviewee, a practitioner or investigator may tend to control personal dynamics by masking nonverbal behavior as an attempt to appear neutral or inconspicuous. It should be remembered, however, that such passivity can be perceived as indicative of dullness, withdrawal, uneasiness, snobbish aloofness, or even deceptiveness. It also should be noted that if a practitioner appears to be insincere or exhibits any deceptive verbal or nonverbal behavior, it likely will be noticed by the interviewee.

Perhaps it is better to achieve a more natural, high degree of confidence, an active element in a cycle of increasingly sophisticated self-presentational strategies and skills. The more practice and refinement of these skills, the more confident and the more likely practitioners are to experience greater interpersonal success.

Everything that occurs during the interview, whether positive, negative, or neutral, is felt by the interviewee. It is the practitioner's responsibility to maintain harmony within this interactive process. The practitioner must never take dignity away from anyone, because it can never be returned. Loss of dignity creates irreparable damage which can become personalized at that time and may never be repaired. The practitioner should never lose sight or stray from the mutual interview objective.

Closing the Interview -- During the concluding phase of the interview, give the interviewee the opportunity to reveal any other information he or she may have. At this time, it also is advisable to repeat significant portions of the interview to confirm with the interviewee that the information is accurate and complete. Confirmation of this process should be reflected in the interviewer's notes and rumors or hearsay statement should be labeled as such. It is important to develop a standardized close for each interview to ensure that the interviewer has gathered the vital data in a comprehensive sense. In the closing segment of the interview, the investigator should:

- Review all responses with the interviewee to affirm a mutual understanding,

- Determine if there is anyone else who should be interviewed,

- Determine if there are any further documents to supplement the investigation,

- Answer any questions the interviewee may have,

- Stress the importance of the continued confidentiality of the investigation,

- Explain in a general manner how the investigation will proceed, and

- Thank the interviewee for his or her cooperation and stress that continued cooperation as the investigation proceeds is expected.

Assess the Interviewee's Credibility

Interviewee credibility is an essential component for the success of any investigation. An astute investigator will be cognizant of behavior indicators of truthfulness and deceit, and it is imperative to include such observations in the overall evaluation of each interaction during an investigation. As each interview closes, it is wise to spend a few moments reflecting on the entire interview. The investigator should note the verbal and nonverbal interaction communicated during the interview and list specific impressions of the interviewee's body language. Some primary considerations during this reflection process are:

- The interviewee's overall demeanor,

- The interviewee's reactions to allegations,

- The interviewee's level of confidence,

- The interviewee's version of the event,

- The consistency of the chronology and descriptions of the event,

- The plausibility of interviewee's interpretation of events, and

- The ease or difficulty of the interviewee's disclosure.

Some contingency considerations for the investigator to deliberate upon during the reflection process are corroborating evidence and circumstantial evidence.

Corroborating Evidence -- Corroborating evidence or direct information that illustrates that something has happened is of ultimate concern for the investigator. During an interview, the investigator should take specific note of whether the interviewee actually made any admissions or cited a reason for doing the act in question. Note if the interviewee specifically denied anything or if his or her statements conflicted with any written information previously collected. Consider, also, whether the interviewee's version of the event was similar or different from another's version, and list any possible supporting witnesses.

Circumstantial Evidence -- Consider circumstantial evidence or things that the interviewee has said or done in other comparative situations which would lead the investigator to believe whether or not the facts in dispute actually happened.

The Investigation Summary -- Following the interview, the investigator should prepare a written memorandum addressed to the interviewee which summarizes the interview. A cover letter should request the interviewee to verify the accuracy and completeness of the memorandum with a signature or to return the document with a letter clarifying information that is not accurate or clear.

The interview witness also should sign a statement which sets forth the significant results of the interview. The investigator should organize the record of the entire investigation, prepare a summary, and draw conclusions for recommendations. This summary should contain the following points:

- The date when the investigation began and the date of completion;

- A statement of the investigation objective or purpose;

- The name/s of person/s conducting the investigation;

- The name of the person initiating the investigation;

- A dated statement indicating that the person raising the issue and the investigated employee both were asked and agreed that the person conducting the investigation, in their opinion, would be competent, objective, and fair;

- The names of all persons interviewed (witnesses and those having relevant information);

- A listing of all documents reviewed;

- Final decisions, a plan of action, and the date implemented;

- Notations about conflicting or inconsistent testimony;

- Notations about the credibility of all those interviewed and the criterion on which this was assessed; and

- Statements about why those interviewed were credible or questionable.

This listing contains the key factual findings of the investigation and supports the credibility of the decision-making process. The investigator is reminded that the investigation summary should only report findings and analysis and not reflect the content of conversations or written communiqués. These statements should be written in an objective, neutral style.

Drawing Conclusions

When analyzing facts and interview results, the investigator should draw upon all basic life experiences and an all inclusive set of foundational skills of logic in order to reach conclusions. At this stage of the investigation, it is important for the investigator to critically evaluate the data gathered at every stage of the investigation. In the event that disciplinary action or termination is warranted, the investigator must consider the entire body of evidence, statements of the witnesses, reputations of the witnesses, and possible motivation for any witness to fabricate information or be less than truthful. Thus, the investigator must investigate each complaint to the fullest extent possible, carefully document each interaction, and treat each interaction as consistently as possible. To draw conclusions on what actually happened, the investigator must:

1) Examine the objective facts,

2) Consider the subjective matter of the entire investigation, and

3) Compare and contrast all interactions which occurred during the investigative process.

These three components of the decision-making process can be compartmentalized into four groupings:

1) Time frame,
2) Past history,
3) Motivation, and
4) Credibility.

Each element briefly is discussed below:

Time frame -- Some considerations related to the time frame of events leading to an investigation are: Was the issue raised in a timely manner? How and why was the issue raised? Were there any peculiarities concerning the timing or sequencing of events?

Past History -- Does either the accused/suspect or the complainant have a past history of similar issues? If so, why has there been a repetition? Or is this the first event for either the accused/suspect or the complainant?

Motivation -- Is there a motive for the person raising an issue to fabricate facts regarding the event? What is the motivation, if any, for the accused/suspect? Is there motivation for any witness to fabricate facts?

Credibility -- Has the credibility of all those interviewed been substantiated or is there some doubt in the investigator's mind as to the truthfulness of the testimony during anyone's interview?

Comparative Points -- Based on the findings and analysis of the entire investigation, the investigator may draw conclusions. Some basic emphasis should include the following points:

- How do company policies, guidelines, and philosophies apply to the situation?

- Are there any bottom-line factual conclusions?

  "As a result of this investigation, it has been concluded that you have made multiple, personal long distance phone calls that were billed to the company."

- Present and describe any issues that were not resolved

- What action, if any, is recommended?

Options for Action -- In regard to options for action, the investigator should identify the best case possibilities to recommend. The investigator's goal may be to modify behavior or eliminate the problem. Whichever the goal, the investigator should consider:

1)   How can this goal best be met? and

2)   Will the proposed option work to meet this goal?

There is never just one way to meet a goal, and each situation may call for a different action. Listed below in Figure 10.6 is a set of actions that may be recommended.

Implementing the Recommended Action

There are several more essential steps following the investigator's conclusions and recommendations. Reporting the results of the investigation and implementing the recommended action should ensure proper protocol. These two activities should be contemplated cautiously with or in connection to the following criteria:

Figure 10.6
RECOMMENDED ACTION CHOICES

- No action
- Transfer
- Suspension
- Demotion
- Termination

- Reduction in salary
- Counseling/educational program
- Written warning
- Corrective action plan
- Verbal warning

Preliminary Investigative Report -- The preliminary investigative report should be written to ensure that all information is present and accounted for and to further ensure that nothing is missing. The report should include a list of all documents, a summary of all interviewees including all witnesses' testimonies, and evaluations of the credibility of all interviewees. Everything that possibly can be verified should be verified -- all records should be checked and corroborating statements obtained when ever possible.

Legal Counsel -- The investigator should consult with legal counsel regarding the application of relevant law and to obtain an opinion regarding the preliminary report.

Conclusions -- The summary of the preliminary investigative report should provide conclusions regarding the facts of the case, the evidence which substantiates the conclusions, and recommendations for appropriate action.

Notification of Results

It is the investigator's responsibility to inform those who have a business need to know of the resolution and recommended action. In this case, need to know can be defined as: necessary in order to make a decision regarding the truth of the allegation or the proper disciplinary action.

Notifying the Subject of the Investigation -- A private meeting should be called with the subject of the investigation for the purpose of describing the course of the investigation, the results, and recommended action. The investigator should be prepared to explain how and why the results were reached and anticipate and be prepared to answer the employee's questions. Questions to consider are:

- Will the results be put in the employee's personnel file?

- Who else in the company will be informed of the results?

- How will this influence the employee's future with the company?

- Can the employee work with certain employees after this?

- Can the employee be transferred to another division or department?

- Is there an allowance for an appeal?

- The investigator should conclude the interview with the employee by describing the protocol regarding who to contact with future questions or information regarding the investigation.

Notifying the Complainant -- It is essential to inform the complainant who initially raised the issue of the investigator's findings and recommendations. The following points should be covered:

- What conclusions were reached, how, and why.

- What action is being taken, and who will be implementing the action.

- What the complainant should do if she or he experiences any retaliation, especially in the areas of sexual, racial, or ethnic harassment.

- Describe the appeals process if the complainant decides to appeal.

- Describe the policy for confidentiality by the complainant regarding the investigation, findings, and actions.

- Ask the complainant if there are any further questions or any further information that should be discussed prior to closure.

Final Investigation File

The final investigation file should contain the variety of documents that have been produced or collected during the investigation. Only final copies of such documents should be placed in the final investigation file, and all drafts should be destroyed. No other file containing such information should be kept, and all computer files and disks containing information regarding the investigation should be eliminated. The file should be labeled as "Need-to-Know -- Confidential," and access to this file limited to only those with a legitimate business reason to know. Unless required by law, the information in the final investigation file should not be released to anyone outside of the company. While the actual contents of any given file may vary depending on the circumstances of the investigation, the file should show the key steps that were taken to investigate and respond to the problem. If the investigation is considered to be within the realm of "attorney-client privilege," all documents within the file should be so noted with a stamp stating "attorney-client privilege." The following documents should be included in the final investigation file:

- Written notification from the employee raising the issue/s,

- Issue confirmation to the employee raising the issue/s,

- Suspension notice -- or action notice,

- Investigation summary,

- Results and notifications;

- Documentation and documents necessary to support key facts and conclusions in the investigation summary, and

- Written documentation of electronic communications regarding the investigation which may be important to demonstrate the steps taken during the investigation.

Allowing for an Appeal

The company may wish to have a pre-established process for an appeal of an investigation's conclusions. Advantages to offering an appeal process are: It demonstrates the employer's commitment to fairness, it could allow for the introduction of further evidence, and it can serve as a viable mechanism to release or dissipate the anger of the targeted employees. The appeals process further allows the employer a way to minimize his or her liability for an improper investigation and reduce the risks of future mistakes. Some post-investigative procedures an employer may wish to consider are:

- A copy of the results of the investigation should be provided to the accused/suspect to provide him/her an opportunity to respond in a proper manner;

- Delay any recommended action against an employee if the results of the investigation are unclear or appealed;

- Keep the information and communication within the realm of only those who have a business need to know;

- Maintain separate records of investigations -- this type of information should not be kept in the employee personnel files;

- Take precautions to ensure that no retaliation is taken against witnesses of any complaining employees; and

- If, after the completion of the investigation, an error is discovered, consider reopening the investigation.

If an employee files an appeal to review the decisions made in an internal formal investigation, encourage the employee to provide you with a written summary of what should be reviewed. Some items in the written summary might include:

- Any new information or anything that was not considered in the internal investigation,

- Specific comments she or he may have regarding the thoroughness or impartiality of the investigation, and

- Any specific comments she or he may have regarding the investigation being conducted in accordance with company policy.

Appeal Confirmation
A confirmation of appeal should be provided in the form of written notification to the employee requesting an appeal. This is done to provide the person responsible for handling the appeal and the employee requesting the appeal an opportunity to list all the issues to be reviewed. This action is designed to save time and energy for everyone and to ensure that the issues are clearly understood. The confirmation memo should include:

- The date the appeal was filed, the name of employee requesting the appeal, and the name of person to whom the request was made;

- A listing of all issues requested to be reviewed;

- A statement confirming with the employee that she or he has shared all of the information or evidence to be reviewed or will do so at this time; and

- A summary of the initial discussion with the employee filing the appeal, what she or he will be expected to do, and what is expected from the person conducting the appeal.

Appeal Summary -- The appeal process may range from a review of the final investigation file to a repetition of portions of the investigation. The process should include a review of the facts, a review of additional data, an analysis, and a recommended course of action. These findings and conclusions should be documented in an appeal summary, and a final appeal file should be assembled to contain the following documents:

- **Raising the Appeal Issue/s** -- Written notification from the employee requesting the appeal;

- **Appeal Confirmation** -- The statement which identifies the objective and purpose of the appeal;

- **Appeal Summary** -- A summary of the entire appeal process including the analysis, findings, and conclusions;

- **Results Notifications** -- Written notifications describing the results and suggested actions to the complainant and the investigated employee;

- **Documentation** -- Interview notes and supporting documents to describe key facts or conclusions in the appeal summary;

- **Final Investigation File** -- A copy of the final investigation file should be available and protected; and

- **Communications** -- Written or electronic communications regarding the appeal should be given only to individuals on a business need-to-know basis.

Investigating Specific Issues
This section supplementary addresses the particular legal duties related to investigating specific issues such as:

1)   Employee violence,
2)   Fraud and theft,
3)   Drug and alcohol usage, and
4)   Sexual harassment.

The pertinent issues related to each of these categories are listed below:

Workplace Violence -- An employer is obligated to provide a safe workplace, and failure to comply with this duty may result in workers' compensation liability for employee injuries and deaths that result from violence by co-workers or third parties. Employers are not just liable for employees but also customers, vendors, or any person in the workplace who may be in danger from an employee's violent behavior. In some situations, employees also have a right to bring civil actions against an employer for injuries sustained and are allowed to seek both punitive and compensatory damages. Compensatory damages are limited to payment for actual losses and "pain and suffering," while punitive damages are designed to "punish" the employer and can result in very large monetary awards to the complainant. It therefore is imperative to understand the legal duties and issues related to workplace investigations involving suspicion or allegations of illegal or dangerous activity. The following is a listing of items to consider before conducting an investigation related to workplace violence:

- Is this an issue to be referred to law enforcement authorities?

- Should mental health authorities be notified?

- Should the violating employee be immediately suspended or dismissed?

- If the employee is not suspended, does he or she pose a risk of injury to others or property?

- If the employee is not suspended, is there a risk of negative public image or media reports?

- If the employee is not suspended, will his or her presence intimidate or bother other employees?

- Should employees, customers, vendors, clients, or other public persons be advised of potential danger?

- Before suspending an employee, determine that the action does not have a discriminatory effect on protected classes.

- It should be a top priority to proactively secure sensitive and essential information to prevent theft or sabotage.

- It should be top priority to proactively know how to identify a potentially violent employee and understand the warning signs, *i.e.*, verbal threats, physical actions, bizarre thoughts, and obsessive behavior that a troubled employee may exhibit before the act of violence occurs.

- The employee handbook should contain a policy for reporting clues to violence if observed by a co-worker.

- If a potential for violence is reported, it is critical to initiate an immediate investigation rather that wait for violence to occur or escalate.

Fraud and Theft

It is the employer's duty to exercise "due diligence" in preventing and detecting criminal conduct by employees and agents. Self-policing in the prevention and detection of fraud and theft has led to greater consideration by the courts in legal cases. Some "due diligence" guidelines for fraud and theft prevention are as follows:

- The employer must establish compliance standards and procedures designed to reduce the prospect of criminal activity.

- High-level management should bear the responsibility to oversee compliance of such standards and procedures.

- The employer must effectively communicate the standards and procedures to all employees and agents via training programs and disseminating publications.

- The employer must monitor compliance of standards in order to detect criminal conduct.

- The employer must consistently enforce the standards with appropriate disciplinary measures.

- The employer must not hire or delegate a task or procedure to any individual known to have a propensity to engage in illegal activity.

Investigating Theft or Fraud -- It is difficult to prove theft or fraudulent activities. Therefore, such investigations must be thoroughly and carefully executed. It is recognized that different levels of sophistication for the investigation will be determined by the magnitude of the crime committed. It is critical to maintain a consistent and comprehensive documentation system that includes time cards, bookkeeping journals, cash records, inventory sheets, and related information. Search and surveillance policy should provide the employer with permission to search specifically-identified property and accommodate the employee with a "reasonable expectation" of privacy. The investigator should never threaten the accused/suspect in order to obtain an admission or restitution.

Drug and Alcohol Usage

The Drug Free Workplace Act compels federal contractors to provide a drug-free workplace by publishing a statement notifying employees that the unlawful manufacture, distribution, dispersion, possession, or usage of controlled substances in the workplace is prohibited. Employers not compelled by the act realize the proactive advantages of this philosophy and have established drug-free awareness programs and make good faith efforts to maintain a drug-free workplace. Employers must notify employees (preferably in the employee handbook) that, as a condition of employment, each employee must:

1)   Abide by the terms of the statement, and

2)   Notify the employer of any criminal drug conviction for the violation occurring in the workplace no later than five days after each conviction.

Employers must impose an "appropriate personnel action" on, or require the "satisfactory participation" in, an employee assistance program by the guilty employee. Investigations are essential for compliance of this law.

Legal Aspects of Drug and Alcohol Investigations -- The investigator should be aware that any investigation related to alleged drug or alcohol abuse must conform to specific state laws on drug testing. He must also consider employee rights to privacy. An employee's "reasonable expectation" of privacy may limit an employer's investigation. The company's employee handbook should contain a comprehensive policy on drug and alcohol usage and testing in and out of the workplace. The Drug Free Workplace Act and Americans with Disabilities Act combine to form federal legislation which regulates workplace drug and alcohol testing. Some primary policies on workplace drug and alcohol usage are:

- Any employer may prohibit the use of drugs or alcohol at work as well as employees being under the influence at work.

- Employers may require employee compliance with the Drug Free Workplace Act of 1988, as well as regulated industries' standards, much like the Department of Defense.

- A test for illegal drugs is not controlled by the ADA, because it is not considered a medical examination.

- Information regarding the medical condition of an employee obtained from a drug test must be treated confidentially, with the exception of the drug test results.

- A user of illegal drugs or alcohol who is not disabled is not protected by the ADA.

- If an employee is participating in, or has successfully completed, a drug rehabilitation program and no longer is using illegal drugs, he or she is considered disabled under the ADA.

- If an employee is observed with specific characteristics, *i.e.*, slurred speech, incoherent conversation, stumbling, staggering, dilated eyes, *etc.*, he or she may be disciplined -- not for drug or alcohol use, but for reporting to work unfit and unable to perform work.

Investigations With Law Enforcement Support

A company may determine that it is appropriate to call for law enforcement assistance. In this regard the investigator must be aware that:

- Once law enforcement is involved in an investigation, the employer turns over all control to the law enforcement agency.

- Law enforcement agencies are subject to stricter constitutional standards than are private companies or employers.

- Once police are involved, the employer risks losing discretion for discipline, *i.e.*, the lower internal standard of "reasonable doubt" increases to a higher standard of "probable cause."

- Law enforcement involvement constitutes an escalation of the magnitude of the investigation which may have significant ramifications to the employer and company.

- An employer or company may be held liable for the acts of the involved law enforcement agency.

Investigating Sexual Harassment

The Civil Rights Act of 1991 has placed great pressure on employers to eliminate all forms of discrimination and harassment in the workplace. Sexual harassment as the subject of an internal investigation has some specific characteristics and issues. There is an increased need for confidentiality, safeguarding against retaliation, and for training and policy issues. There actually are three steps an employer may take as proactive action against sexual harassment: prevention, investigation, and remedial action. Each of these points are discussed below:

Preventing Sexual Harassment -- A company can position itself for successful defense of possible sexual harassment litigation and prevent future occurrences if it develops a program to make employees aware of their rights, ensures protection of their rights, and allows for swift action to protect those rights when violations occur. Listed below are some guidelines for the prevention of sexual harassment in the workplace:

- A policy regarding sexual harassment should be written and disseminated to all employees;

- All employees should receive formal training on the various forms of sexual harassment, so they can be reasonably expected to comply with company policy;

- A means of confidential reporting of sexual harassment should be developed -- this procedure should ensure that the complainant will be protected from retaliation;

- There should be prompt, thorough, and discreet investigations of all sexual harassment complaints; and

- If sexual harassment actually has occurred, prompt, and appropriate corrective action is mandated.

The Equal Employment Opportunity Commission (EEOC) Guidelines provide that:

> "An employer should take all steps necessary to prevent sexual harassment from occurring, such as affirmatively developing the subject, expressing strong disapproval, developing appropriate sanctions, informing employees of their right to raise and how to raise the issue of harassment under Title VII, and developing methods to sensitize all concerned" (29 CFR Section 1604.11[f]).

Timely, Complete, and Judicious Investigation -- There is an affirmative duty to investigate any and all formal or informal complaints of sexual harassment. Generally, a human resources director is designated to handle sexual harassment complaints and to conduct the investigation within the company policy. Sexual harassment investigations should accomplish the following:

- Determine whether or not sexual harassment has actually occurred;

- Gather information for related employment decisions;

- Reduce damages and consequences related to the complaint;

- Protect all other employees from potential sexual harassment;

- Determine strategy for defense of potential litigation;

- Determine interim corrective action; and

- Organize the record of the investigation, summarize it, and draw conclusions.

A copy of the investigation results should be placed in the personnel files of each of the principal parties. However, the full investigative records should be filed separately in a confidential secured file, and should not be placed in the personnel file.

Corrective Action for Sexual Harassment -- At the conclusion of the investigation, the employer must decide upon a course of corrective action and notify the principal parties of the results. If the investigation found that sexual harassment has occurred, corrective action is warranted and can include oral and written warnings, suspensions, terminations, or demotion. If the investigator determines that the complainant contrived the event, the employer must determine a course of action appropriate for the complainant.

Question Formulation Matrix

The reader is reminded that a general section on question formulation has been presented in Chapter Eight. The following section presents a question formulation matrix to serve as an example of a question formulation and delivery technique. This matrix format is designed to direct a line of questioning with the six-step management strategy for self-disclosure.

Truthful vs. Suspect Answers -- The delivery technique distinguishes between a *truthful* and a *suspect* answer for a series of typical incident-investigation interview questions. *Truthful* answers and *suspect* answers are qualified with explanatory delivery and nonverbal cues. The question delivery format then moves from a suspect answer with the assistance of selected *suspect answer, response-management* statements, to a *revised, question follow-up* technique.

Response Management Statements -- The suspect answer and response management statements are preparatory to conditioning the interviewee to feel safe enough to disclose information. These responses tend to minimize the importance of a question, or at least provide a rationalization to allow the candidate to disclose information.

Revised Question Follow-Up -- The revised question is a rephrased question which reflects the response management statement. The question is rephrased so that it is less threatening and safer to answer. Thus, the matrix can be applied within the framework of the six-step management strategy for self-disclosure. This question-delivery technique employs the *suspect answer responses* to assist the practitioner in reaching the *critical moment*, while the revised question follow-up actually can be selected as the *strategic question*, to elicit the omitted or falsified information from the candidate. While a complete set of question guidelines can be developed for application to an entire interview, only select topics are presented here as a representative instructional sample.

Question Formulation Matrix Design

The following question formulation matrix series is intended to illustrate the basic framework design for the entire investigative interview. Each individual matrix is graphically divided to progressively demonstrate the following:

1)   (Q) Opening question styles and inquiry variations;

2)   (TA) Truthful answer illustrations;
        (SA) Suspect answer illustrations;

3)   (RM) Response Management styles and prequestion condi-
        tioning statements;

4)   (RQ) Revised follow-up question variations.

QUESTION FORMULATION MATRIX

INQUIRY AREA	1	INCIDENT INVESTIGATIONS
Focus area	A	Disclosure -- Completion

Opening Question

Q 1	Have you any other details about this incident?
Q 2	Is there anything more you can tell us about this situation?
Q 3	Did you see anything else that may be relevant?
Q 4	Did anything else happen?

Truthful Answer Illustration

TA 1	No! (Immediate response -- without hesitation.)
TA 2	No, I don't! (Direct response.)
TA 3	No. That's when I called my supervisor.

Suspect Answer Illustration

SA 1	(Slight pause) ... no.
SA 2	(Elongated response) n...o.
SA 3	No...not that I can remember. (Qualified yes answer.)
SA 4	Well...no.

Suspect Answer Response Management

RM 1	Certainly, (name), its difficult to remember every detail of an incident like this, but sometimes things that seem unimportant are important.
RM 2	It's not easy to remember everything in exactly the order it happened. Sometimes the mind plays tricks on us.
RM 3	Your cooperation is most appreciated, but as you know, it's really important that we find out as much as we can about what happened.

Revised Question Follow-Up

RQ 1	What other things happened, even if you don't think it was important?
RQ 2	Thinking the incident over again, what did you leave out that we need to know to conduct a fair investigation?
RQ 3	Having given yourself more time to remember, what else can you remember about what happened?

QUESTION FORMULATION MATRIX

INQUIRY AREA	1	INCIDENT INVESTIGATIONS
Focus area	B	Witness Interview

Opening Question

Q 1   Did you see (name) break the lock to the office?

Q 2   Was (name) the person who broke the lock?

Q 3   Did (name) break the lock while you were in the room?

Truthful Answer Illustration

TA 1   No, I was on the phone. (Direct, to the point.)

TA 2   I don't know.

TA 3   Yes.

Suspect Answer Illustration

SA 1   No. Not really. (Qualified answer.)

SA 2   No. (Soft withdrawn answer.)

SA 3   No. (Slight pause.)

Suspect Answer Response Management

RM 1   It's not easy to talk about your co-workers when they aren't here, but we're just trying to find out what happened.

RM 2   No one is perfect, and all of us make our fair share of mistakes in life. I certainly have (smile). I just need to find out what happened.

RM 3   The world is certainly not a perfect place. Everyone makes a mistake or two. That's why we are just human beings.

Revised Question Follow-Up

RQ 1   (Name), with all circumstances considered, how did (name) manage to break that lock?

RQ 2   (Name), based on all the information, what happened to the lock on the door to the office?

RQ 3   Having taken some time to think about what happened, where were you when (name) broke the lock?

QUESTION FORMULATION MATRIX

INQUIRY AREA	1	INCIDENT INVESTIGATIONS
Focus area	C	Suspect Questioning

Opening Question

Q 1	Were you driving too fast when the accident took place?
Q 2	You were driving a bit over the speed limit when it happened, weren't you?
Q 3	Do you think you were going too fast when it happened?

Truthful Answer Illustration

TA 1	Absolutely not.
TA 2	No. I always follow the speed limit. (Very direct response and direct eye contact.)
TA 3	No.

Suspect Answer Illustration

SA 1	(Slight pause) ...No.
SA 2	No. (Briefly breaks eye contact.)
SA 3	No. Not much. (Qualified answer.)

Suspect Answer Response Management

RM 1	You know, (name), we all drive a little fast from time to time -- that's just human nature.
RM 2	Sometimes, (name), people drive faster than they realize. I know I've caught myself doing so from time to time.
RM 3	We all make mistakes when we're driving -- that's why accidents happen. We're just human after all.

Revised Question Follow-Up

RQ 1	Thinking back on it, do you think you might have been driving faster than you usually do?
RQ 2	Considering what you were doing at the time, is it likely that you were going too fast?
RQ 3	(Name), is it likely that you made a mistake or just weren't paying attention and were driving over the speed limit?

UNICOM Model for Employment Investigations Summary

The UNICOM Model for Employment Investigations is based on the importance of understanding interactive verbal and nonverbal communication for effective interviewing, legal requirements for compliance with employment law, and the dynamics of managing the trilogy of interactive activities for investigators. The chapter outlined a strategy for employment investigations and discussed pertinent points of the investigative process. An extensive list of kinds of issues requiring investigations was presented. The attributes of an effective investigator were addressed as well as the pros and cons of interviewing cooperative, neutral, or noncooperative witnesses. Employee-generated documentation vs. employer-generated documentation was addressed as well as the function of a standardized form for documentation for the entire investigative process. The five Ws (Who, What, When, Where, and Why) were suggested for consideration prior to the investigative interview, and question formulation techniques were presented. Points required for drawing conclusions were listed as well as recommended action choices. The final investigation file was described and strategies for handling an appeal were suggested.

CHAPTER ELEVEN

UNICOM_{SM}
MODEL FOR POST-EMPLOYMENT INVESTIGATIONS

The purpose of this chapter is to instruct the human resource manager and administrator of the importance of proactive planning. The old adage of the value of 20/20 hindsight is most applicable to post-employment investigations. When conducting workplace investigations, human resource managers must be scrupulously fair, because everything they say and do that even resembles biased or prejudiced action can be used against them and the reputation of their companies. A post-employment investigation, in almost every case, would follow an internal formal investigation within the preemployment or employment stage. These investigations may have been for any number of reasons but most generally are for:

- Self-audit and prevention purposes designed to ensure employee honesty;

- Pre-disciplinary measures instigated by a complaint or employee grievance, *i.e.*, sexual harassment;

- Suspicion of white-collar crime violations, *i.e.*, embezzlement, misappropriation, or divulging trade secrets;

- Suspicion of employee deviant behavior (see Chapter Three and Appendix B);

- A legal charge or lawsuit or regulatory allegation/complaint; and

- An employee's right to appeal a decision.

It is estimated that over 95% of all employment lawsuits are settled out of court. However, the cost of these actions has been found to average about $100,000 per case. Even though a company is sued and has been completely fair and has acted within the law, when considering the businesses factors and legal causes, it may decide that settlement is less costly and more prudent than litigation. Other reasons for settlement is that the law may change significantly and quickly; it is more prudent to settle than risk losing, and settlement may prevent bad publicity.

Negligent Investigation -- A New Legal Theory

A new legal theory, "negligent investigation," has emerged from the employment doctrine and can be brought into action as a result of a haphazard or incomplete workplace investigation leading to an employee's termination. The major benefit of conducting a proper internal workplace investigation is that it may protect against termination lawsuits, even if the results of the investigation are proven wrong.

Safe Workplace vs. Employee Rights -- Today's corporation or employer is faced with ambiguity and conflict in an effort to ensure employees' rights and to operate a safe workplace where unlawful behavior cannot be tolerated. In such cases as discrimination against the eight protected classes or outright sexual harassment, an internal, formal investigation is mandated by law. But when an employer suspects deviant behavior (*i.e.*, leaked trade secrets, an accountant who flashes newfound wealth, an executive who returns from lunch with a distinct aroma of alcohol) the decision to investigate requires a judgment call which most often is based on the company's need to safeguard employees and to protect its property and competitive status. This section addresses many of those issues and provides suggestions for proactively managing those circumstances.

Preventing Wrongful Discharge

It has been determined that wrongful termination law covers the entire employment relationship from beginning to end and that, if an employer or company has been consistently fair with all employees, there is less likely to be a lawsuit. If there is a suit, it generally is the company's fairness standards that determine the outcome of the case. Judges have placed significant limitations on management's right to dismiss employees at will. The best time for employers to consider the woes of wrongful discharge is during the preemployment stage as a new employee is hired and terms of a working relationship are established. Some suggestions are as follows:

Discuss Terms of Job Before Contract is Offered -- It is recommended that recruiters and interviewers discuss all the terms, conditions, and responsibilities of a job with an applicant up front, no matter what type of job is offered. It establishes positive relations with employees and minimizes breach of contract and wrongful discharge lawsuits. A company can dictate the terms of a job before the contract is offered, but it is too late after an employee has been dismissed. Therefore, the entire preemployment process must be carried out to the letter of the law. A brief sequential checklist of preemployment tasks are listed below:

- **Job description** -- An updated job description should be developed to include all aspects of the job advertised.

- **Advertising the position** -- The job advertisement should be posted internally and, if appropriate, through contacting recruiting agencies.

- **Prepare legal application forms** -- Ensure that the application does not ask illegal questions such as national origin, sex, age, race, color, marital status, health or disability, *etc.*

- **Review resumes** -- Watch for time gaps between past positions.

- **Pre-screen applicants** -- A telephone interview is helpful, if properly designed and managed with the overall recruiting and screening process.

- **Prepare interview** -- Plan the environment and format, set the times, write interview questions, and plan for consistency to efficiently manage resources and control costs.

- **Conduct interview** -- Follow employment law to the letter and apply the UNICOM Trilogy of Interactive Activities method.

- **Conduct necessary preemployment tests** -- Follow law, employment practices, and guidelines, and be aware of disparate impact implications.

- **Conduct background and reference checks** -- A thorough background and reference check is the best proactive precaution against negligent hiring.

- **Make the employment offer** -- The employment offer should be a written document spelling out the terms of employment and is considered a legal contract.

- **Notify rejected applicants** -- Rejected applicants need to know that they were considered under the letter of employment law.

- **Begin employment with a new-employee trial period** -- A trial period rather than probationary period is preferred in the event the new employee does not meet expectations and is terminated.

Each of these tasks must be managed proactively and in a planned manner within the realm of employment law.

Written Contracts and Documentation -- A verbal agreement and a handshake only indicates that employer and employee have agreed on a working relationship. A written contract can spell out important points that can avoid misunderstandings and disputes. Secondly, a written contract can involve the arbitration clause which can compel an employee to resolve a dispute by arbitration rather than litigation, thus making a company's defense less burdensome and less expensive. Some pointers to consider are listed below:

- Treat all employees fairly and consistently. The best way to prove people are treated fairly is to show that all are treated the same.

- Keep consistent documentation. It will prevent unintentional discrimination.

- For every decision regarding who will be hired, promoted, trained, and terminated, it is important to articulate and record a legitimate business reason.

Avoiding Fraudulent Concealment or Misrepresentation -- It is important to be absolutely truthful with all employees. Answer questions as specifically as possible and don't lie or answer in half-truths to conceal the truth. Document questions raised by applicants to avoid later accusations regarding the transaction or interaction.

Management Malpractice

It may seem that employees, in many respects, have more rights than an employer. Even after the working relationship is over, employees are entitled to benefits financed, in part, by the employer. For example, in most cases the terminated employee is entitled to unemployment insurance, workers' compensation for job injuries, and a social security retirement pension.

Employee Handbooks -- Personnel policies and employee handbooks are critical and legal documents. These documents should include all the provisions, rules, and guidelines necessary to set the mode of employee conduct for human resource managers and all employees. They also should detail how misconduct will be handled. In the majority of the states, the employee handbook is considered a legal contract between the company and employee. Employee handbooks should include four significant areas:

- **Welcome Statement** -- The welcome statement should not contain any promises that the company cannot keep or commitments that could be considered by the courts to be above the minimal standards of fairness.

- **Discipline Policy** -- If a company states that, before termination, employees will (must or shall) receive three warnings, it may be binding in a lawsuit. Rather, if a company states that, before termination, warnings may or could be given, it provides flexibility to omit some of those steps, depending upon the circumstances.

- **Termination Policy** -- A company can provide most protection by stating that it reserves the right to terminate all employees at will.

- **Employee Acknowledgment Section** -- The last page of the handbook should be an employee acknowledgment form. A copy of this form should be left in the handbook while a signed original is placed in the employee's personnel file to serve as an employment contract between employee and employer.

Wages, Hours, and Overtime -- The Fair Labor Standards Act (FLSA) governs overtime pay and minimum wages. Policy related to these areas should be clearly understood by both management and workers and recorded in the personnel file.

Independent Contractors -- The Internal Revenue Service has determined 20 factors to differentiate between an employee and an independent contractor. Substantial penalties can be adjudicated for employers who misclassify employees as subcontractors for up to three years.

Worker's Compensation, Health, and Safety Laws -- Company policy should be drawn to ensure that issues such as worker's compensation and health and safety rules are consistent with the law and regulatory policy.

Performance Appraisals and Employee Discipline -- Guidelines should be covered by the employee handbook so that each case can be treated in a standardized manner yet be individualized to meet the unique needs of each situation. All interaction between the human resource personnel and employees should be recorded and filed in an appropriate, secure place, available only to those with a business need to know. Performance appraisals are considered critical documents and should be conducted on a regular basis to create a clear record of an employee's job history.

Documentation and Personnel Files -- Employers maintain a staggering amount of records ranging from personnel files to equal employment documentation to a listing of toxic substances in the workplace. It is every employer's duty to ensure that information compiled in an individual's record is accurate, timely, relevant, and complete. Third-party access to such documents should be barred. With the preparation of each document, the human resource manager should assume that a judge is going to see it. It is essential to get employee's signatures on all warnings, performance appraisals, and other important documents.

Record Keeping -- Accurate record keeping is essential to show diligence especially in the event of a lawsuit or claim filed by an employee or former employee. It is advised that employers assume that a judge will see all documents. The EEOC may audit records at any time and demand a record of:

- All help-wanted ads,

- The names and gender of all employees hired,

- The names and gender of all applicants for all positions, and

- The actual job applications and resumes of all employees and applicants.

False Imprisonment

It generally is accepted that employers can question employees in an effort to discover illegal or deviant behavior provided that the questioning is conducted during normal business hours; there are no threats forcing the employee to remain in the room; and the questioning serves a legitimate, reasonable purpose. However, employees have certain rights during such interviews, including the right:

- To an explanation regarding the purpose of the interrogation or interview,

- To insist on the presence of a representative at the interview,

- To limit questions to relevant matters,

- To refuse to sign any written statements,

- To remain silent,

- To consult an attorney before speaking, and

- To leave the room at any time.

If a company conducts an investigative interview incorrectly, grim legal consequences may ensue.

Invasion of Privacy

Employers face a dilemma of protecting an employee's rights of privacy and exercising reasonable care in hiring and retaining employees. The violation of a person's constitutionally protected right to privacy can occur in the preemployment and employment arenas. During the preemployment phase, employers have a duty to take reasonable care in hiring individuals who may pose a threat of injury to fellow employees and the public. During the employment phase, employers have those same duties in retaining employees. Negligent-hiring and negligent-retention suits have been made against employers for murders, rapes, sexual assaults, physical assaults, personal injuries, and property losses allegedly committed by an unfit employee.

Preemployment Application -- Preemployment actions must guard against invasion of privacy in such areas as interviewing; checking references; investigating of medical, criminal, and credit or bankruptcy records; and preemployment testing.

Employment Application -- Employees are protected by privacy law at home and at work, and employers cannot unreasonably invade their personal lives. However, employers, simultaneously, have the right to protect themselves if employees' personal lives affect their ability to work and threaten the safety of the workplace. Employment management and monitoring actions must guard against invasion of privacy in such areas as search and surveillance and drug and alcohol testing. Courts have established a four-step process to analyze whether an employer's action is an illegal invasion of privacy:

- **Zone of Privacy** -- The most personal zone of privacy includes a person's body, mind, and home. The next most personal zone includes personal belongings such as clothing, purse, briefcase, and car. Less personal zones are the workplace desk and work area, while the least personal zone is considered to be the general workplace and parking lot.

- **Reasonable Expectation of Privacy** -- Depending on which zone of privacy is affected, the reasonable expectation of privacy can be determined. The more personal the zone of privacy, the higher the expectation of privacy.

- **Reason to Invade Privacy** -- Employers must have a compelling interest, or reasonable suspicion before invading areas that have a high expectancy of privacy. A rational basis is required before invading areas of lower expectations of privacy. These reasons may include reasonable suspicion of theft, reasonable suspicion of intoxication, plant security, work performance, workplace safety, trade secrets, bribery, and conflict of interest.

- **Means Reasonably Related to Ends** -- If an employer has a compelling or rational reason to invade privacy, the means rationally must relate to the end sought. Thus, the need of an employer to obtain information is weighed against the extent to which an employee's privacy is invaded.

Controlling Drug and Alcohol Use in the Workplace -- The Federal Drug-Free Workplace Act requires companies to develop drug-awareness programs, and establish a drug-free workplace policy. In recent years, drug testing has become a proactive practice for many companies. Six types of drug tests are acknowledged:

1) Preemployment -- to screen applicants,

2) "For cause" -- testing employees upon reasonable suspicion of intoxication,

3) Post-accident,

4) Regularly scheduled tests,

5) Unannounced random tests, and

6) Follow-up tests -- to confirm that an employee is maintaining sobriety after testing positive.

Drug testing may not be conducted in a discriminatory manner, *i.e.*, if applicants or employees are to be tested, all must be, from janitor to CEO, and all must follow the invasion of privacy standards listed above.

The company rules should contain clear policy, based on the mandate for a drug-free workplace, on the use of drugs and alcohol in the workplace. It also is the employer's responsibility to provide alternative means of transportation for employees who attend company functions where alcoholic beverages are served. Employees should be advised of company policy against excessive consumption of alcoholic beverages at company-sponsored parties or events. Also, instruct servers to limit employees' consumption, and to serve only nonalcoholic beverages during the final hour of any such gatherings.

Controlling Deviant Behavior in the Workplace -- Since it is an employer's duty to provide a safe workplace for employees and clients, the possibility of deviant and especially violent behavior carefully should be considered. The rules set forth in the employee handbook should be enforceable, and behavior must be monitored within legal techniques. The human resources or employee relations department, as well as all supervisors, should be forewarned of all incidents of employee violence. It is suggested that the negligent retention theory be used whenever applicable as additional grounds for the employment termination of unfit or incompetent workers.

Keeping Trade Secrets -- A trade secret is defined as information, including a formula, pattern, compilation, program, device, technique, or process, that has value because it is not generally known to competitors. Examples of trade secrets are: salary information, product specifications, inventions, customer lists, vendor lists, unpublished works, software, sales and marketing plans, pricing information, and customized computer programs. Thirteen proactive methods for keeping a trade secret are as follows:

1) Treat trade secrets as private and confidential.

2) Write procedures for handling trade secrets including employee-confidentiality agreements.

3) Reveal trade secrets only to employees with the need to know and provide training on their duty of confidentiality.

4) If secrets are revealed to anyone outside the company, require them to sign confidentiality agreements.

5) Mark such information as "confidential" or "secret," but do not mark things as secret that are not.

6) Keep trade secrets in a secure place, have a check-in and check-out procedure, and keep a log of all activity. Conduct an audit or inventory regularly.

7) Establish a security system which includes entrance guards, badge requirements, briefcase inspections, a prohibition on cameras, and card-key or locked security doors into sensitive areas. Insist that employees use personal keys and not allow other employees into locked areas.

8) Keep a visitor log, issue ID tags, and escort all visitors to ensure that visitors do not enter secured areas.

9) Use security measures for computer-stored secrets. Do not allow any breach of computer security.

10)   Monitor and control access to photocopy machines.

11)   Destroy or shred all waste materials related to trade secrets.

12)   Conduct new hire and exit interviews which emphasize legal obligations to maintain secrecy.

13)   Treat employees fairly and pay competitively to prevent motivation to steal trade secrets.

Legal Termination of Employees -- An at-will employee can be fired at any time, for any reason, or for no reason at all. However, if an employee/employment contract states that the employment is for a specific period of time, that employment is not at will. In this case, the employee can only be fired at the end of the contract, unless the employer has a "good cause" for termination. Some examples of good cause for termination are listed below:

● Unsatisfactory work performance;

● Insubordination or refusing a direct order;

● Use or possession of alcohol or drugs at workplace;

● Violence at the workplace;

● Theft from the company or employees;

● Harassment, sexual, racial, or other;

● Possession of weapons at the workplace;

● Gambling at the workplace; and

● Disobeying workplace safety procedures.

Employee Layoff Liability -- Layoffs, as a result of a plant closing, lack of business, or reorganization rarely lead to wrongful termination suits. However, an employer can be sued for discrimination if the layoff impacts one group more than others. For employers under the Worker Adjustment and Retraining Notification (WARN) Act, adequate warning must be given prior to a layoff. There are three areas that can lead to wrongful termination suits:

1)   **Legitimacy of the Decision to Layoff** -- Lack of business, plant closing, or reorganization. The term "layoff" may mean a company is required to reinstate employees

if their positions come open again later. However, "reduction in force" may refer to a permanent loss of employment with no opportunity for reinstatement.

2) **Criteria of Selection Employees for Layoff** -- A company should have a written policy to establish criteria for selecting employees for layoff. Examples of typical criteria are:

    a) **Seniority** -- employees may be laid-off in reverse order of seniority,

    b) **Job Titles** -- job classifications or departments may be eliminated,

    c) **Skill Sets** -- employees with the least skills and abilities may be laid-off first, and

    d) **Merit** -- employees who have poor performance may be laid off first.

3) **Adverse Impact** of any of eight groups protected by EEO law.

Sexual Harassment Issues -- Companies are required to take all steps necessary to prevent harassment including posting a policy, training managers, and establishing a grievance procedure. The courts have established four factors necessary to prove sexual harassment, and all four must be shown for a victim to win a case:

1) The act must be explicitly sexual,

2) The act must be repeated or gross,

3) The act is unwelcome by the victim, and

4) The employer knew or should have known it was occurring and did nothing to stop it.

EEOC regulations require a company to take all steps necessary to prevent harassment. Five proactive measures are suggested:

1) Affirmatively raise the issue,

2) Express strong disapproval of harassment,

3)   Develop appropriate penalties for harassers,

4)   Inform employees of their right to raise and method to raise the issue, and

5)   Develop methods to sensitize all employees.

Employee Appeal Rights

Discharged employees have the right to appeal to the courts for relief under several different agreements, such as discrimination suits and unjust dismissal suits.

Discrimination Suits -- Employers must guard against all forms of discrimination in the preemployment and employment phases. The magnitude of the ramifications involving discrimination are so great that entire books are written for each area of possible discrimination. The need for human resource managers and administrators to understand and follow employment law cannot be overstated.

Unjust Dismissal Suits -- If employees cannot allege that their dismissal violated a particular law, they can now use one of three arguments to sue or appeal:

- **The firing conflicts with public policy** -- *i.e.*, the employee was terminated because he or she refused to do something wrong or unethical in order to retain a job.

- **The firing violated an employment contract** -- Whether a written or implied contract, courts are calling certain managerial indications, such as a benefit that says the firings are only for just causes, evidence of a contract.

- **The firing was unfair** -- There is an employer obligation to act in good faith in using the power to terminate.

Two caveats employers must be cognizant of are:

1)   No disciplinary action should be taken until a complete investigation has been conducted and sufficient evidence of wrongdoing has been substantiated; and

2)   Documentation that illustrates that an investigation has been thorough, careful, and fair will sustain challenges to findings and actions.

It therefore becomes a priority for human resource managers to create policies and procedures on how to handle a variety of investigative situations long before an employment crisis occurs or the first complaint is filed.

Convert Terminations Into Resignations

Perhaps the best method of guarding against post-employment lawsuits and appeals is to convert terminations into resignations. This procedure provides the terminated employee the opportunity to truthfully say that he or she resigned from the last job, rather than living with the stigma of being "fired." It also mitigates any potential claims for defamation or unfair terminations because the employee has agreed to the resignation. Because not all terminations should be converted into resignations, each case should be considered individually. In the event it is possible to convert the termination into a resignation, the employee and employer can enter into a valid separation agreement which includes a proper waiver and release of all potential claims by the employee against the employer. Some considerations for the employer who offers the option of resigning in lieu of termination are:

- Advise employees that a voluntary resignation may assist them in an attempt to gain new employment;

- Consider the feasibility of offering outplacement assistance to gain future employment;

- Remind the employee that voluntary resignation in the face of certain discharge will not preclude him or her from receiving unemployment benefits;

- Document the circumstances leading to the employee's separation, including the opportunity to resign in lieu of termination.

Obtain Release From Resigning or Terminating Employees

Another important precaution for employers to implement to protect themselves from lawsuits is to obtain a release statement from resigning or terminating employees. Such releases should be drafted in consultation with an attorney. It also is suggested that the employee be given an opportunity to consult with an attorney before signing the release. The employee should not be forced or coerced into signing a release and should be provided ample time for consideration.

Handling Post-Employment References

Post-employment reference procedures are handled differently depending upon which side of the hiring fence the employer stands. If the employer is in the hiring mode, the reference goal is to obtain complete reference information to minimize potential liabilities for negligent hiring. On the other hand, if the employer is providing a reference for a past-employee, the goal is to cautiously provide a limited amount of information as a way of avoiding liability for defamatory post-employment references. Whether providing references for past employees or past independent contractors, some specific cautionary tactics are as follows:

- Make sure the company has a written post-employment reference policy so that all personnel who are responsible for providing references have specific guidelines.

- Post-employment reference policy should require that all post-employment references be furnished only by the human resources or employee-relations department.

- Always verify that the party requesting information has a bona fide need to know and avoid responding to oral requests for post-employment reference information.

- When possible, limit reference information to verification of dates of employment and positions held by the former employee.

- Do not provide reasons for a former employee's separation from employment.

- Respond only to questions asked by the prospective employer -- do not volunteer any information.

- Always obtain a signed termination release from the employee waiving all claims against the employer in connection with the disclosure of employment data.

- If a favorable reference is promised to a departing employee, an unfavorable reference should not be provided.

- Document all references provided by specifically noting who made the request for information, how the request was made, how the information was provided, and what information was provided.

- Do not provide opinions -- limit references to objective and documented facts.

- Do not provide information based on unverifiable hearsay.

- Always refer the task of reference provision to persons with firsthand information regarding the former employee. Do not provide second-hand information unless it is based on documented reliable information. In addition, if second-hand facts are provided, advise the employer that the information is not based on personal knowledge.

- Confer with legal counsel regarding inquiries of past employees having a potential relationship relevant to negligent hiring behavioral issues, as well as history or knowledge of past criminal or deviant behavior.

Averting Other Post-Employment Tortious Charges

It is of major concern for an employer to realize that he or she can be held liable for the actions of a former employee. For instance, post-termination tort actions may originate as a result of the commencement of a civil or criminal proceeding against employees, enforcement of restrictive covenants, and inducing current employers to terminate a former employee's present employment. Suggestions for avoiding these types of post-employment tortious claims are listed below:

- Always evaluate requests by managers and officials to institute criminal proceedings against employees who have filed lawsuits against the employer.

- Never file a civil or criminal suit against any employee without probable cause to believe that the employee engaged in the alleged misconduct.

- Never file a criminal charge against employees without first conducting a thorough, internal investigation and obtaining sworn statements supporting the charges and verifying the facts underlying the allegations.

- Always confer with in-house and/or outside legal counsel before filing a criminal charge against a current or former employee.

- In the event criminal charges are filed against an employee, one or more suitable representatives of the employer should appear during each of the court proceedings.

- Never file professional misconduct charges against an employee before fully investigating and verifying facts supporting the allegations.

- Never file civil proceedings against an employee without first considering the likelihood that employee will file a counterclaim for malicious prosecution.

- Never introduce "no competition" covenants that are unconscionable or otherwise unreasonable. Always confer with legal counsel before introducing or enforcing contract clauses.

- Avoid recommending or inducing another employer to fire an employee.

- Avoid interfering with the selection of employees by other employers.

- Never allow supervisors or managers to use a post-employment   reference as an opportunity for retaliation against a former employee.

- Always make post-employment references objective and factual. Avoid opinions and speculations, even if requested by the prospective employer.

Guarding Against Post-Employment Charges

This chapter has reviewed the steps, procedures, and precautions a company or employer must take to avoid the charges related to negligent hiring, negligent retention, negligent termination, and management malpractice. The purpose of this presentation was to instruct the human resource practitioner in proactive planning with the purpose of avoiding entanglements that potentially could lead to lawsuits involving one or more of the above-mentioned torts.

The chapter discussion communicates that many of the necessary steps for the avoidance of post-employment liability must take place long before an applicant is even hired. Proper record-keeping procedures and documentation maintenance during the pre-employment and employment of an individual also was highlighted as important to the process -- as is the professional, fair, and considerate treatment of the employee during the termination or layoff procedure.

CHAPTER TWELVE

UNICOM_{SM}
APPLICATION SUMMARY

The Application Component of Part III introduces investigative models for preemployment investigations, employment investigations, and post-employment investigations. Each model is based on the fundamentals of the UNICOM strategy.

Workplace Investigation Algorithm

This chapter provides an instructional algorithm for a model employment investigation (Figure 12.1) in an effort to provide the human resource practitioner with an illustration of the processes through which the overall investigation must pass. The purpose of the algorithm is to demonstrate the step-by-step methodology of the investigation in an effort to aid the investigator in collecting relevant and up-to-date information in an objective fashion in order for the results of the investigation to be reliable and defensible.

The purpose of a workplace investigation is to determine whether company policies and procedures or even state or federal laws have been violated and catalogue such evidence proving or disproving an allegation for future use. The investigator must determine the validity of complaints or charges made and whether a rule, policy, or law has been violated while keeping in mind the fact that an accused/suspected person should morally share the constitutionally guaranteed rights of a person presumed innocent unless otherwise established.

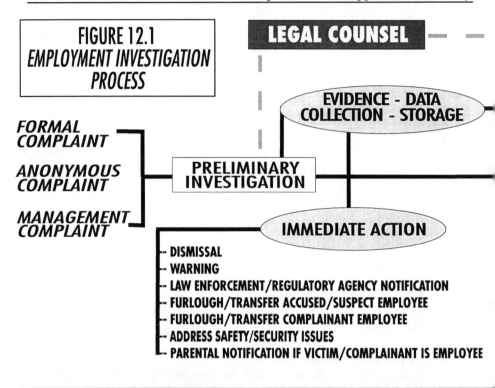

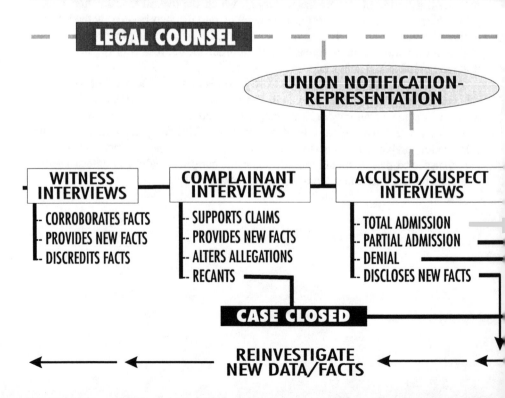

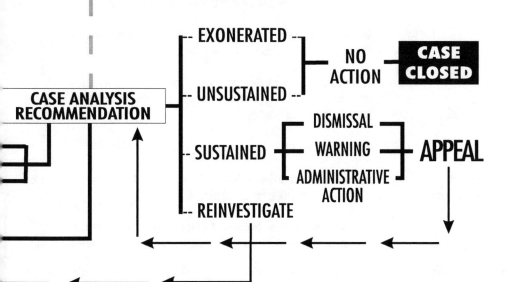

LEGAL COUNSEL

FORMAL INVESTIGATION

- DESIGN INVESTIGATION STRATEGY
- SELECTION OF INVESTIGATOR(S)
- ESTABLISHING REPORTING GUIDELINES
- REVIEW OF COMPANY POLICIES
- REVIEW OF EMPLOYMENT PRACTICES
- REVIEW FOR UNION RESTRICTIONS
- REVIEW FOR EMPLOYEE AGREEMENTS

DATA & INFORMATION COLLECTION

- RECORD SEARCH OF ACCUSED/SUSPECT
- RECORD SEARCH OF COMPLAINANT
- RECORD SEARCH OF WITNESSES
- SEARCH FOR ADDITIONAL WITNESSES
- SEARCH FOR ANY SIMILAR/ RELATED UNREPORTED INCIDENTS

LEGAL COUNSEL

CASE ANALYSIS RECOMMENDATION

- EXONERATED
- UNSUSTAINED

NO ACTION

CASE CLOSED

- SUSTAINED

DISMISSAL
WARNING
ADMINISTRATIVE ACTION

APPEAL

- REINVESTIGATE

Chapter Summary Points

For Preemployment Application -- The following set of questions should be contemplated prior to preemployment selection, hiring new employees, or advancing employees to another level of employment:

1) Were the questions legal, job-related, and consistently asked of each candidate?

2) Was each candidate given "equal opportunity" to satisfy job requirements?

3) Were all resumes checked for unexplained gaps in employment or education history?

4) Were all interviews held in a private, quiet setting free of potential interruptions?

5) Was written permission obtained from the candidate to allow verification of past employment, education, background checks of credit, criminal, and work history?

6) During the interview, did the practitioner probe for more information about gaps or inconsistencies in employment history and reasons for leaving previous positions?

7) Were the applicant's personal and professional references carefully checked?

8) Were reference-checking interviews carefully documented? Were unanswered requests also documented.

9) Did the practitioner try to obtain specific descriptions of the applicant's character and abilities.

10) If the applicant was disabled, were reasonable accommodations discussed regarding the job per the Americans with Disabilities Act?

11) Was a background check completed for the applicant?

For Employment Application -- The following set of questions should be contemplated prior to and following each investigation:

1) Was a written plan developed prior to the investigation detailing who will be interviewed, the sequence of those

interviews, and how other documentary evidence is to be obtained?

2) Was the investigator credible, sufficiently trained, unintimidating, impartial, discreet, and competent?

3) Have all documents obtained in the investigation been carefully reviewed to ensure that evidence and information is reliable and complete?

4) Was the investigated employee cognizant of employment policy or law related to the wrongdoing prior to such behavior?

5) In the event the wrongdoing was not a criminal charge, has the employee been given an opportunity to change habits or behavior?

6) If the employee had abused drugs or alcohol, has the employee been offered assistance for rehabilitation or counseling?

7) Has the employee had an opportunity to present his or her case in a nonthreatening environment?

8) Has the credibility of all testimony been considered?

9) Has the investigator emphasized confidentiality and proceeded discreetly throughout the investigation.

10) Have all appropriate individuals been interviewed?

11) Has the investigator maintained a file of information resources, including interview notes, documents obtained, a timeline of occurrences, and other pertinent information?

12) Has the investigation file been stored in a secure place and guarded against unauthorized access to such confidential information?

13) Has an attorney been consulted to outline the parameters of the interview procedures, especially concerning which questions are appropriate and which are not?

14)   Has the plan of action been continually under review to ensure flexibility and to make changes depending upon the scope of the investigation?

15)   Have the persons being interviewed (either witnesses or suspects) been allowed to review any written statements and make changes to them?

16)   Have the interviewees been informed that their testimony may become public.

17)   Have the employees' rights to privacy been violated?

18)   Were the interviews conducted in a private place under relaxed, nonintimidating circumstances?

19)   Was the investigation carefully monitored by the employer during each stage of the process, from the initial complaint through remedial action and follow-up at the conclusion?

Post-Employment/Employee Termination -- In an employee termination situation, the following questions might be considered:

1)   Did the employer have a clear rule or policy against the type of behavior which led to the firing?

2)   Is the rule or policy reasonably related to the orderly, efficient, and safe operation of the employer's business?

3)   Did the employer provide all employees with a reasonable opportunity to learn the rules or policies?

4)   Has the employer administered and enforced rules or policies consistently and without discrimination among all employees?

5)   Did the employer fairly investigate the circumstances related to the alleged offense?

6)   Did the employer obtain sufficient evidence?

7)   Does the employee have a past history of similar behavior?

8)   Was it proper to discharge the employee or should the employee have received a warning or suspension?

9)   Did the employer do anything to contribute to the employee's act, *i.e.* provoke anger by remarks?

10)   Were witnesses credible in proving the case?

11)   Were there mitigating factors to explain the employee's behavior?

12)   Was the termination fair under all circumstances?

APPENDIX A

GLOSSARY OF TERMS
FOR WORKPLACE INVESTIGATIONS

ABUSE OF PROCESS -- A cause of action which arises when one party intentionally misuses the legal process to injure another.

ACTIONABLE -- That for which a legal action will stand, furnishing a legal ground for such action. The fact or facts which give a person a right to judicial redress or relief against another.

ACTUAL DAMAGES -- Compensation for actual injuries or loss awarded to an employee found to be treated illegally or improperly. Examples include backpay and front pay as well as out-of-pocket expenses such as medical bills, costs due to forced sale of property, and other foreseeable losses.

ADA -- AMERICANS WITH DISABILITIES ACT -- Passed by Congress in 1990, it protects from discrimination people who suffer from a permanent impairment of a life function, like walking, seeing, or breathing.

ADEA -- AGE DISCRIMINATION IN EMPLOYMENT ACT OF 1967 -- A federal law that applies to all employers with 20 or more regular employees. It prohibits discrimination against those in age groups over 40 but less than 70.

ADMISSIBLE -- Pertinent and proper to be considered in a court of law in reaching a decision.

ADMISSIBLE EVIDENCE -- Evidence introduced during legal proceedings having such a character that a court or judge is bound to receive it; that is, allow it to be introduced at a trial.

ADMISSION -- Confessions, concessions, or voluntary acknowledgment made by a person regarding the existence of certain facts.

ADVERSE IMPACT -- A substantially different rate of selection in hiring, promotion, or other employment decisions that works to the disadvantage of members of a race, sex, or ethnic group. A substantially different rate is less than 4/5 or 80% of the selection rate for the group with the highest selection rate.

ADVERSE WITNESS -- A witness who provides evidence on a material matter prejudicial to the person then examining him.

AFFIDAVIT -- A written statement of fact made voluntarily and confirmed by oath or affirmation of the person making it.

AFFIRMATIVE ACTION PLAN (AAP) -- A written plan calling for an assertive program to combat employment standards or procedures which tend to discriminate on the basis of sex, race, age, color, religion, or national origin. Affirmative action not only deals with overtly discriminatory practices, but also with those practices which are fair in form but discriminatory in effect.

AGE DISCRIMINATION IN EMPLOYMENT ACT -- Legislation prohibiting discrimination against people over 40-years-old.

AGENT -- A person authorized by another (principal) to act for or in place of him; one who is entrusted with another's business.

AIDS -- Acquired Immune Deficiency Syndrome.

ALJ -- ADMINISTRATIVE LAW JUDGE -- One who presides at an administrative hearing with power to administer oaths, take testimony, rule on questions of evidence, regulate the course of proceedings, and make agency determination of fact.

ALLEGATION -- An assertion, complaint, claim or statement of a person charging another party of a wrongdoing.

AMERICANS WITH DISABILITIES ACT (ADA) -- Legislation prohibiting discrimination against people with disabilities.

APPEAL -- A process whereby the losing party of a legal proceeding may appeal to a higher court to determine the correctness of the decision. In the case of employment, the losing party may appeal to management regarding what may have been unfair decision-making practices.

ARBITRATION -- A method of settling a labor-management dispute by holding a formal hearing in the presence of an impartial third party who renders a decision. The decision may or may not be binding upon the parties.

ARBITRATION AGREEMENT -- An agreement between two conflicting parties to enter into an arbitration process for a final decision regarding their dispute.

ARREST -- An action to deprive a person of his liberty by legal authority. Taking, under real or assumed authority, custody of another for the purpose of holding or detaining him to answer a criminal charge or civil demand.

ASSAULT AND BATTERY -- Battery is the willful and unlawful use of force or violence upon the person of another. Assault is the threat to commit a battery where the threat places the other in apprehension of imminent harm. During a workplace investigation, an employer who physically detains or attempts to detain an employee or threatens or uses physical force against an employee may commit either or both criminal violations (see false imprisonment).

ATTORNEY-CLIENT PRIVILEGE -- A client's legal privilege to refuse to disclose and to prevent any other person from disclosing confidential communications between the client and his attorney. The privilege protects all communications between the attorney and client made for the purpose of furnishing or obtaining legal advice or assistance. This privilege permits an attorney to refuse to testify as to communications from the client to him, though it belongs to the client, not the attorney and, hence, the client may wave it.

ATTORNEY WORK PRODUCT -- The "attorney work product" doctrine protects the documents and theories prepared by an attorney in the course of an investigation if litigation is pending or is anticipated.

AWARD -- A judicial decision to compensate the winning party in a lawsuit.

BONA FIDE -- In good faith, honestly, and without fraud or deceit.

BFBP -- BONA FIDE BENEFIT PLAN -- Hiring practices that permit the consideration of certain qualifications (*i.e.*, age, religion, or national origin) necessary to performance of the job.

BFES -- BONA FIDE EXECUTIVE SYSTEM -- Protects an executive position and allows special treatment as a condition of an executive position as opposed to lower level positions.

BFOQ -- BONA FIDE OCCUPATIONAL QUALIFICATION -- Specific qualification/s required by the job description or considered as a business necessity.

BFSS -- BONA FIDE SENIORITY SYSTEM -- Protects someone in a seniority position.

BREACH OF CONTRACT -- Failure, without legal excuse, to perform any promise which forms the whole or part of a contract.

BURDEN OF PROOF -- The necessity or legal duty in the law of evidence of affirmatively proving a fact in dispute concerning an issue raised between the parties in a legal proceeding.

BUSINESS NECESSITY -- A qualification that is essential to fulfilling a position for a specific business need.

CAUSE OF ACTION -- The fact or facts which give a person the legal right to judicial redress or relief against another.

CIRCUMSTANTIAL EVIDENCE -- Testimony not based on actual personal knowledge or observation of the facts in controversy, but of other facts from which deductions are drawn, showing indirectly the facts sought to be proved.

CIVIL ACTION -- A legal action brought to enforce, redress, or protect an individual's private rights. In general, all types of actions other than criminal proceedings.

CIVIL COURT -- Generally, any court which presides over noncriminal matters.

CIVIL LIBERTIES -- Personal, natural rights guaranteed and protected by Constitution; *e.g.* freedom of speech and press, freedom from discrimination, *etc.*

CIVIL RIGHTS ACT OF 1964 -- This act (as amended by the Equal Employment Opportunity Act of 1972) prevents discrimination in employment on the basis of race, color, religion, sex, or national origin and applies to private sector employers having at least 15 employees each day for 20 weeks of one year, unions, employment agencies, educational institutions, and state and local government.

CLASS ACTION -- An action is a representative action brought in the form of a lawsuit based upon a primary or personal right belonging to the plaintiff and other person in his class.

COLLECTIVE BARGAINING -- A method of determining conditions of employment by the negotiation between representatives of an employer and union representatives of the employee. The results of the bargaining are set forth in a collective bargaining agreement.

COMMON LAW -- Law which evolves from reported case decisions which are relied upon for their precedential value. In general, it is a body of law that develops and derives through judicial decisions, as distinguished from legislative enactments.

COMPENSATORY DAMAGES -- A monetary sum representing actual harm suffered or loss incurred which is awarded to a complaining party

COMPLAINT -- A legal document which initiates a lawsuit. It alleges the facts and causes of action upon which the plaintiff relies to collect damages.

CONFLICT OF INTEREST -- The ethical inability of a person to work with a client or employee because of competing loyalties.

CONSEQUENTIAL DAMAGES -- A measure of damages referring to the indirect injuries or losses that a party suffers.

CONSOLIDATED OMNIBUS BUDGET RECONCILIATION ACT (COBRA) -- Legislation allowing employees to continue insurance benefits after termination.

CONSUMER CREDIT PROTECTION ACT -- Provides that an employer may not discharge an employee because the employee's earnings have been subjected to garnishment for any one indebtedness.

CONSUMER REPORT -- Any written or oral information bearing on a person's credit history, character, reputation, or mode of living prepared by a reporting agency.

CONVICTION -- The result of a criminal trial which ends in a judgment that the accused is guilty as charged.

CORROBORATING EVIDENCE -- Direct evidence that something has happened or about an issue.

COURT OF APPEALS -- The first court to review a judge or jury decision to ensure it complies with the law. Court of appeals decisions are precedent only for the district in which the court sits.

COVENANT -- An agreement or promise of two or more parties. Any agreement or contract.

CREDIBILITY -- The believability of a witness as perceived by a judge, jury, or the interviewer.

DAMAGES -- An award, usually monetary, to the winning party in a lawsuit as compensation for the wrongful acts of another.

DECEPTION -- An inaccuracy of a truth, accomplished by falsification, omission, or distortion or any combination thereof concerning the existing facts of a matter.

DECISION -- The determination of a case or matter of a judicial body.

DEFAMATION -- An intentional false communication, either published or publicly spoken, that injures personal reputation or good name, such as holding up a person to ridicule, scorn, or contempt in a respectable and considerable part of the community. This may be criminal as well as civil.

DEFAULT JUDGMENT -- A judgment entered against a party who has failed to defend against a claim or lawsuit that has been brought by another party.

DEFENDANT -- A person being sued in a lawsuit.

DEFINITE TERM OF EMPLOYMENT -- Employment for a fixed period of time.

DEMEANOR -- The body language or nonverbal behavior of someone.

DEPARTMENT OF LABOR -- Government agency which enforces overtime and minimum wage laws.

DEPOSITION -- Pretrial testimony under oath before a court reporter but no judge. Usually, one side's attorney calls witnesses from the other side and questions them about their testimony. The process can last from a few hours to days.

DIRECT COMPENSATION -- Payment for employee performance in terms of productivity or amount of time worked.

DISCHARGE -- The dismissal of an employee, who may have broken rules or policy of management, or who is incompetent, or for a good reason.

DISCHARGE WARNING -- A written notice given to an employee stating that he or she will be discharged if further violations or infractions to rules occur or if unsatisfactory work continues.

DISCIPLINARY LAYOFF -- Suspension, sometimes temporary, of an employee who has violated rules or policy of management. It is meant to serve as a warning and notice of possible termination if the employee's future behavior does not improve.

DISCLAIMER -- A clause in sales, service, or other contract which attempts to limit or exonerate one party from liability in the event of a lawsuit.

DISCOVERY -- The process during a lawsuit before trial where each side asks the other to answer written questions (interrogatories) and provide copies of relevant documents.

DISCRIMINATION -- An unfair labor practice under federal and state labor laws related to hiring, promoting, or firing because of race, creed, color, religion, national origin, sex, disability, or pregnancy.

DRUG FREE WORKPLACE ACT -- Legislation requiring anti-drug policy for the workplace.

DUCHENNE SMILE -- A universal smile that expresses genuine happiness. It is named after Gullaume Benjamin Amand Duchenne (1862), who first reported this smile phenomenon.

DUE PROCESS -- The Fifth and Fourteenth Amendments provide that no citizen shall be deprived of life, liberty, or property without due process of law.

DURESS -- Unlawful threats, pressure, or force that induces a person to act contrary to his or her intentions.

EEO -- Equal Employment Opportunity for all protected classes, *i.e.*, national origin, race, color, sex, religion, age, and the disabled.

EEOC -- EQUAL EMPLOYMENT OPPORTUNITY COMMISSION -- An agency established to administer the provisions Title VII of the Civil Rights Act of 1964 (as amended by the EEO Act of 1972).

EMPLOY -- To engage in one's service, to hire, to use as an agent or substitute in transacting business, to commission and entrust with the performance of certain acts or functions or with the management of one's affairs. When used in respect to a servant or hired laborer, the term is equivalent to hiring, which implies a request and a contract for a compensation.

EMPLOYEE -- A person in the service of another under any contract of hire, express or implied, oral or written, where the employer has the power or right to control and direct the employee in the material details of how the work is to be performed. One who works for an employer; a person working for salary or wages.

EMPLOYEE ASSISTANCE PROGRAM (EAP) -- A program provided by employers, voluntarily, to counsel employees with personal problems, including substance abuse.

EMPLOYER -- One who employs the services of others; one for whom employees work and who pays their wages or salaries.

EMPLOYMENT AT WILL -- Employment which does not provide an employee with job security, since the person can be fired on a moment's notice with or without cause.

EMPLOYMENT CONTRACT -- An agreement or contract between employer and employee in which the terms and conditions of one's employment are provided.

EQUAL EMPLOYMENT OPPORTUNITY ACT OF 1972 -- This act gave the EEOC the ability to take cases directly to the court system.

EQUAL PAY FOR EQUAL WORK -- A legal principle designed to establish pay rates based on quantity or quality of work and not on such unrelated factors as race, sex, or religion.

ERISA -- EMPLOYEE RETIREMENT INCOME SECURITY ACT OF 1974 -- Prohibits discrimination among employees and governs pension plans and employee benefit plans such as disability, medical insurance, and severance pay.

ESSENTIAL FUNCTIONS ON THE JOB -- Covered by the Americans with Disabilities Act, essential functions are referenced under Title 1, Section 101 (8), which states:

The term "qualified individual with a disability" means an individual with a disability who, with or without reasonable accommodation, can perform the essential functions of the employment position that such an individual holds or desires. For the purposes of this Title, consideration shall be given to the employer's judgment as to what functions of a job are essential and, if an employer has prepared a written description before advertising or interviewing applicants for the job, this description shall be considered evidence of the essential functions of the job.

EVIDENCE -- Any species of proof, or probative matter, legally presented at the trial of an issue, by the act of the parties and through the medium of witnesses, records, documents, exhibits, concrete objects, *etc.*, for the purpose of inducing belief in the minds of the court or jury as to their contentions.

EXCLUSIVE REMEDY -- Employees cannot sue in court for certain wrongs because their exclusive remedy is restricted to rights under a particular law: *i.e.,* workers' compensation is the exclusive remedy for employees injured at work.

EXECUTIVE ORDER 11246 -- Presidential order establishing Affirmative Action.

EXHIBIT -- Tangible evidence used to prove a party's claim.

EXIT AGREEMENT -- An agreement often signed between employers and employees upon resignation or termination of an employee's services.

FACT-FINDING -- A method of impasse resolution that involves investigation of a labor-management dispute by a neutral third party, whether it be an individual, board, or panel. Usually, the fact-finder's report is advisory, although in some cases the decision may become binding upon parties.

FAIR CREDIT REPORTING ACT OF 1970 -- This act protects applicants and employees from the dissemination of inaccurate or misleading personal information by consumer reporting agencies and imposes certain restrictions on both the reporting credit agency and user of the consumer report.

FALSE CONSENSUS BIAS -- Also known as the egocentric bias, it suggests that interviewers might be too willing to conclude that their views of a particular applicant are shared by other interviewers.

FALSE IMPRISONMENT -- The unlawful restraint by one person of the physical liberty of another. Confinement, harm, and the apprehension of the person are required elements. "Imprisonment" does not necessarily mean incarceration *per se.* A person may be falsely imprisoned if his or her actions are restrained on an open street, if the person is required to accompany another against his or her will, or if the only egress from the room is blocked by another.

FAMILY AND MEDICAL LEAVE ACT OF 1993 -- Allows employees to take up to 12 weeks of unpaid leave during any 12-month period to care for family members or because of a serious health condition of the employee.

FEP -- FAIR EMPLOYMENT PRACTICE -- Encompasses a broad range of issues including labor relations and standards, employment benefits, employment at will, workplace safety, and EEO.

FEPC -- FAIR EMPLOYMENT PRACTICE COMMISSIONS -- Are state governed entities which handle employment claims and file EEOC charges.

FLSA -- FAIR LABOR STANDARDS ACT OF 1938 -- One of the broadest pieces of legislation in the United States regulating the following: employee status, child labor, minimum wage, overtime pay, record keeping.

FOIA -- FREEDOM OF INFORMATION ACT OF 1966 -- Provides for making information held by federal agencies available to the public unless it comes within one of the specific categories of matters exempt from public disclosure.

FOS -- FACTORS OTHER THAN SEX -- Job performance issues which may be involved in discriminatory selection practices, *i.e.*, job requirements such as lifting, which could prohibit women from holding certain positions.

4/5'S RULE -- Adverse impact typically is evaluated by the 4/5's rule: That any protected group must pass a selection procedure at a rate of no less than 80% of the passing rate of the majority group. Example: The passing rate of a majority group is 50% on a selection procedure. Passing rate of a minority group must then be 50% x 80% = 40% to meet the condition of the 4/5's rule.

FOURTH AMENDMENT -- The Fourth Amendment prohibits unreasonable searches and seizures by the government.

FRAUD -- An intentional, false representation of a matter of fact, whether by words or conduct, by false or misleading allegations, or by concealment of that which should have been disclosed and which deceives or is intended to deceive another.

FRINGE BENEFITS -- Non-wage benefits or payments received by or credited to employees, in addition to wages, which often provide income for time not worked, *i.e.*, vacations, holiday pay, medical insurance, and pensions.

GOOD CAUSE -- Good cause connotes a fair and honest cause or reason, regulated by good faith on the part of the party exercising the power.

GRIEVANCE -- A formal complaint to management usually by an employee regarding work practices. If a grievance cannot be settled at the supervisory level, it is appealed to higher levels of management authority or legal means.

GROUND -- A foundation or basis; points relied on; *e.g.* "ground" for bringing a civil action or charging a criminal defendant, or foundation for admissibility of evidence.

HEARSAY -- Generally a term applied to that species of testimony stated by a witness who relates not what he knows personally but what others have told him or what he has heard said by others.

HEARSAY EVIDENCE -- Testimony in court of a statement made out of court, the statement being offered as an assertion to show the truth of matters asserted and, thus, resting for its value upon the credibility of the out-of-court person originally making the assertion.

I-9 -- A form required to be presented to all new employees in which they prove they legally are entitled to work in the United States.

IMMIGRATION REFORM AND CONTROL ACT -- Legislation prohibiting employers from hiring people not legally entitled to work in the United States.

IMPLIED CONTRACT -- An agreement that is tacit rather than expressed in clear and definite language; an agreement inferred from the conduct of the parties.

IMPRESSION MANAGEMENT -- An attempt to exercise control over selected communicative behaviors and cues for purposes of making a desired impression.

INDEMNIFICATION -- Protection or reimbursement against damage or loss. The indemnified party is protected against liabilities or penalties from the party's actions; the indemnifying party provides the protection or reimbursement.

INDEMNIFY -- To save harmless; to secure against loss or damage; to give security for reimbursement of a person in case of an anticipated loss falling upon him.

INDEPENDENT CONTRACTOR -- A person who contracts with another to do something for him, but who is not controlled by the other nor subject to the other's right to control with respect to his physical conduct in the performance of the undertaking.

INFLICTION OF EMOTIONAL DISTRESS -- A legal cause of action in which a party seeks to recover damages for mental pain and suffering caused by another.

INFORMAL RESOLUTION -- Resolution of a problem or issue without a full formal internal investigation.

INJUNCTION -- A court order restraining a party from doing or refusing to do an act.

INTUITION -- The ability to *know* something without any apparent cognitive processing or even to *know* something without any observable data to rely upon.

INVASION OF PRIVACY -- The unwarranted appropriation or exploitation of another person by publicizing his private affairs, with which the public has no legitimate concern, or wrongful intrusion into his private activities in such a manner as would cause mental suffering, shame, or humiliation to a person of ordinary sensibilities.

INVESTIGATION -- The act or process of systematically investigating or making inquiry for the purpose of ascertaining fact.

JOB -- A specific arrangement of tasks, duties, and responsibilities that must be performed for the organization to achieve its goals.

JOB ANALYSIS -- A systematic process for gathering information about a job.

JOB CLASSIFICATION -- A method of arranging jobs into various categories or classes based on training, experience, or skill.

JOB DESCRIPTION -- Written summaries of the basic tasks, duties, and responsibilities of jobs.

JOB DESIGN -- The arrangement of task contents to satisfy organizational and human requirements.

JOB ENLARGEMENT -- The process of changing the job to allow employees more discretion over their work and increased involvement in planning, decision making, and controlling activities related to the job's tasks.

JOB ENRICHMENT -- The process of changing the job to allow employees more discretion over their work and increased involvement in planning, decision making, and controlling activities related to the job's tasks.

JOB ENVIRONMENT -- Unique job situations (tasks, duties, responsibilities) that require certain skills, rules, knowledge, and attitudes.

JOB EVALUATION -- The process by which the worth of jobs to the organization is assessed relative to all other jobs in the organization.

JOB EXPECTATION TECHNIQUE -- A variation of the team-building process that focuses on clarifying roles, expectations, and responsibilities of managers and subordinates.

JOB INSTRUCTION TRAINING -- A set of coordinated procedures for conducting on-the-job training developed by the War Manpower Commission during World War II.

JOB ROTATION -- The process of having an employee perform several different jobs, moving from one to the other in some prearranged logical sequence over some period of time.

JOB SAFETY ANALYSIS -- A process of identifying job hazards.

JOB SECURITY -- Contract provisions such as the union shop, seniority, and so on, which preserve the union's status and the members' jobs.

JOB SHARING -- A program in which two people share one job.

JOB SPECIALIZATION -- The process of breaking work down into smaller sets of related tasks.

JOB SPECIFICATIONS -- Written summaries of the skills, background, and qualifications necessary for an employee to perform the job in a satisfactory manner.

JOB STANDARDS -- The expected performance for each job duty described in the job description.

JOB UPGRADING -- Reclassifying a job from a lower classification to a higher classification to reflect a change in duties or requirements for performing the job. It is distinguished from promotion in which an employee is moved from a job to a higher classified job.

JOB VALUE -- Values attached to the kind of work one does based on the minimum qualification factors required by the job and minimum effort factors demanded by the job.

JUDGMENT -- A verdict rendered by a judicial body. If money is awarded, the winning party is a "judgment creditor," and the losing party is the "judgment debtor."

JUDGMENTAL ACCURACY -- The extent that a judgment of an attribute is congruent with some criterion measure.

JURISDICTION -- The authority of a court to hear a particular matter.

KINESICS -- Body language including movements of the hand, arm, head, foot, leg, postural shifts, gestures, eye movements, and facial expressions.

KSAs -- KNOWLEDGE, SKILLS, AND ABILITIES -- Determined to be prerequisites for a position as described in the job description and job specifications.

LAYOFF -- A temporary or indefinite separation from work usually due to a change in demand for work. Generally, the employee retains status as employee as opposed to discharge or firing when the worker is permanently separated from the job.

LEAKAGE -- A deception clue that can be seen in micro-facial movements and imperfectly formed simulations of smiles and frowns which are caused by an attempt to control or censor expressions.

LEGAL DUTY -- The responsibility of a party to perform certain acts.

LETTER OF ENFORCEMENT -- An enforceable contract in form of a letter.

LETTER OF PROTEST -- A letter sent to document a party's dissatisfaction.

LIABLE -- Legally responsible for or legally in the wrong.

MAJOR LIFE ACTIVITIES -- ADA defines major life activities as those functions that involve care for one's self, performing manual tasks, walking, seeing, hearing, speaking, breathing, learning, and working.

MALICIOUS INTERFERENCE WITH CONTRACTUAL RIGHTS -- A legal cause of action in which one party seeks to recover damages against another who has induced or caused the party to terminate a valid contract.

MALICIOUS PROSECUTION -- A legal cause of action in which a party seeks to recover damages after another instigates or institutes a frivolous judicial proceeding, usually criminal, which is dismissed.

MASKING SMILES -- Those smiles in which there are muscular traces of disgust, anger, fear, sadness, or contempt thought to be the consequences of lying.

MISAPPROPRIATION -- The unlawful taking of another's personal property.

MISREPRESENTATION -- A legal cause of action which arises when one party makes untrue statements of fact that induce another party to act and be damaged as a result.

MOTIVATION -- The willful desire to direct one's effort (behavior) toward achieving given goals.

NATIONAL INSTITUTE OF OCCUPATIONAL SAFETY AND HEALTH -- A government agency which performs and analyzes measures of workplace safety.

NATIONAL LABOR RELATIONS ACT (NLRA) -- A law created to give employees the protected right to join and form unions and to engage in collective bargaining. The act does not include agricultural laborers, domestic servants, employers' children and spouses, independent contractors, supervisors and managers, government employees, and railroad and airline employees. Legislation concerning labor unions.

NATIONAL LABOR RELATIONS BOARD -- The agency which enforces the labor laws.

NATIONALITY -- The status acquired by belonging to, or being associated with, a nation or state. It arises by birth or naturalization.

NEED TO KNOW -- Employment-related information is held confidential and available to only those with a "need to know."

NEGLIGENCE -- The omission of an action which a reasonable man, guided by ordinary considerations that customarily regulate human affairs, would do; or engaging in an action which a reasonable and prudent man would not do.

NEGLIGENT HIRING -- The failure to exercise reasonable care in the selection of a job applicant in view of the risk created by the position.

NEGLIGENT RETENTION -- This occurs when an employer keeps on the job an unfit employee who later commits a crime involved with the job or even indirectly is related to the employment situation.

NEGLIGENT TERMINATION -- This occurs when an employee is terminated from a position without reasonable care or consideration of law.

NONCOMPETITION CLAUSE -- A restrictive provision in a contract which limits an employee's right to work in that particular industry after she or he ceases to be associated with the present employer.

NOTARY PUBLIC -- A person authorized under state law to administer an oath or verify a signature.

OCCUPATIONAL SAFETY AND HEALTH ACT OF 1970 -- This act created mandatory standards of safety and health such that even the most recalcitrant employer would take steps to protect the health and well-being of its employees.

OFCCP -- OFFICE OF FEDERAL CONTRACT COMPLIANCE PRO-GRAMS -- Audits companies receiving government contracts and grants to determine their compliance to rules.

OPTION -- An agreement giving a party the right to choose a certain course of action.

ORAL CONTRACT -- An enforceable verbal agreement.

ORDER-OF-INTERVIEWS EFFECT -- When the first interview becomes the gauge for the following interviews.

OSHA -- OCCUPATIONAL SAFETY AND HEALTH ADMINISTRATION -- The enforcement agency for the Occupational Safety and Health Act which was created to develop and enforce safety and health standards.

OTETA -- OMNIBUS TRANSPORTATION EMPLOYEE TESTING ACT OF 1991 -- Called for drug and alcohol testing of transportation industry employees in safety-sensitive positions.

OWBPA -- OLDER WORKERS BENEFIT PROTECTION ACT OF 1990 -- leaves only one defense for age-based discrimination in applicable benefit plans -- actuarial cost differences based on age.

PARALANGUAGE -- Content-free vocalization which includes voice pitch, volume, frequency, stuttering, filled pauses, silence, interruptions, and speech rate.

PARTY -- A plaintiff or defendant in a lawsuit.

PAST PRACTICE -- A manner of considering a grievance by viewing past history of how similar issues or conflicts were resolved.

PDA -- PREGNANCY DISCRIMINATION ACT OF 1978 -- Forbids virtually any discrimination based on pregnancy and protects women who seek abortion, covers abortion as a disability if there is potential danger to the mother, and covers as disability medical complications to an otherwise uncovered abortion.

PERFORMANCE APPRAISAL -- The process of measuring the degree to which an employee accomplishes work requirements.

PERJURY -- Committing false testimony while under oath.

PERSONNEL DEPARTMENT -- A division of an organization that coordinates human resource planning, recruitment, and selection, wage and salary administration, training, and labor relations. Activities might also include problem-solving, consultation with operating managers, participation in designing and implementing corporate policy, evaluation and development of mid- and top-level managers, and contribution to the design of organizational structures and objectives.

PERSONNEL MANAGER -- A person who recruits, interviews, and selects employees; provides a channel for communication and counseling for all employees; and tries to create the most effective working ambiance for employees.

PHYSICAL DEPENDENCE -- The feeling that drugs are needed to achieve a feeling of well-being.

PHYSIOGNOMY -- The study of the language of the face.

PLAINTIFF -- The party who initiates or files a lawsuit.

POLYGRAPH PROTECTION ACT OF 1989 -- Prohibits private sector employers from using polygraphs, voice print devices, and other technologies in selecting and testing employees with certain exceptions.

POWER OF ATTORNEY -- A document executed by a party allowing another to act on his or her behalf in specified situations.

PRAGMATICS -- The study of communicational affects of behavior which recognizes that all behavior, including speech, is communication and that all communication, including communicational cues, influences behavior.

PRECEDENT -- A past case that sets the judgment by other courts.

PRIMA FACIE CASE -- Such as will prevail until contradicted and overcome by other evidence. A case which has proceeded upon sufficient proof to that stage where it will support a finding if evidence to the contrary is discarded.

PRIMA FACIE EVIDENCE -- Evidence good and sufficient on its face. Such evidence as in the judgment of the law is sufficient to establish a given fact, or the group or chain of facts constituting the party's claim or defense, and which, if not rebutted or contradicted, will remain sufficient.

PROBABLE CAUSE -- Correct or reasonable belief that the facts on which a claim is based exist, that the claim may be valid under applicable law, or that the advice of counsel was given in good faith and after disclosure of all known relevant facts.

PROXEMICS -- Interpersonal spacing, distance, and territory.

PSYCHOLOGICAL DEPENDENCE -- Marked by a growing tolerance of a drug's effects so that increased amounts of a drug are needed to obtain a desired effect and by the onset of withdrawal symptoms over periods of prolonged abstinence.

PUNITIVE DAMAGES -- Money awarded as punishment for another's wrongful acts.

QUALIFIED PRIVILEGE -- The elements of qualified privilege are: good faith by the defendant; an interest or duty to be upheld; a statement limited in its scope to the purpose; a proper occasion; and publication in a proper manner and to the proper parties only, to those who "need to know."

QUANTUM MERIT -- An equitable principle whereby a court awards reasonable compensation to a party who performs work, labor, or services at another party's request. It also is referred to as "unjust enrichment."

REALISTIC JOB PREVIEW -- A recruitment procedure in which the applicant may observe the performance of the job or actually perform the work.

REASONABLE-MAN DOCTRINE -- The standard which one must observe to avoid liability for negligence is the standard of the "reasonable man" under all circumstances, including the foreseeability of harm to one such as the plaintiff.

REASONABLE-WOMAN STANDARD -- The standard by which conduct may be measured in cases where a female party's gender is relevant, *i.e.*, workplace conduct that constitutes sexual harassment may be determined by reference to whether a "reasonable woman" would be offended.

REFERENCES -- Persons or past employers who may be contacted for an evaluation of an applicant's ability and/or work history. Their use may have more credibility for managerial and professional personnel because the hiring employer may be familiar with the person giving the reference.

RELEVANT INFORMATION -- Information that is acceptable legally and ethically as a basis for judging applicant qualifications.

RETALIATORY DISCHARGE -- An employment termination might be considered retaliatory if it is the result of an employer "punishing" an employee for engaging in a protected activity. These activities might include:

1)   Filing a discrimination charge;
2)   Opposing unlawful employer practices; or

3) Testifying, assisting, or participating in an investigation, proceeding, or litigation against the employer under any of the labor relations, OSHA, workers' compensation, or unemployment compensation acts.

SELF-CRITICAL ANALYSIS PRIVILEGE -- Protects a corporation from having to disclose information gathered in an investigation.

SEVERANCE PAY (DISMISSAL PAY) -- A lump sum paid to an employee who separates from a job due to the elimination of the position or a reduction in workforce.

SEX-PLUS ISSUES -- Issues related to sex discrimination such as asking a female applicant questions about her marriage and children but not asking the same questions to male applicants.

SEXUAL HARASSMENT -- A type of employment discrimination including sexual advances, requests for sexual favors, and other verbal or physical conduct of a sexual nature in the course of employment prohibited by Title VII of the 1964 Civil Rights Act.

SLANDER -- The speaking of base and defamatory words which tend to prejudice another in terms of personal reputation, community standing, office, trade, business, or means of livelihood.

STANDARD OF CARE -- In the law of negligence, that degree of care which a reasonably prudent person should exercise in the same or similar circumstances.

STANDARD OF PROOF -- The burden of proof required in a particular type of case, as in a criminal case where the prosecution has the standard or "proof beyond a reasonable doubt," and in most civil cases where "proof by a fair preponderance of the evidence" is required.

STATUTE -- A law created by a legislative body.

STATUTE OF LIMITATIONS -- The length of time a person has to file a lawsuit. Can range from 30 days to four years, depending on the type of claim.

SUBPOENA -- A written legal document requiring a person or witness to appear at a legal proceeding.

SUMMATION -- The final phase of a trial when both attorneys summarize their respective positions of their clients or case.

SUMMONS -- A written legal document served upon the defendant to provide notification of a lawsuit.

SUPERVISORY ANALYSIS -- A method of job analysis requiring supervisors to record the activities, tasks, duties, and responsibilities of the jobs over which they have authority.

SUPREME COURT -- The highest court in the United States and the highest court in each state (except New York). All state supreme court decisions are precedent and binding on the lower courts in that state and may influence courts in other states. U.S. Supreme Court cases are binding on all courts.

SURVEILLANCE -- A watch kept over a person, group, *etc.*, especially over a suspect, prisoner or the like; supervision or superintendent, care, control management.

TESTIMONY -- An oral presentation of evidence by a witness under oath.

TIME IS OF THE ESSENCE -- A legal term defining the requirements of timeliness.

TITLE VII OF THE U.S. CIVIL RIGHT ACT OF 1964 -- Legislation prohibiting discrimination on the basis of national origin, color, race, sex, and religion.

TORT -- A private or civil wrong or injury, including action for bad faith breach of contract, for which a court will provide a remedy in the form of an action for damages.

TOTAL DISABILITY -- A physical disability that prevents a person from performing all the substantial acts necessary for the person's job or occupation.

TRIAL COURT -- The court of original jurisdiction where all evidence is first received and considered.

TRUTH -- The state or character of being true; fundamental reality; a verified or indisputable fact, accepted fact, truism, or platitude.

UNFAIR DISCHARGE -- Termination of an employee's employment without legal justification.

UNFAIR LABOR PRACTICES -- Behaviors by employers or unions that interfere with employees' rights to engage in collective bargaining.

UNIFORM GUIDELINES -- Published in 1978 by the EEOC to provide guidance to employers on how to comply with the Civil Rights Act in employment decisions.

VERDICT -- A decision by a jury or a judge.

WHISTLE-BLOWER ACTS -- Federal and state statutes designed to protect employees from retaliation for the disclosure of an employer's misconduct.

WITNESS -- A person who testifies at a judicial proceeding or hearing. An employee who testifies about an issue or behavior during an internal, formal workplace investigation.

WORK ENVIRONMENT -- Physical conditions under which employees must work and the general treatment they receive.

WORK SAMPLE -- Performance testing in which an applicant performs a real or simulated portion of work which will be performed on the job.

WORKERS' COMPENSATION -- Monetary compensation paid to an employee for injuries sustained during the course of employment.

APPENDIX B

COMMON ACTS OF EMPLOYEE DEVIANCE

Employee deviance is described as any counterproductive behavior that may cause, either directly or indirectly, loss of resources, assets, profits, goodwill, and/or time to the employing company. Some deviant behaviors are common or possible for any type of occupation. These include, but are not limited to: sexual harassment, drug and alcohol abuse, drug trafficking, and carrying concealed, unlicensed, or unauthorized weapons.

This appendix illustrates the common acts of employee deviance for some notable and highly populated industry groups. A review of the deviant behaviors for these representative groups can assist the human resource practitioner or investigator in assimilating the vulnerabilities and risks inherent for other groups and occupations not listed.

Automobile Servicing/Sales Personnel	
• accepting gratuities • collusion with parts department personnel/factory reps • collusion with regional management • excessive charges • falsifying inspections • falsifying job hours • falsifying warranty work • insurance collusion/fraud • intentional damaging of a customer's property • job falsifying/padding for parts/service time • kickbacks from suppliers	• senior citizen fraud/abuse • substituting lower quality parts and overcharging • switching/theft of customer parts • switching/theft of parts/equipment with parking lot vehicles • theft of company parts/supplies/inventory • theft of employee tools/property • theft of general company property • theft of money/cash payments • theft by not reporting sales from services • theft of parts • theft of tools/equipment

Bank Management Personnel

- altering personal bank records
- conducting personal transactions
- customer discourtesy
- embezzlement of accounts/deposits
- loan collusion
- money laundering
- selling customer lists
- senior citizen abuse/fraud
- theft of overages
- theft of premiums
- theft of teller funds
- unauthorized disclosure of customer data

Bank Security Personnel

- accepting gratuities
- bribery
- customer/employee discourtesy
- excessive force
- inattentive part-time personnel providing security services
- kickbacks from security vendors/suppliers/contract services
- sleeping on job
- theft from teller money pools/drawers
- theft of premiums/property/certificates
- unauthorized access/disclosure of account information

Bank Teller Personnel

- customer discourtesy
- falsification/alteration of personal bank records
- keeping overages
- theft of fellow teller funds
- theft of premiums
- unauthorized disclosure of confidential customer information

Convenience Store Clerk Personnel

- collusion with vendors
- credit card fraud/trafficking
- customer discourtesy
- falsification of advertised sales
- falsifying theft/robbery reports to management/police
- falsifying/altering gas pump/price records
- falsifying time/ work records
- illegal betting/organized gambling
- manipulation/theft of dispensed drinks sales
- not ringing up sales
- overringing sales/overcharging
- sleeping on job
- telephone abuse
- theft of money by falsifying voids/returns
- theft of overages
- theft/shorting of deposits
- unauthorized discounts/privilege abuse
- unauthorized early closings
- unauthorized give-away of merchandise to friends
- unauthorized persons on premises
- underringing sales

Convenience Store Management Personnel

- abuse of complimentary/gratuity policies
- collusion with regional/upper management
- coupon fraud
- credit card fraud
- employee payroll fraud/collusion
- falsifying gas pump/company records
- falsifying receiving records
- gambling/betting/trafficking on premises
- gas pump price manipulation
- not ringing up sales
- overringing sales/overcharging
- selling unauthorized merchandise
- sleeping on job
- theft of charity donations
- theft of deposits
- theft of money by falsifying voids/returns/misrings
- unauthorized discounts/privileges abuse
- unauthorized food consumption
- underringing sales
- vendor kickbacks/fraud

Correctional Guard Personnel

- abuse of authority
- betting/gambling/bookmaking
- bribes/gratuities
- conflicts of interest with inmate personnel
- contraband trafficking
- excessive force
- failure to report incidents/ dereliction of duty
- information trafficking
- permitting inmate misconduct/ illegal activities/abuse
- prescription drugs/medication/ trafficking
- selling communications/cellular phone trafficking
- theft from inmates
- theft of supplies/equipment
- theft/sale of institutional food
- unauthorized granting of privileges

Food/Drink Serving Personnel

- collusion with staff
- customer discourtesy
- falsifying returns
- falsifying time records
- overringing sales
- selling personal merchandise
- theft of bulk merchandise
- theft of supplies/equipment
- theft of tips
- unauthorized consumption
- unauthorized giveaways
- underringing sales

Food Handlers/Cooks/Serving Personnel

- collusion with food purveyors
- collusion with wait staff
- customer discourtesy
- failure/falsifying spoilage records
- gambling
- theft of bulk food
- theft of equipment/supplies
- unauthorized food orders
- unauthorized food consumption

Law Enforcement Personnel

- abuse of authority
- accepting gratuities
- bribery
- business referrals/steering
- conducting personal business on duty
- conflicts of interest
- damage to department vehicles/intentional
- dereliction of duty
- disclosing confidential information for gain
- discourtesy
- discrimination
- drug/alcohol use/abuse
- excessive force
- extortion
- falsifying/manufacturing evidence
- falsifying on-duty injuries
- falsifying reports/records
- falsifying vehicle breakdowns
- gambling/betting/trafficking
- inattention to duty
- kickbacks
- perjury
- sexual harassment
- sexual impropriety
- sleeping on duty
- theft of confiscated property
- theft of crime scene property
- theft of equipment/supplies
- theft of evidence
- unauthorized disclosure of criminal records

Manufacturing Personnel

- collusion with competition
- falsifying injury claims
- falsifying production reports
- falsifying time records
- falsifying workman comp. claims
- family leave bill abuse
- gambling
- gang extortion activity of employees/supervisors/ management/owners
- inattention to detail
- intentional work stoppage/sabotage
- medical benefits abuse
- pranks/horseplay
- prostitution
- safety violations
- racial/ethnic harassment
- reckless acts/behavior
- theft from fellow employees
- theft of products/components
- theft of supplies/equipment and tools
- vandalism

Public Transportation Personnel

- customer discourtesy/abuse
- excessive/false breaks
- failure to make passenger stops
- failure to record fares
- failure to report accidents/vehicle damage
- failure to turn in lost property
- falsifying breakdowns
- falsifying police reports -- robbery/ theft
- falsifying safety records
- gambling/betting/trafficking
- meter tampering
- safety violations/reckless operation
- selling transfers
- senior citizen abuse/theft/fraud
- switching vehicle equipment parts
- theft of fares
- theft of fuel
- theft of parts/equipment/tools
- unauthorized discounts
- unauthorized passengers

Restaurant Management Personnel

- coupon fraud
- falsifying management/police reports
- gambling/betting/bookmaking
- giveaways of merchandise
- kickbacks/gratuities for work assignments
- kickbacks/suppliers/vendors
- overringing sales
- theft of bank deposits/shortages
- unauthorized discounts
- underringing sales

Retail Sales Clerks

- altering/damaging of computer/ accounting systems
- coupon fraud
- customer discourtesy
- damaging merchandise
- discount abuse
- failure to report shoplifting
- falsifying time records
- giveaways of merchandise
- not ringing up sales
- overringing sales
- refund fraud
- shoplifting collusion
- switching price tags
- unauthorized borrowing of merchandise
- unauthorized discounts
- underringing sales

Retail Sales/Management Personnel

- collusion with employees
- discount abuse
- failing to ring up sales
- giveaways of merchandise
- gratuities/kickbacks for preferential work assignments
- gratuities/kickbacks from vendors
- intentional damaging merchandise
- overlooking employee misconduct for *quid pro quo* favors
- overringing sales
- refund fraud
- switching price tags
- time theft/falsifying time records
- unauthorized absences
- unauthorized giveaways of merchandise
- unauthorized markdowns
- unauthorized/misuse of purchasing authority
- unauthorized personal use of merchandise/company property
- underringing sales
- vendor kickbacks

Security Personnel

- bribery/gratuities to permit violations/misconduct
- collusion to commit theft
- concealed/unlicensed/unauthorized weapon
- customer discourtesy
- damage of equipment/intentional
- entering unauthorized areas/desks/lockers
- excessive force
- falsifying reports/reporting systems
- failure to make rounds
- failure to report security violations
- failure to report damage to vehicles/equipment
- failure to turn in found property
- illegal surveillance of employees/customers
- impersonating a police officer
- intimidation of employees
- libel/slander
- manufacturing conditions to justify budget allocation
- manufacturing incident reports
- permitting unauthorized persons on premises
- sexual harassment
- telephone abuse/fraud
- theft from contract/employer premises
- theft of supplies/equipment
- unlawful constraint/false arrest/battery
- unlawful searches/privacy intrusion

Shipping/Receiving Personnel

- collusion with customers
- criminal intelligence collection of customer lists/shipping data
- damaging merchandise/intentional
- falsifying injury claims
- misdirecting shipments intentionally
- shorting shipments
- sleeping
- theft of excess/overloads of merchandise/product
- work slowdowns/stoppages by intentional damaging/sabotage

Supervisory Personnel

- fraudulent time keeping/fraud
- gratuities/kickbacks from vendors
- gratuities/kickbacks for work assignments/time thefts
- overlooking employee misconduct for *quid pro quo* favors
- payroll abuse/fraud

Truck Drivers/Delivery Personnel

- bribing dispatchers for job assignments
- damaging cargo intentionally
- damaging equipment
- damaging vehicle intentionally
- drug/substance use/abuse
- equipment abuse
- falsifying mileage/expenses
- falsifying theft/robbery reports
- falsifying transportation records
- failure to report vehicle damage
- gambling
- reckless conduct/competitive driving/speeding with other drivers
- selling stolen property
- shipper/driver collusion
- theft of cargo from terminal area/docks
- theft of cargo/overloads
- theft of COD's
- transporting contraband
- transporting stolen property
- unauthorized hauling of cargo
- unauthorized occupants/ passengers
- unauthorized passengers
- unauthorized stops/layovers
- unauthorized use of vehicle/ loads/cargo

Vending Route Personnel

- extortion/placement of machines
- failure to report damage to equipment/vehicles
- falsifying break-ins
- falsifying counters/rigging counters
- falsifying money shortages
- falsifying refunds
- falsifying spoilage/tests
- giveaway of merchandise
- personal unauthorized use/ consumption
- supplying with personal merchandise
- theft from competitor vendors
- theft of money overages
- unauthorized passengers
- unauthorized use of keys
- unauthorized use of vehicle

Warehouse/Inventory Personnel

- damaging/falsifying inventory systems
- damaging merchandise intentionally
- gambling/betting/bookmaking
- reckless behavior/pranks/horseplay
- safety violations
- theft by substitution of merchandise
- theft of merchandise by concealment
- vandalism

APPENDIX C

BIBLIOGRAPHY
REFERENCES AND SUGGESTED READING

ACA (1984). *Glossary of compensation terms*, Scottsdale, AZ: The American Compensation Association.

Allen, J. G. (1993). *Complying with ADA: A small business guide to hiring and employing the disabled.* New York, NY: John Wiley & Sons, Inc.

Almquist, E. (1979). *Minorities, gender, and work.* Lexington, MA: Lexington Books.

AMA (1987). Scientific issues in drug testing. *Journal of American Medical Association,* 257(22):3112.

Anderson, S. (1992). Effective policies for prevention and investigation. *HRfocus* (Feb):11.

Arthur, D. (1994). *Workplace testing: An employer's guide to policies and practices.* New York, NY: AMACOM.

Arthur, D. (1991). *Recruiting, interviewing, selecting, & orienting new employees.* New York, NY: AMACOM.

Arvey, R. D., Faley, R. H. (1988). *Fairness in selecting employees.* Reading, MA: Addison-Wesley Publishing Co.

Ash, P. (1991). A history of honesty testing. In J. W. Jones (ed.) *Preemployment honesty testing* (pp. 1-19). New York, NY: Quorum Books.

Ash, P. (1974). Convicted felons' attitudes toward theft. *Criminal Justice and Behavior,* 1:21-29.

Ash, P. (1971). Screening employment applicants for attitudes toward theft. *Journal of Applied Psychology,* 55(2):161-164.

ASPA and ACA (1988). *Elements of sound base pay administration,* 2nd ed., Alexandria, VA: The American Compensation Association and the American Society for Personnel Administration.

Asquith, N., & Feld, D. E. (1995). *Employment testing manual: 1995 cumulative supplement.* Boston, MA: Warren, Gorham & Lamont.

Asquith, N., & Feld, D. E. (1993). *Employment testing manual: 1993 cumulative supplement.* Boston, MA: Warren Gorham Lamont.

Avery, R. D., & Champion, J. E. (1982). The employment interview: A summary and review of recent research. *Personnel Psychology*, 35:281-322.

Avery, R. D., & Foley, R. (1988). *Fairness in selecting employees.* 2nd ed. Reading, MA: Addison-Wesley Publishing Co.

Bagozzi vs. St. Joseph Hospital (1991). Mich. N. W. 2d.

Balinsky, B., & Burger, R. (1959). *The executive interview: A bridge to people.* New York, NY: Harper.

Bailey, F. L. (1988, Oct). *A checklist for private employers and polygraph examiners.* Washington, DC: American Polygraph Association.

Baird, L. S., Schneier, C. E., & Beatty, R. W. (1988). *The strategic human resource management sourcebook.* Amherst, MA: Human Resource Development Press.

Bass, B. M. (1990). From transactional to transformational leadership. *AMA Quarterly Review*, Winter.

Bates, N. D. (1992). *Negligent hiring liability.* Farmingham, MA: Liability Consultants, Inc.

Bates, N. D. (1992). Violence in healthcare: Legal implications. Farmingham, MA: Liability Consultants, Inc.

Bates, N. D. (1988). Reducing liability's toll. *Security Management* (Oct):75-77.

Bates, N. D. (1989). Understanding the liability of negligent hiring. *Security Management* (Special Supplement):7A.

Bates vs. Doria (1986). 502 N.E.2d 454 (Ill. App. 3 Dist.).

Bell, A. H. (1989). *The complete manager's guide to interviewing: How to hire the best.* Homewood, IL: Dow Jones-Irwin.

Bender, M. (1993). *Employment Law Deskbook.* New York, NY: Shave & Rosenthal.

Bernardin, H. J. (1988). Police Officer. In S. Gael's. (ed.) *The job analysis handbook for business, industry, and government* (Vol. 1, pp. 1242-1254). New York, NY: Wiley.

Bernieri, F. J., & Rosenthal, R. (1991). In R. S. Feldman & B. Rime's (eds.) *Fundamentals of nonverbal behavior* (pp. 401-431). Cambridge: Cambridge, MA: University Press.

Birdwhistell, R. L. (1970). *Kinesics and context: Essays on body motion communication.* Philadelphia, PA: University of Pennsylvania Press.

Bishop vs. Okidata Inc. (1994). No. 94-1931 (DC NJ 10/3/94).

BLS (1989). Survey of employer anti-drug programs. January. Bureau of Labor Statistics Washington, DC.

Blank, W. E. (1982). *Handbook for developing competency-based training programs.* Englewood Cliffs, NJ: Prentice-Hall, Inc.

Bond, C. F., Jr., Kahler, K. N., & Paolicelli, L. M. (1980). The miscommunication of deception: An adaptive perspective. *Journal of Experimental Social Psychology*, 21:331-345.

Bond, C. F., Jr., Omar, A., Mahmoud, A., & Bonser, R. N. (1990). Lie detection across cultures. *Journal of Nonverbal Behavior*, 14(3):189-204.

Bond, J. (1994). Domestic violence: A health care crisis. *Planning For Health*, 24(4):6-7.

Branch, J. A. (1988). *Negligent hiring practice manual.* New York, NY: Wiley.

Brinkerhoff, R. O. (1987). *Achieving results from training.* San Francisco, CA: Josey-Bass.

Bromiley, P., & Curley, S. P. (1992). Individual differences in risk taking. In J. F. Yates (ed.) *Risk-taking Behavior.* New York, NY: John Wiley & Sons.

Brown, S. S. (1992). The case of the incompetent employee. *Supervisory Management* (Nov).

Buck, R. W., Baron, R., & Barrette, D. (1982). Temporal organization of spontaneous nonverbal expression: A segmentation analysis. *Journal of Personality and Social Psychology*, 42:506-517.

Buck, R. W., Baron, R., Goodman, N., & Shapiro, B. (1980). Utilization of spontaneous nonverbal expression: A segmentation analysis. *Journal of Personality and Social Psychology*, 39:522-529.

Bureau of Justice Statistics (1992). Drugs, crime and the Justice System: A national report. Washington, DC: U.S. Department of Justice.

Bureau of National Affairs (1988). *Individual employment rights manual*, 35 (515):101-110.

Buros, O. K. (1978). *The eighth mental measurements yearbook.* Highland Park, NJ: Gryphon Press.

Byars, L. L., & Rue, L. W. (1993). *Human resource management,* 4th ed. Homewood, IL: Richard D. Irwin, Inc.

Carrell, M., Kusmets, F., & Elbert, N. (1991). *Personnel: Human resource management,* 4th ed. Columbus, OH: MacMillan Publishing Co.

Campion, M. A., Pursell, E. D., & Brown, B. K. (1988). Structured interviewing: Raising the psychometric properties of the employment interview. *Personnel Psychology*, 41:25-42.

Caple, J. (1991). *The ultimate interview.* New York, NY: Main Street.

Carlson, S. (1993). Workplace violence common. *The Denver Post,* Section I, p. 1.

Caruth, D. L., Mondy, R. W., & Noe, R. M. III. (1990). *Staffing the contemporary organization,* New York, NY: Quorum Books.

Cascio, W. F. (1991). *Applied psychology in personnel management,* 4th ed. Englewood Cliffs, NJ: Prentice-Hall, Inc.

Cascio, W. F. (1989). *Human resource planning employment and placement.* ASPA-BNA Series #2. Washington, DC: The Bureau of National Affairs, Inc.

Cascio, W. F. (1987). *Costing human resources: The financial impact of behavior in organizations,* 2nd ed. Boston, MA: Kent Publishing Co.

Cherrington, D. J. (1991). *Personnel management,* 3rd ed. Needham Heights, MA: Allyn & Bacon

Clarkson, K. W., Miller, R. L., Jentz, G. A., & Cross, F. B. (1992). *West's business law: Text cases, legal and regulatory environment* (5th ed.). St. Paul, MN: West Publishing Co.

Clutterham vs. Coachman Industries, Inc. (1985). 169 Call. App. 3d 1223.

Coath vs. Jones (1980). 419 A.2d 1249 (Pa. Super.).

Cody, M. J., Marston, P. J., & Foster, M. (1984). Deception: Paralinguistic and verbal leakage. In R. N. Bostrom's (Ed). *Communication yearbook 8* (pp. 464-490). Beverly Hills, CA: Sage.

Commerce Clearing House (1991). *Equal employment opportunity manual for managers and supervisors.* 2nd ed. Chicago, IL: CCH, Inc.

Connecticut Telephone and Electric Corporation (1950). 22 Lab Atb.632.

Corker vs. Appalachian Regional Healthcare, Inc. (1989). U.S. District Court, SC. W. Va. 33 ATLA L. Rep. 264.

Corley, R. N., Reed, O. L., & Shedd, P. J. (1990). *The legal environment of business* (8th ed.). New York, NY: McGraw-Hill Publishing Co.

Council on Education in Management. (1994). *How to conduct an internal investigation.* Walnut Creek, CA: Council on Education in Management.

Covey, S. R. (1991). *Principle-centered leadership.* New York, NY: Fireside.

Craig, R. L. (1987). *Training and development handbook -- A guide to human resource development,* 3rd ed. New York, NY: McGraw-Hill Co.

Day, D. V., Silverman, S. B. (1989). Personality and job performance: Evidence of incremental validity. *Personal Psychology,* 41(1), 225-36.

DeAngelis vs. Jamesway Department Store (1985) NJ 501 A.2d 561.

Deerings West Nursing Center, A Division of Hillhaven Corporation vs. Scott (1990). The Texas Court of Appeals, 787 S. W. 2d 494 (Tex. app. El Paso 1990).

Deming, J. (1991 July). Rescuing workers in violent families. *HR Magazine,* p. 46.

Dessler, Gary. *Personnel/human resource management,* 5th ed. Englewood Cliffs, NJ: Prentice-Hall, Inc.

deTurck, M. A., & Miller, G. R. (1985). Deception and arousal: Isolating the behavioral correlates of deception. *Human Communications Research,* 12:181-201.

Devereux, E. C., Jr. (1968). Gambling. *International Encyclopedia of Social Sciences,* 6:53-62.

Dipboye, R. L. (1991). *Selection interviews: Process perspectives.* Cincinnati, OH: South-Western Publishing Co.

Dipboye, R. L. (1982). Self-fulfilling prophecies in the selection recruitment interview. *Academy of Management Review,* 7:579-587.

Dipboye, R. L., & Macan, T. (1988). A process view of the selection/recruitment interviews. In R. S. Schuller, S. A. Youngblood, & V. L. Huber (eds.) *Readings in personnel and human resource management* (pp. 217-232). St. Paul, MN: West Publishing.

Dittman, A. T. (1971). The role of body movement in communication. In A. W. Siegman & S. Feldstein's (eds.) *Nonverbal behavior and communication* (2nd ed.) (pp. 37064). Hillsdale, NJ: Lawrence Eribaum Associates.

Dothard vs. Rawlinson -- U.S. Supreme Court (1977). 433 U.S. 321, 97 S. CT. 2720, 53 L Ed. 2d 786.

Douglas, J. E., Feld, D. E., & Asquith, N. (1989). *Employment Testing Manual.* Boston, MA: Warren, Gorham & Lamont, Inc.

Downs, C. W., Smeyak, G. P., & Martin, E. (1980). *Professional interviewing.* New York, NY: Harper & Row.

Drake, J. D. (1982). *Interviewing for managers: A complete guide to employment interviewing,* New York, NY: AMACOM.

Draper vs. U.S. Pipe and Foundry Co. (1992). 6th Cir. F.2d.

Druckman, D., Rozelle, R. M., & Baxter, J. C. (1982). *Nonverbal communication: Survey, theory, and research.* Beverly Hills, CA: Sage.

DuBois, P. H. (1970). *A history of psychological testing.* Boston, MA: Allyn and Bacon.

Dubrin, A. J. (1988). *Human Relations: A job oriented approach.* Englewood Cliffs, NJ: Prentice Hall.

Dyer, L. (1988). *Human resource management: Evolving roles and responsibilities.* ASPA-BNA Series #1. Washington, DC: The Bureau of National Affairs, Inc.

EBRI Staff (1990). *Fundamentals of employee benefit programs,* 4th ed., Washington, DC: Employee Benefit Research Institute.

EEOC vs. Atlas Paper Box Co. (1989). 6th Cir. 868 F.2d 1487.

Ekman, P. (1985). *Telling lies: Clues to deceit in the marketplace, marriage, and politics.* New York, NY: Norton.

Ekman, P. (1973). Universals and cultural differences in facial expressions of emotion. In J. Cole (ed.) *Nebraska Symposium on Motivation.* (pp. 207-283) Lincoln, NE: University of Nebraska Press.

Ekman, P. (1972). *Emotion in the human face.* Cambridge, MA: Cambridge University Press.

Ekman, P., Friesen, W. V., & Scherer, K. R. (1976). Body movement and pitch in deceptive interaction. *Semiotica,* (16):23-37.

Exline, R. V. (1974). Visual interaction: The glances of power and preference. In S. Weitz (ed.) *Nonverbal communication* (pp. 65-92). New York, NY: Oxford Press.

Falcone, P. (1994). Holistic questions measure the 'whole' candidate. *HRfocus,* (Mar):13.

Fallon vs. Indian Trail School (1986). 500 N.E.2d 101 (Ill. App. 2 Dist.).

Fear, R. A. (1984). *The Evaluation Interview* (3rd ed.). New York, NY: McGraw-Hill Book Co.

Fear, R. A., & Chiron, R. J. (1990). *The evaluation interview* (4th ed.). New York, NY: McGraw Hill Publishing Co.

Fernandez, J. P. (1991). *Managing a diverse work force: Regaining the competitive edge.* Lexington, MA: Lexington Books.

Fernandez, J. P., & Bassman, E. (1988). *Looking beyond tomorrow; Strategic issues.* Basking Ridge, NJ: AT&T.

Festinger, L. (1957). *A theory of cognitive dissonance.* Evanston, IL: Row, Peterson.

Fine, S. A. (1988). Human service worker. In S. Gael's. (ed.) *The job analysis handbook for business, industry, and government* (Vol. I. pp. 1163-1180). New York, NY: Wiley.

Fischhoff, B. (1992). Risk taking: A developmental perspective. In J. F. Yates (ed.) *Risk-taking behavior* (pp. 133-162). New York, NY: John Wiley & Sons, Ltd.

Fitz-Enz, J. (1984). *How to measure human resource management.* New York, NY: McGraw-Hill Book Co.

Fitz-Enz J. (1990). *Human value management.* San Francisco, CA: Jossey-Bass, Inc.

Focke vs. United States (1982). 597 F. Supp. 1325.

Freedman, R. D. (1992). Back to the basics of interviewing. *HRfocus* (Jan).

Freedman, W. (1994). *Internal company investigations and the employment relationship.* Westport, CT. Quorum Books.

Frierson, J. G. (1992). *Employer's guide to the Americans with Disabilities Act.* Washington, DC: The Bureau of National Affairs, Inc.

Friesen, W. V. (1972). Cultural differences in facial expression in a social situations: An experimental test on the concept of display rules. Unpublished doctoral dissertation. San Francisco, CA: University of California.

Garod, J. J. (1983). Master's liability for the torts of his servant. *The Florida Bar Journal* (Nov):597-600.

Garrett, A. (1982). *Interviewing: Its principles and methods.* Milwaukee, WI: Family Service America.

Gatewood, R. D., & Field, H. S. (1990) *Human resource selection,* 2nd ed. Chicago, IL: The Dryden Press.

Giles vs. Shell Oil (1985). 487 A.2d 610 (D.C. App.).

Goodale, J. G. (1994). *One to One: Interviewing, selecting, appraising, and counseling employees.* Englewood Cliffs, NJ: Prentice Hall.

Goodale, J. G. (1982). *The fine art of interviewing.* Englewood Cliffs, NJ: Prentice-Hall, Inc.

Goldberg, A. C. (1992). What you can and cannot ask. *HRfocus* (July).

Gomez-Mejia, L. R. (1989). *Compensation and benefits,* (ASPA-BNA Series #3), Washington, DC: The Bureau of National Affairs, Inc.

Green, P. C. (1983). *Behavioral interviewing.* Memphis, TN: Behavioral Technology, Inc. (Brochure).

Green, R. M., Reibstein, R. J. (1992). *Employer's guide to workplace torts.* Washington, DC: Bureau of National Affairs, Inc.

Green, R. M., & Reibstein, R. J. (1988). *Negligent hiring: Fraud, defamation, and other emerging areas of concern.* Washington, DC: Bureau of National Affairs. Special Report.

Gregory, D. L. (1988). Reducing the risk of negligence in hiring. *Employee Relations Law Journal,* 14, 31-40.

Griggs vs. Duke Power Co. (1971). 401 U.S. 88.

Gutman, A. (1993). *EEO law and personnel practices.* Newbury Park, CA: Sage.

Haerle, C. M. (1984). Negligent hiring liability. *Minnesota Law Review,* 68(4):1303-1327.

Hahn, J. M., & Smith, K. M. (1990). Wrongful discharge: The search for a legislative compromise. *Employee Relations Law Journal* 15(4):515-540.

Hale, J. L., & Stiff, J. B. (1990). Nonverbal primacy in veracity judgments. *Communication Reports,* 3:75-83.

Half, R. (1986). *Robert Half On Hiring.* New York, NY: New American Library.

Hanson, C. (1994). Internal surveillance. *Minneapolis Star Tribune,* June 1:2D.

Hanson, G. (1991). To catch a thief: The legal and policy implications of honesty testing in the workplace. *9 Minn Law Review,* 497-398.

Hart & Houck (1992). Skeletons in the corporate closet. *Business Law Today* (May/June):4.

Hawks, R. L., & Chiang, C. N. (1986). *Urine testing for drugs of abuse.* NIDA Research Monograph, 73.

Henderson, R. L. (1994). *Compensation management: Rewarding performance,* 6th ed. Reston, VA: Reston Publishing, Co., Inc.

Hill, M. F., Jr., & Wright, J. A. (1993). *Employee lifestyle and off-duty conduct regulation.* Washington, DC: BNA Books.

Hills, F. S. (1987). *Compensation decision-making,* Chicago, IL: The Dryden Press.

Hocking, J. E., & Leathers, D. G. (1980). Nonverbal indicators of deception: A new theoretical perspective. *Communication Monographs,* 47:119-131.

Hodson vs. First Federal Savings and Loan Assoc. (1975). 455 F.2nd 818, 5th Circuit.

Hoffman, D. (1994). American Pie. *Learning 94,* (Feb.) Springhouse, PA: Springhouse Corporation.

Hollinger, R. C. (1989). *Dishonesty in the workplace: A manager's guide to preventing employee theft.* Park Ridge, IL: London House Press.

Hollinger, R. C., & Clark, J. P. (1983). Deterrence in the workplace: Perceived severity, perceived certainty, and employee theft. *Social Forces,* 62:398-418.

Hollinger, R. C., & Clark, J. P. (1982). Formal and informal social controls of employee deviance. *The Sociological Quarterly,* 23:333-343.

Hollinger, R. C., & Clark, J. P. (1982b). Employee deviance: A response to the perceived quality of the work experience. *Work and Occupations,* 9:97-114.

Hollinger, R. C., Dabney, D., & Gluck, L. (1993). *1993 National Retail Security Survey: Final report.* Gainesville, FL: University of Florida.

Howe, R. (1991). Minding your own business: Employer liability of invasion of privacy. *7 Lab. Lawyer* 315: 387-388.

HR NEWS (1995). Supervisors may be liable under the ADA. *HR News* (Jan):12.

Hughes, G. L., & Prien, E. P. (1989). Evaluation of task and job skill linkage judgments used to develop test specifications. *Personnel Psychology,* 42(2):283-292.

Hunter, J. E., & Hunter R. F. (1984). Validity and utility of alternative predictors of job performance. *Psychological Bulletin,* 96(1):72-98.

Husband, J. M., & McCorrison, A. (1990). *Privacy: The manager's guide to minimizing exposure to violations of employee's right to privacy.* Walnut Creek, CA: Borgman Associates.

Inbau, F. E., Reid, J. E., & Buckley, J. P. (1986). *Criminal interrogation and confessions* (3rd ed.). Baltimore, MD: Williams & Wilkins.

Ingber, C. J. (1993). A duty to protect. *Security Management,* (Dec):63-67.

Ivancevich, J. M., & Glueck, W. F. (1989). *Foundations of personnel,* 4th ed. Homewood, IL: Richard D. Irwin, Inc.

Jacron Sales Co. vs. Sindorf (1976). Maryland App. 350 A.2d 688.

Janz, T. (1982). Initial comparisons of patterned behavior description interviews versus unstructured interviews. *Journal of Applied Psychology,* 67:577-580.

Janz, T., Hellervik, L., & Gilmore, D. C. (1986). *Behavior description interviewing: New, accurate, cost-effective.* Boston, MA: Allyn and Bacon.

Jaspan, N. (1974). *Mind your own business.* Englewood Cliffs, NJ: Prentice Hall.

Jayne, B. C. (1993). Interviewing strategies that defeat deceit. *Security Management* (Dec):37-42.

Johnson, M. A., & Kaupins, G. (1993). Lies, damn lies and the selection interview: Don't take them lies lying down. *Industrial Management*, 35(3):23-24.

Jones, J. W., Arnold, D., & Harris, W. G. (1990). Introduction to the model guidelines for preemployment integrity testing. *Journal of Business and Psychology*, 4(4):525-532.

Jones, J. W., Ash, P., & Soto, C. (1990). Employment privacy rights and pre-employment honesty tests. *Employee Relations Law Journal*, 15(4):561-576.

Jones, J.W., & Joy, D. S. (1991). Empirical investigation of job applicants' reactions to taking a preemployment honesty test. In J. W. Jones (ed.) *Preemployment honesty testing* (pp. 121-131), New York, NY: Quorum.

Jones, J. W., & Terris, W. (1991a). Selection alternatives to the preemployment polygraph. In J. W. Jones (ed.) *Preemployment honesty testing* (pp. 39-52). New York, NY: Quorum.

Jones, J. W., & Terris, W. (1991b). Integrity testing for personnel selection: An overview. *Forensic Reports*, 4:117-140.

Jones, T. L. (1993). *The Americans with Disabilities Act: A review of best practices.* New York, NY: The American Management Association.

Jossem, J. H. (1991). Investigating sexual harassment complaints. *Personnel*, 68(7):9-10.

Kauffman, N. (1992). The 1-2-3s of interviewing in today's economy. *Supervisory Management* (Nov).

Kaul, P. A. (1992). Prepare for the best interview you've ever conducted. *Association Management*, (Nov):27-31.

Kearsley, G. (1984). *Training and technology.* Reading, MA: Addison-Wesley Publishing Co.

Kestenbaum vs. Pennzoil Co. (1988). New Mexico Supreme Court 706 P. 2d 280.

King, D. (1992). *Get the facts on anyone.* New York, NY: Prentice Hall.

Knapp, M. L., Hart, R. P., & Dennis, H. S. (1974). An exploration of deception as a communication construct. *Human Communication Research*, 1:15-29.

Knowles, M. (1990). *The adult learner: A neglected species*, 4th ed. Houston, TX: Gulf Publishing Co.

Kotter, J. P. (1990). *A force for change.* New York NY: The Free Press.

Kouzes, J. M., & Posner, B. Z. (1987). *The leadership challenge.* San Francisco, CA: Jossey-Bass, Inc.

Kraut, R. (1978). Verbal and nonverbal cues in the perception of lying. *Journal of Personality and Social Psychology*, 36:380-391.

Kuhn, R. A. (1991). How to hire and keep quality employees. In N. H. Snyder, O. A. Broome, Jr., W. J. Kohoe, J. T. McIntyre, & K. E., Blair (eds.) *Reducing employee theft: A guide to financial and organizational controls.* New York, NY: Quorum Books.

Laird, D. (1985). *Approaches to training and development,* 2nd ed. Reading, MA: Addison-Wesley Publishing Co.

Landy, F. J. (1989). *Psychology of work behavior.* Pacific Grove, CA: Brooks-Cole.

Latham, G. P., & Saari, L. M. (1984). Do people do what they say? Further studies on the situational interview. *Journal of Applied Psychology*, 69:569-573.

Latham, G. P., Saari, L. M., Pursell, E. D., & Campion, M. A. (1980). The situational interview. *Journal of Applied Psychology*, 65:422-427.

Lawler, E. E., III (1981). *Pay and organizational development*, Reading, MA: Addison-Wesley Publishing Co.

Lear Siegler, Inc. vs. Stegall. (1987). 360 S.E.2d 619, 184 Ga. App. 27.

Leathers, D. G. (1992). *Successful nonverbal communication: Principles and applications* (2nd ed.). New York, NY: Macmillan Publishing Co.

Ledvinka, J. (1991). *Federal regulation of personnel and human resource management.* 2nd ed. Boston, MA: Kent Publishing Co.

Lenneberg, E. H. (1967). *Biological foundation of language.* New York, NY: Wiley.

Levin-Epstein, M. D. (1984). *Primers of equal employment opportunity.* Washington, DC: The Bureau of National Affairs.

Lindo, D. K. (1993). Are you asking for a lawsuit. *Supervision* (Dec):17-19.

Link, F. C., & Foster, D. G. (1980). *The kinesic interview technique.* Anniston, AL: The Interrotec Press.

Lipman, M. (1973). *Stealing: How America's employees are stealing their companies blind.* New York, NY: Harper's Magazine Press.

London House (1975). *The Personnel Selection Inventory.* Park Ridge, IL: London House.

London House (1988). *Human Resource Inventory.* Park Ridge, IL: London House.

LoPresto, R. L., Mitcham, D. E., Ripley, D. E., Humpelett, P. Collyer, R. M., & Eastus, V. I. (1993). *Reference checking Handbook.* Alexandria, VA: Society for Human Resource Management.

MacHovec, F. J. (1989). *Interview and interrogation.* Springfield, IL: Charles C. Thomas.

Malorney vs. B&L Motor Freight, Inc. (1986). 496 N.E.2d 1086, 146 Ill. App.ed 265.

Mangione, T. W., & Quinn, R. P. (1975). Job satisfaction, counterproductive behavior, and drug use at work. *Journal of Applied Psychology*, 1:114-116.

Manhardt, P. J. (1989). Base rates and tests of deception: Has I/O psychology shot itself in the foot? *The Industrial and Organizational Psychologist*, 26(2):48-50.

Mansfield vs.Susman Refrigerator Co. (1997). 68 LA 565, 569.

Marderosian, G. (1985). Tort law -- Employer liable for negligent hiring after cursory investigation of a prospective employee. *Suffolk University Law Review*, 19:371-378.

Mars, G. (1982). *Cheats at work: An anthropology of workplace crime.* London: George Allen & Unwin.

Martin, D. C., & Bartol, K.M. (1987). Potential libel and slander issues involving discharged employees, *Employee Relations Law Journal*, 13(1):43-60.

Martin vs. Texaco Refining & Marketing Inc. (1991) Cal. App. Dept. Super Ct.

Matarazzo, J. D., & Wiens, A. N. (1972). *The interview research on its anatomy and structure.* Chicago, IL: Aldine-Atherton.

Mathis, R. L., & Jackson, J. H. (1994). *Human resource management.* 7th ed. St. Paul, MN: West Publishing Co.

McCaffery, R. M. (1992). *Employee benefit programs: A total compensation perspective,* 2nd ed. Boston, MA: PWS Kent Publishing Co.

McDaniel, M. A. (1988, April). Employment interviews: Structure, validity, and unanswered questions. Paper presented at the Third Annual Convention of the Society for Industrial and Organizational Psychology.

McDaniel, M. A. , Schmidt, F. L., & Hunter, J. E. (1988). A meta-analysis of the validity of methods for training and experience in personnel selection. *Personnel Psychology,* 41:238-313.

McLean, J. W., & Weitzel, W. W. (1991). *Leadership: Magic, myth, or method?* New York, NY: AMACOM.

Mehrabian, A. (1972). *Nonverbal communication.* Chicago, IL: Aldine Atherton.

Mehrabian, A. (1971). Nonverbal betrayal of feelings. *Journal of Experimental Research in Personality,* 5:64-75.

Mercer, M. W. (1993). *Hire the best and avoid the rest.* New York, NY: AMACOM

Mercer, M. W. (1991). *Abilities and Behavior Forecaster Tests.* Chicago, IL: Mercer Systems, Inc.

Miller, G. R., & Stiff, J. B. (1993). *Deceptive communication.* Newbury Park, CA: Sage.

Milkovich, G. T., & Boudreau, J. W. (1993). *Personnel: Human resource management,* 7th ed. Homewood, IL: Richard D. Irwin, Inc.

Minum, M. (1988). Employer liability under the doctrine of negligent hiring: Suggested methods for avoiding the hiring of dangerous employees. *Delaware Journal of Corporate Law,* 13(2):501-532.

Mitchell, G. (1992). *The trainer's handbook: The AMA guide to effective training.* New York, NY: American Management Association.

Mitchell, J. V., Jr. (ed.) (1985). *The ninth mental measurements yearbook.* Lincoln, NE: Buros Institute of Mental Measurements.

Mondy, R. W., & Noe, R. M. III (1990). *Personnel: The management of human resources,* 4th ed. Needhan Heights, MA: Allyn & Bacon.

Moore vs. St. Joseph Nursing Home, Inc. (1990). Michigan Appellate Court 459 N. W. 2d 100 (Mich. App. 1990).

Morrall, (1987). Knowing the law offers the best defense. *108 Savings Institutions,* 80:84.

Morris, D. (1985). *Bodywatching.* New York, NY: Crown Publishers, Inc.

Muchinsky, P. M. (1987). The use of reference reports in personnel selection: A review and evaluation. *Journal of Occupational Psychology,* 52:287-297.

Mullaney, C. P. (1989 June). Torts in the courtroom: Defamation, emotional. *Trial,* 40-45.

Mulvey vs. State of Connecticut (1991). N. W. 2d.

Munsterberg, H. (1913). *Psychology in industrial efficiency.* Boston, MA: Houghton Mifflin.

Murphy, K. R. (1987). Detecting infrequent deception. *Journal of Applied Psychology,* 72(4):611-614.

Murphy, K. R. (1989). Maybe we should shoot ourselves in the foot: Reply to Manhardt. *The Industrial-Organizational Psychologist,* 26(3):45-46.

Nadler, L., & Wiggs, G. D. (1986). *Managing human resource development.* San Francisco, CA: Jossey-Bass, Inc.

National Law Journal (1991). Nov. 25:15

National Treasury employees Union vs. Von Raab. U.S. Supreme Court (1989). 109 S. Ct. 1384.

Newport News Shipbuilding and Dry Dock Company vs. EEOC, U.S. Supreme Court (1983). 462 U.S. 669, 103 S.Ct. 2622, 77 L Ed. 2d 89.

O'Bannon, R. M., Goldinger, L. A., & Appleby, G. S. (1989). *Honesty and integrity testing: A practical guide.* Atlanta: Applied information Resources.

O'Greene, J., O'Hair, D. H., Cody, M. J., & Yen, C. (1985). Planning and control of behavior during deception. *Human Communication Research,* 11(3):335-364.

O'Hair, H. D., Cody, M. J., & McLaughlin, M. L. (1981). Prepared lies, spontaneous lies, Machiavellianism and nonverbal communication. *Human Communication Research,* 7:325-339.

Odiome, G. S., & Rumlet, G. A. (1988). *Training and development: A guide for professionals.* Chicago, IL: Commerce Clearing House.

Ofsanko, F. J., & Napier, N. K. (1990). *Effective human resource techniques: A handbook of investigators.* Alexandria, VA: Society for Human Resource Management.

Orpen (1985). Patterned behavior description interviews versus unstructured interviews: A comparative validity study. *Journal of Applied Psychology,* 70:747-776.

O'Toole, C. B. (1994). Workplace Investigations. Minneapolis, MN: Norwest Center.

Ouellette, R. W. (1992). Preventing violence through nonverbal communication. *Hotel/Motel Security and Safety Management* (May): pp. 5-8.

Parliman, G. C. (1990). Proposed congressional limitations upon the use of unsupervised waivers of ADEA claims. *Employee Relations Law Journal,* 15(4):541-550.

Pillar, C. (1993). Special reports on electronic privacy: Bosses with x-ray eyes, *Macworld,* (July):118-120.

Pimentel, R., Bissonnette, D., & Litito, M. J. (1992). *Employee benefit planning,* 2nd ed. Englewood Cliffs, NJ: Prentice Hall.

Ponticas vs. K.M.S. Investments (1983). 331 N.W.2d 907.

Porter, M. E. (1985). Competitive advantage. New York, NY: The Free Press.

Prentice, R. A., Winslett, B. J. (1987). Employee references: Will a "no comment" policy protect employers against liability for defamation? *American Business Law Journal,* 25:207-239.

Pruitt vs. Pavelin (1984). 685 P.2d 1347 (Ariz. App.).

Rafilson, F. M. (1991). Development of a standardized measure to predict employee productivity. In J. W. Jones (ed.) *Preemployment honesty testing* (pp. 146-158). New York, NY: Quorum Books.

Redeker, J. R. (1989). *Employee discipline: Policies and practices.* Washington, DC: The Bureau of National Affairs, Inc.

Reilly, R. R., & Chao, G. T. (1982). Validity and fairness of some alternative employee selection procedures. *Personnel Psychology*, 35(1):1-62.

Reuter (1993, Sept). Violence in workplace costs business billions. *The Reuter Business Report*.

Reynolds Metal Co. vs. Mays (1989). Alabama Sup. Ct. 547 So. 2d 518, 5 IER 1820.

Rice, J. D. (1978). Privacy legislation: Its effect on pre-employment reference checking. *Personnel Administrator*, 40:46-51.

Risser, R. (1993). *Stay out of court: The manager's guide to preventing employee lawsuits.* Englewood Cliffs, NJ: Prentice Hall.

Rose, R. C. (1992) Guerrilla interviewing. *Inc.* (Dec):145-147.

Rosenbloom, J. S., & Hallman, G. V. (1986). *Employee benefit planning,* 2nd ed. Englewood Cliffs, NJ: Prentice Hall.

Rulon-Miller vs. IBM (1984). 1st Dist. Ct. App. 208 Cal. Rptr. 524.

Ryan, A. M., Lasek, M. (1991). Negligent hiring and defamation: Areas of liability related to pre-employment inquiries. *Personnel Psychology*, 44(2):293-319.

Ryan, A. M., & Sackett, P. R. (1987). A survey of individual assessment practices by I/O psychologists. *Personnel psychology*, 40(3):455-488.

Rynes, S., Gerhart, B. (1990). Interviewer assessments of applicant "fit": An exploratory investigation. *Personnel Psychology*, 43(1):221-245.

Sack, S. M. (1993). *The hiring & firing book: A complete legal guide for employers.* Merrick, NY: Legal Strategies, Inc.

Sack, S. M. (1993). Fifteen steps to protecting against the risk of negligent hiring claims. *Employment Relations Today*, 20(3):313-320.

Sackett, P. R., Burris, L. & Callahan, C. (1989). Integrity testing for personnel selection: An update. *Personnel Psychology*, 42:491-529.

Sackett, P. R., & Harris, M. M. (1985). Honesty testing for personnel selection: A review and critique. In H. J. Bernardin & D. A. Bownas (eds.) *Personality assessment in organizations.* New York, NY: Praeger.

Sapir, A. (1993). The L.S.I. Course on Scientific Content Analysis (SCAN). Phoenix, AZ: L.S.I. (Brochure).

Schein, E. H. (1992). *Organizational culture and leadership,* 2nd ed. San Francisco, CA: Jossey-Bass, Inc.

Schlei, B. L., & Grossman, P. (1983). *Employment Discrimination Law,* 2nd ed. Washington, DC: The Bureau of National Affairs, Inc.

Schmitt, M. J. (1980). Employer owes a duty to the general public to use reasonable care in hiring and retaining employees: Evans vs. Morsell. *Baltimore Law Review*, 9, 435-452.

Schmitt, N. (1976). Social and situational determinants of interview decisions: Implications for the employment interview. *Personnel Psychology*, 29:79-101.

Schmitt, N., & Borman, W. C. (1992). *Personnel selection in organizations.* San Francisco, CA: Jossey-Bass, Inc.

Schneier, C. E., Beatty, R. W., & Baird, L. S. (1987). *The performance management sourcebook.* Amherst, MA: Human Resource Development Press.

School Board of Nassau County, Florida, vs. Arline, U.S. Supreme Court (1987). 107 S.Ct. 1123.

Schuler, R. S. (1990). *Managing human resources in the information age.* SHRM-BNA Series #6. Washington, DC: The Bureau of National Affairs, Inc.

Schuler, R. S., Beutell, N. J., & Youngblood, S. A. (1989). *Effective personnel management,* 3rd ed. St. Paul, MN: West Publishing Co.

Scott, W. D. (1916). Selection of employees by means of quantitative determinations. *Annuals of the American Academy of Political and Social Sciences,* 65:182-193.

Shepard, I. M., Dustin, R. L., & Russell, K. S. (1989). *Workplace privacy: Employee testing, surveillance, wrongful discharge, and other areas of vulnerability.* Washington, DC: The Bureau of National Affairs, Inc.

Sherman, A. W., Jr., & Bohlander, G. W. (1991). *Managing human resources.* 9th ed. Cincinnati, OH: South-Western Publishing Co.

SHRM Learning System: (1994). Selection and Placement; Training and Development; Compensation and Benefits; Employee and Labor Relations; Health, Safety, and Security; International Human Resource Management. Minneapolis, MN: Golle & Holmes Custom Education.

Silver, M. (1987 May). Negligent hiring claims take off. *ABA Journal,* 72-78.

Singer Shop-Rite vs. Rangel (1980). 174 N.J. Super. 442, 416 A 2d 965 (App. Div.), cert denied, 85 N.J. 148, 425 A 2d 299.

Skinner vs. Railway Labor Executives Association, U.S. Supreme Court (1989). 109 S.Ct 1402.

Slowik, D. W. (1995). *Universal interviewing and communications: A preemployment application.* Evergreen, CO: Evergreen Press.

Slowik, D. W. (1993). *Crimes against the elderly.* Evergreen, CO: Evergreen Press.

Smart, B. D. (1989). *The smart interviewer: Tools and techniques for hiring the best.* New York, NY: John Wiley & Sons.

Snyder, N. H., Broome, O. W. Jr., Kehoe, W. J., McIntyre, J. T., & Blair, K. E. (1991). *Reducing employee theft: A guide to financial and organizational controls.* New York, NY: Quorum Books.

Society for Human Resource Management (1994). *Conducting an effective internal investigation.* Alexandria, VA: Society for Human Resource Management.

Society for Industrial and Organizational Psychology, Inc. (1987). *Principles for the validation and use of personnel selection procedures* (3rd ed.). College Park, MD.

Spain & Spain (1989). *The Spain Report,* A-1-32. Pittsburgh, PA: Spain & Spain, Inc.

Spense, W. R. (1991). *Substance abuse definition guide.* Waco, TX: Health Edco.

Stiff, J. B., & Miller, G. R. (1986). "Come to think of it...": Interrogative probes, deceptive communication, and deception detection. *Human Communication Research,* 12:339-357.

Stuart, P. (1992 Feb). Murder on the job. *Personnel Journal.*

Supervisory Management (1990). Negligent hiring costs companies. *Supervisory Management* (May):2.

Swan, W. (1989). *Swan's how to pick the right people program.* New York, NY: John Wiley & Sons, Inc.

Terry, C. C. (1984). *Dictionary of the principles of misconduct in the workplace.* Chicago, IL: DeAclen-Terry Publishing Co.

Texas Department of Community Affairs vs. Burdine, U.S. Supreme Court (1981). 450 U.S. 248, 101 S.Ct. 1089, 67 L Ed. 2d 207.

Tranor, M. (1994). Computer privacy issues unresolved, *Natl. Law Journal* S2(Jan).

Tung, R. (1987). *The New Expatriate: Managing human resources abroad.* Cambridge, MA: Ballenger Publisher.

Turner, R. (1988). Compelled self-publication: How discharge begets defamation. *Employee Relations Law Journal*, 14:19-29.

Uniform Guidelines on Employee Selection Procedures (1978). *Federal Register*, Aug. 15, Part IV, 38295-38309.

Ulrich, L., & Trumbo, D. (1965). The selection interview since 1949. *Psychological Bulletin*, 63:100-116.

Vigneau, J. D. (1995). To catch a thief...and other workplace investigations. *HR Magazine* (Jan):90-95.

Wagemarr, W. A. (1992). Risk taking and accident causation. In J. F. Yates (ed.) *Risk-taking behavior* (pp. 257-281). New York, NY: John Wiley & Sons, Ltd.

Wagner, H., & Pease, K. (1976). The verbal communication of inconsistency between attitudes held and attitudes expressed. *Journal of Personality*, 44:1-16.

Wagner, R. (1949). The employment interview: A critical summary. *Personnel Psychology*, 2:17-46.

Wainauskis vs. Howard Johnson Co (1985). Pa. Super. Ct. 488 A.2d 1117.

Wais, M. F. (1990). Negligent hiring. *The Wayne Law Review*, 37 (Fall):237-263.

Walker, J. W. (1980). *Human resources planning.* New York, NY: McGraw-Hill Book Co.

Wall Street Journal (1993). Dec. 16:B6

Warren, Gorham & Lamont. (1994). *Policies and practices.*

Waterman, C. A., & Maginn, T. A. (1993). Investigating suspect employees. *HR Magazine* (Jan):85-87.

Watzlawick, P., Helmick, J., & Jackson, D. D. (1967). *Pragmatics of human communication: A study of interactional patterns, pathologies, and paradoxes.* New York, NY: W. W. Norton & Company, Inc.

Webster, E. C. (1964). *Decision making in the employment interview.* Quebec: Eagle Publishing Co., Ltd.

Weisner, W. H., & Cronshaw, S. F. (1988). The moderating impact of interview format and degree of structure on interview validity. *The Journal of Occupational Psychology*, 61:275-290.

Wendover, R. W. (1993). *Smart hiring for your business.* Naperville, IL: Sourcebooks, Inc.

Wendover, R. W. (1989). *Smart hiring: The complete guide for recruiting employees.* Englewood, CO: The National Management Staff, Inc.

Wernimont, P. F. (1988). Recruitment, selection, and placement. In S. Gael (ed.) *The job analysis handbook for business, industry, and government* (Vol. I, pp. 193-204). New York, NY: Wiley.

Wexley, K. N. (1990). *Developing human resources.* SHRM-BNA Series #5. Washington, DC: The Bureau of National Affairs.

Wilson, C. (1988, December). New developments in selection interviewing. Paper presented at the Training '88 Conference for Human Resource Professionals. New York, NY.

Wright, O. R. (1969). Summary of research on the selection interview since 1964. *Personnel Psychology*, 22:391-413.

Yates, J. F., & Stone, E. R. (1992). The risk construct. In J. F. Yates (ed.) *Risk-taking behavior* (pp. 1-25). New York, NY: John Wiley & Sons, Ltd.

Yeschke, C. L. (1987). *Interviewing: An introduction to interrogation.* Springfield, IL: Charles C. Thomas.

Zalud, B. (1991). National Retail Security Survey, *Security Magazine*.

Zaretsky vs. New York City Health and Hospitals Corp (1991). NY City, NYS 2d.

Zuckerman, M., Coestner, R., & Colella, M. J. (1985). Learning to detect deception from three communication channels. *Journal of Nonverbal Communication*, 9(3):188-194.

Zuckerman, M., DeFrank, R. S., Hall, J. A., Larrance, D. T., & Rosenthal, R. (1979). Facial and vocal cues of deception and honesty. *Journal of Experimental Social Psychology*, 15:378-396.

Zuckerman, M., DePaulo, B. M., & Rosenthal, R. (1981). Verbal and nonverbal deception. Vol. 14, In L. Berkowitz (ed.) *Advances in experimental social psychology* (pp. 1-59). New York, NY: Academic Press.

INDEX